JOINING FORCES

THE PRENTICE HALL SERIES
IN MERGERS AND ACQUISITIONS

BENDANIEL AND ROSENBLOOM   *International Mergers and Acquisitions (future)*

MCCANN AND GILKEY   *Joining Forces: Creating and Managing Successful Mergers and Acquisitions*

JOINING FORCES

Creating &
Managing
Successful
Mergers &
Acquisitions

Joseph E. McCann ● Roderick Gilkey

Emory University

PRENTICE HALL, *Englewood Cliffs, New Jersey 07632*

Library of Congress Cataloging-in-Publication Data

McCann, Joseph E.
   Joining forces.

   Bibliography: p.
   Includes index.
   1. Consolidation and merger of corporations.
   2. Industrial management.   I. Gilkey, Roderick.
   II. Title.
   HD2746.5.M34 1988   658.1'6   87-32685
   ISBN 0-13-510538-2

Editorial/production supervision
and interior design: BARBARA MARTTINE
Cover design: GEORGE CORNELL
Manufacturing buyer: LORRAINE FUMOSO

© 1988 by Prentice-Hall, Inc.
A Division of Simon & Schuster
Englewood Cliffs, New Jersey 07632

The publisher offers discounts on this book when ordered in bulk quantities. For more information, write:

Special Sales/College Marketing
Prentice Hall
College Technical and Reference Division
Englewood Cliffs, NJ 07632

Printed in the United States of America

10 9 8 7 6 5 4 3 2 1

ISBN 0-13-510538-2

PRENTICE-HALL INTERNATIONAL (UK) LIMITED, *London*
PRENTICE-HALL OF AUSTRALIA PTY. LIMITED, *Sydney*
PRENTICE-HALL CANADA INC., *Toronto*
PRENTICE-HALL HISPANOAMERICANA, S.A., *Mexico*
PRENTICE-HALL OF INDIA PRIVATE LIMITED, *New Delhi*
PRENITCE-HALL OF JAPAN, INC., *Tokyo*
SIMON & SCHUSTER ASIA PTE. LTD., *Singapore*
EDITORA PRENTICE-HALL DO BRASIL, LTDA., *Rio de Janerio*

We Dedicate This Book
To Our Families
And Our Mentors:
Eric Trist
and
Len Greenhalgh

CONTENTS

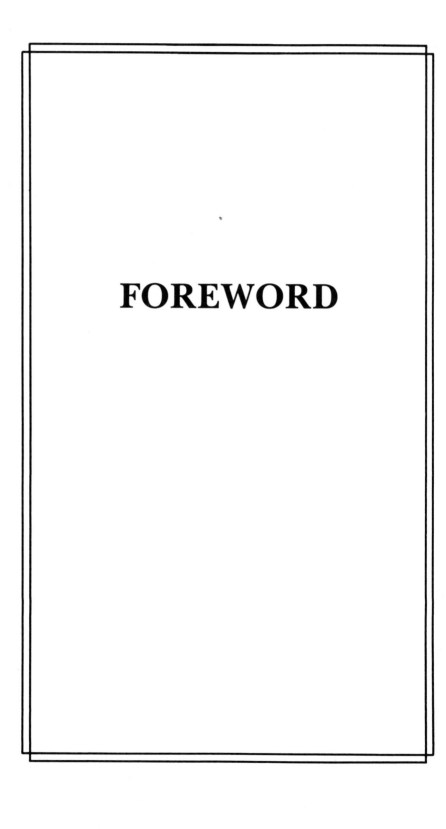

FOREWORD

Mergers and acquisitions are among the most important restructuring tools that American industry is using today to adapt to the forces of economic change. Companies large and small throughout our economy are pursuing mergers to gain size and strength, achieve better balance in operations, raise the technological level of their product lines and obtain efficiencies of scale, better market coverage, and other benefits.

The pace of M&A activity also has risen dramatically. In 1986, mergers and acquisitions in the U.S. reached a record number of more than 3500. That's more than twelve transactions every work day throughout the year with an annual value of more than $200 billion.

So much activity obviously suggests that American companies expect great things from mergers. Yet the record shows that, far more often than not, these high hopes are never realized. In fact, according to the consultant McKinsey & Company, as many as two out of every three mergers or acquisitions fail to live up to initial projections of their value.

What accounts for this dismal showing? One problem— perhaps the most obvious one—is that companies choose the wrong merger partner. This can happen because they are not clear enough about strategic objectives, or because they do not do careful enough pre-merger evaluation of candidate companies. They end up acquiring companies that—because of dissimilarities in business, financial structures and organizations—simply don't mesh with their own.

A second problem, and one that has been receiving far less attention, is that many of these undertakings fail because they cease to receive priority attention from top management once the strategic decisionmaking, candidate selection and negotiations have been successfully concluded. This study by Joseph McCann and Roderick Gilkey breaks new ground in giving appropriate emphasis to the transition and integration phases which conclude the merger process. The book's first-hand testimony and careful analysis make clear that, while these phases are often neglected, success in meeting their many challenges is absolutely crucial to building the long-term operational strength that alone can validate mergers.

For the transition phase, which focuses on the *initial* bringing together of the merging companies, the key ingredients of success are careful planning, purposeful implementation, persuasive selling of the new partnership, and sensitivity to the effects of merger actions on employees. The merging firms must agree about their transition roles and formulate a strategy for beginning to build the new company. Often it makes sense to put this assignment in the hands of a task force of key players from the various function areas of *both* companies. This approach increases the likelihood that the new company will be created out of the very best ideas and talent made available by the merger.

Joining Forces describes each of the transition activities in full detail, discussing cases in which they have been successfully employed—as well as illustrating how the shortchanging of these procedures can derail the most promising merger.

The book does an equally thorough job of discussing the integration phase of the merger process. This phase focuses on the actual combining of the merging companies' component parts—on the selective fitting together of the two firms' organizations, processes and systems, people and cultures. Here McCann and Gilkey give emphasis to such fundamental issues as prioritizing areas for integration, determining what degree of consolidation is appropriate, and ensuring that integration activity does not distract management attention from day-to-day operations. One point that the authors mention deserves to be highlighted: the need to devote ample financial and managerial resources to the integration activity. Skimping at this phase is a false economy.

Managers experienced in mergers and acquisitions know this is an exceptionally demanding and difficult field. Directing the merger process involves mastering a number of complex disciplines as well as grappling with organizational integration and other processes which are not yet fully understood. All of us in business need to learn a lot more about handling mergers and acquisitions. U.S. industry must reverse its poor success record in these transactions and learn to take fuller advantage of the many opportunities they offer for rebuilding faltering industries, advancing our technology, and improving our competitiveness in markets around the globe.

This is why I think business managers will find McCann's and Gilkey's book valuable. *Joining Forces* will add to our knowledge, sharpen our thinking and broaden our understanding about a subject that is vitally important to our companies and our nation's economy.

E. L. HENNESSEY, JR..
Chairman and CEO
Allied-Signal Inc.

PREFACE

Rapid growth and diversification through mergers and acquisitions is standard practice in corporate America, despite disappointingly low success rates. The paradox of high merger/acquisition activity and low success rates perhaps is caused by a few corporations' visible and dramatic success, prompting others to become active acquirers. With success rates estimated as low as 33%, and capital and human costs being very high, it is vitally important to understand how a few successful companies have managed to beat the odds.

Our purpose in writing this book is to describe how successful merger management programs work. Our intent is to understand corporate health—how organizations can respond healthily and adaptively to the challenge of rapid change and still achieve growth. Since so many mergers and acquisitions are disappointments, much of what is written in the press reads like a pathology report. "Corporation X grows too rapidly and flounders, enters into a business it doesn't understand, or clashes with the culture of its new partner." We want to tell a different story, not one of shipwrecked corporations with employees overboard and stockholders marooned, but a story about how a corporation's careful charting of anticipated dangers can lead to a smooth voyage over turbulent waters.

We have studied many corporations trying to find common denominators that contribute to their successful diversification efforts. We report on numerous acquisitions, and we will focus on the Allied-Signal Corporation as an example. But remember, the complexities of modern corporations and today's business environment jeopardize the reliability of any selection method, as does rapid change and unanticipated events.

The Danish philosopher Kierkegaard wrote, "The problem with life is that we understand it backwards, but have to live it forwards." While we can speculate about the future, we have to make judgments based on past lessons and present realities. Such is the case with our sample. In our estimation, the old Allied Corporation has been very successful at assimilating (and accommodating itself) to two major partners, Bendix and Signal. Because of its success, Allied has become a more versatile and adaptive organization, with potential for continued growth. We think it premature to pass final judgment on whether these efforts are fully successful. What we can say is Allied-Signal now faces a more promising future as an advanced technology corporation. It has successfully passed through several phases of dramatic transition to achieve its current vigor. We think the story of Allied-Signal's achievements should be communicated since many of its management practices are worth emulating.

What we have learned from dozens of coast-to-coast interviews can be summarized in three points. First, successful merger/acquisition programs are well conceived. They take into account what we have called the three pillars of success: financial fit, business fit and organizational fit. Since there is never a perfect fit in all three areas, informed leaders must assess the minimum critical fit in each area before proceeding further.

Second, an awareness of the merger/acquisition process and the resultant ability to exercise critical control over it is crucial to success. Change always plays a role in complex business transactions. That role seems to be minimized with experienced players. Successful mergers and acquisitions are the product of proactive, not reactive corporations. While opportunism and serendipity seems to explain a certain number of successful acquisitions, we suspect that such success is in reality the result of careful behind-the-scenes preparation, not chance.

Third, careful transition planning and management are vital to the merger's success. This is the stage where most failures occur. For example, the high costs of an acquisition often leads the acquiring firm to irrational cost conservation, thus endangering the entire venture. A "gold-plated transition program", as one CEO termed it, is not an extravagance. It is a necessity.

A merger/acquisition is only as good as the vision which inspires it. If the vision is well-conceived, it must be shepherded through a complex set of stages in the merger/acquisition process. Finally, the effort must be supported with the necessary capital and human resources to implement the vision, facilitate the transition and maximize its benefits.

Successful business ventures stem from leaders who possess not just ambition, but also wisdom. Such wisdom allows these corporate chiefs to temper their aspirations with a healthy awareness of limitations. They are good at sponsoring needed growth, while preserving necessary stability. They challenge everyone's capacities without overwhelming them, and reach without overreaching.

We have observed that sound corporate growth operates much like the principles governing all organic growth. From embrology we take the epigenetic principle, which states that all growth proceeds from a natural plan, allowing the maturation of an organism from a more simple centralized being to a more differentiated complex one. Each phase of growth occurs in its own time, has its own period of ascendancy and then gives way to a new phase of development. The process is cumulative. Each new phase is dependent on the ones proceeding it. Sponsoring growth from this perspective means helping the organism change while maintaining essential stability. There is inherent growth potential for each organization. Wisdom is understanding both the potential and limits of growth. As noted social observer, Erik Erikson once said, "The plan for growth is all there if we will but let it live."

There is a great need to achieve business growth, diversity and efficiency through mergers and acquisitions if we are to remain productive at home and competitive abroad. As a tool to aid business development, mergers and acquisitions can either facilitate or impede such growth. We hope these tools will be used in an informed and prudent manner, and it is our wish that this book will contribute to the corporate growth effort.

JOSEPH E. McCANN
RODERICK GILKEY

ACKNOWLEDGMENTS

Mergers and acquisitions are truly collaborative events, involving a great variety and number of players. The people who gave their time and effort to this book equally mirror that diversity and number. We are, of course, deeply indebted to Dave Powell, Dennis Signorovitch, Bob Kirk, and Ted Halkyard at Allied-Signal. Other corporate supporters include Bill King at IT Corp., Dan Donovan at Fluor, Don Revelle at Black & Decker, Jack Roberts and Pete Conlin at Bell South Enterprises, Becky Ellenburg at First Atlanta, Harold Flynn at Geonex, George Barsom at ESE, Ed Peddie at SanteFe Healthcare, Diane Heard at C&S Bank. We also received tremendous assistance from Jim Balloun at McKinsey and Joel Koblentz at Egon Zendher International. Dave Jemison at Stanford University, Paul Hirsch at the University of Chicago, and Dean John Robson at Emory were kind enough to share their ideas with us, as well.

Our mentors who helped lay the foundation for our work include Eric Trist and Tom Gilmore, Robert Fulmer at Ibis Inc., and Erik Erikson, Len Greenhalgh, and Howard Wolowitz. Hopefully their infuence shows. Walter Kiechel at *Fortune* and Marty Sikora at *Mergers & Acquisitions* also played critical roles by providing valuable encouragement and counsel.

Several students assisted in research and the early stages

of draft preparation, and these include Mandy Armour, Rick Chocizk, Delynn Davidson, Jed Dodd, Alisa Kutchera, and Tom Butte. They make us glad we are professors. Denise Maloof and Roger Heisler of Emory provided invaluable service in helping edit and organize this manuscript.

We want to particularly thank the following members of the Investment Banking Community: Jim Allwin of Morgan Stanley Inc., Joe Zimmel of Goldman Sachs Inc., and Roger Miller of Salomon Brothers for their invaluable input into this project.

Our thanks also to Jeff Krames at Prentice Hall who made the decision to do the book. Barbara Marttine worked with us in finishing the book, and her professionalism, like that of other Prentice Hall staff, confirmed our wisdom of doing the book with them. It was a pleasure.

"Last but not least", as the phrase goes, we thank our families, particularly Marti and Geri, who lived the book with us, and our children Alex and Sarah, Nicole and Andrea.

1

JOINING FORCES:
THE
PARADOX

The more we thought, read, and talked with executives about mergers and acquisitions, the more curious we became. Tales of corporate raiders and arbitrageurs may have caught our attention first, but it was the underlying numbers that compelled us to dig further. Judging from the number of deals over the past 10 years, mergers and acquisitions have clearly become an important part of corporate strategy for an unprecedented number and variety of firms. Hostile takeovers and "greenmail" schemes excluded, there are clear legitimate reasons for mergers and acquisitions. It is relatively easy to identify those reasons, and the next chapter puts this activity in perspective.

But it was not just volume that intrigued us. While apparently an important instrument of corporate strategy, mergers' and acquisitions' dismal success rates proved even more striking. In general, success has not been good at all, and we will briefly highlight some research about success rates. Here, then, is the paradox we encountered: If mergers and acquisitions are so important to corporate strategy today, then why are success rates so poor?

Joining Forces is the result of our two-year effort to investigate this paradox and offer specific ways to improve the success rate of mergers and acquisitions. Our basic premise is that there are two major determinants of success: the foundation on which a deal is built, and the quality of the process used to execute it, particularly the last stages of that process—the so-called transition and integration stages.

Volume of Activity

The numbers are staggering no matter which way you look at them. For example, there were, on average, about 11 mergers and acquisitions taking place every working day in the first part of 1985.[1] For all of 1985, 3001 deals were recorded—a 12-year record and an 18 percent increase over 1984.[2] Despite tax reform uncertainty, higher stock prices which made firms more expensive to acquire, and an unsettled international economy, 1986 proved a record-breaking year, with more than 3300 deals. And, rather than declining, there were more deals reported in the first 10 weeks of 1987 than in the same period for 1986. The pace did slacken somewhat in the balance of 1987, indicated by a drop in the total dollar value of such deals—the first drop since 1982.[3]

However, it appears a time to catch one's breath, not abandon the chase. Indeed, the pace and level of activity have been so great that Alfred Rappaport, a Northwestern University professor and merger valuation expert, reported that volume may be dropping simply because there are not as many eligible companies left in some basic industries.[4] Still, even in industries where merger-acquisition activity was frantic—food processing, for example—firms may remain attractive acquisition possibilities because their stock prices may still be below their underlying value. Total dollar volume may be down as the billion-dollar "mega-mergers" taper off, but the continuing high volume of "smaller" deals indicates that much smaller firms have joined the game. Rapidly growing high technology and service firms hitting the *Inc. 100* are, for example, reporting sharply increased acquisition activity over their counterparts from 1982 and 1983.[5]

Europe has also caught merger fever. Contrary to traditional business practices in Great Britain, many firms there are aggressively pursuing takeovers of each other. In a study of merger practices in England, Egon Zehnder International and the

London Business School reported that more than 1000 British firms had changed hands in 1986—a record except for two recession years, 1972 and 1973.[6] Australians Robert Holmes à Court and John D. Elliott joined the fray in bold takeover attempts of British firms.

In North America, foreign firms are also visibly but quietly buying U.S. firms at record levels.[7] While American firms did not take advantage of the 1980's relatively cheap prices of foreign firms, European and Asian firms did. Establishing a presence in U.S. markets has become a strategic goal in the present protectionist trade climate. This can add another dimension to acquisition problems: integrating two domestic firms is usually difficult enough without adding cross-cultural factors.[8]

Impact and Success Rate

While dollar values and deal numbers may be impressive, other numbers illustrate the impact of this activity even more profoundly. As Clemens P. Work pointed out in a 1985 *U.S. News & World Report* article, the top 100 mergers in 1984 involved firms with a total of 4.5 million workers or 4.3 percent of the nation's workforce. Even if only one-tenth were affected by their firm's merger, Work says, that would mean the worklives of 450,000 people have already been altered.[9] The impact has not just been on line and staff. Tarnow International, an executive search firm, reported in *Manhattan, Inc.* that 24 of 65, or 37 percent, of the *Fortune 500* CEOs who left their jobs in 1986 left because of mergers and acquisitions.[10]

There is, as pointed out in Chapter 5, a whole industry that has grown not just to support but also to encourage merger-acquisition activity. Stories abound about Wall Street investment banking firms and about takeover artists like Ichan, Pickens, Posner, and Lorenzo. They have become both admired and despised. Despite 1986's dramatic scandals involving many of Wall Street's "best and brightest," talented MBA's from the country's best business schools remain entranced by Wall Street. In their eyes, investment banking offers a quick, adventurous trip to early fortune. The diversion of this talent from more mundane yet essential line management jobs in manufacturing, and the distraction caused by focusing on these very aggressive players, makes the U.S.'s struggle to compete globally even more difficult.

The size of the fees these players earn, the fortunes made and undone, and their highly publicized scandals and cat fights dazzle and distract us from the larger underlying message. Our interest in mergers and acquisitions arose when it became clear that they have developed into a major phenomenon, capable of either seriously damaging or helping American industries' adaptation to fundamentally new forces. Examples of such forces include the globalization of competition, maturing products and stagnant industries, new technologies, and a shift toward a service economy. There are encouraging signs that firms are adapting positively, indicated by the level of new venture initiation and comparable efforts for new venture innovation within corporations. Strategic alliances such as partnerships and joint ventures are also being initiated at unprecedented levels, although with mixed success.[11]

Mergers and acquisitions are, however, simply one of several means to a desired end that can and must be weighed against other strategic options and choices. They are, when one considers how deep the required joining of forces between firms must be, an extreme form. Figure 1-1 illustrates this collaborative dimension and how other options compare.

We want to offer a basic recommendation before diving headlong into the study of mergers and acquisitions. Managers should first explore the full range of strategic options for joining

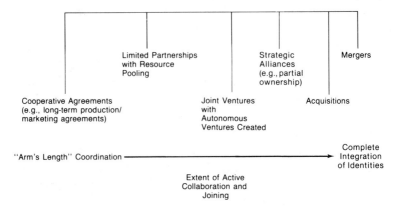

Figure 1-1 A continuum of collaborative options.

forces. Another option, such as a joint venture, may achieve a desired collaboration level with lower cost and commitment than a merger.

Mergers and acquisitions are initiated for many reasons, as covered in Chapter 2. The buying and selling of businesses is, of course, one way for financial entrepreneurs like Bill Simon to amass personal fortunes. They are, more importantly, a way for firms to abruptly change direction by shedding unwanted businesses and adding new ones. Growing an entire business from scratch internally is expensive and takes time. The temptation to buy capacity in an acquisition or to collaborate to improve the competitive advantage of both firms is intuitively appealing.

If mergers and acquisitions are potentially useful means for helping firms adapt, then why aren't they more successful? Data and expert opinion say they fail miserably. The success rate—the extent to which a deal later meets the expectations of either or both firms involved—is estimated by some observers like McKinsey & Co. to be about 33 percent, which means two out of three mergers or acquisitions fail to meet initial expectations![12] In a 1987 *Harvard Business Review* article, Michael Porter reported that, in a study of 33 large corporations, over half of which had their acquisitions in new industries and more than 60 percent in entirely new fields, 74 percent of the unrelated acquisitions were subsequently divested.[13]

The Two Determinants of Success

Why such poor results? There has been increasing interest in this question.[15] While certainly interested in why they fail, we also want to ask how some firms succeed. What do they do to build their odds for success?

Failure and success stories are not hard to find, and we found much to learn from both. Despite a very public and heralded merger between Dart Industries and Kraft Foods, for example, Dart & Kraft announced in late 1986 that they would be splitting up. The trials and tribulations of Peoples Express, also in 1986, concluded with its purchase by Texas Air. On the other hand, one of the largest, most widely applauded, and apparently successful mergers was between Allied and Signal beginning in late 1985. Many other mergers also appear to be going well, and we were curious to know more about how they were done.

It is now clear to us that mergers and acquisitions fail to meet initial expectations for one or both of the following reasons. Either can be fatal. First, they may be structurally flawed in their underlying foundation—what we call the *Three Pillars of Success*: business fit, financial fit, and organizational fit. Second, they may fail because the merger-acquisition process itself is inherently flawed, particularly in the last and extremely important transition and integration stages. Much of this book is devoted to better understanding these last two stages.

We set out on an adventure of reading, talking with merger-acquisition experts in investment banking, law, and consulting firms, and senior executives in both large and small firms in the country. This is not the easiest topic for candid, publishable remarks, and in more than one case comments had to be "off the record." Executives in BellSouth, Black & Decker, Browning-Ferris, C & S Banks, Fluor Corporation, Geonex Corporation, International Technology Corp., SantaFe Healthcare, and, of course, Allied-Signal were particularly forthcoming and helpful. From these interviews, added to extensive interviews with executives in Salomon Bros., Morgan-Stanley, Robinson-Humphrey Co., L.F. Rothschild, McKinsey & Co., Egon Zehnder International, and research staff in the AFL-CIO, patterns began to emerge. One of us also facilitated three acquisition efforts while writing this book, two of which eventually happened.

Our research revealed the importance of mergers and acquisitions in helping transform both entire industries and firms in their attempts to adapt to dramatic change. It is easy to become distracted by the hoopla surrounding hostile takeovers, so-called "mega-mergers," and publicly embarrassing divestitures from poorly executed diversification strategies. We tried to stay away from it. We were not interested in studying unfriendly takeovers and raids. Break-ups of firms acquired in hostile takeovers are, rightly or wrongly, an endangered practice that will be less common in the future.

Instead, we were interested in how two firms could join forces to pursue ends neither could pursue as effectively alone. Penn State professor Barbara Gray calls this desire to join forces "the essence of collaboration." Chapter 2 contains information that places current merger-acquisition activity in perspective by first taking a historical look at previous activity and then examining some of the common reasons why firms do merge and acquire.

We quickly found that success depends on many variables—several simply beyond the control of the two firms involved. The process is inherently problematic because assumptions must be made about many of these variables and their significance. Mergers and acquisitions are still an art, although the science is quickly improving. Nonetheless, a merger is a bit like cooking with a recipe you heard was good, but you have to guess some of its ingredients. Because the configuration of these variables is different in each deal, everyone we talked to said no two deals were ever identical. True in one sense, but we found enough basic patterns across many deals to suggest that models, while general, could still be built and used to gain insight into and perhaps improve practice.

The assumptions that must be made during the process are truly strategic. They may or may not be sound, and the process, by its very nature, prevents their early safe testing. Secrecy and arm's-length negotiations are two-edged swords. We found that the choice of assumptions most directly affects the fit between the three pillars which form the very foundation for success. These pillars are discussed in detail in Chapter 3.

Perhaps most important, the process itself requires active management and monitoring. A major theme of this book is that success, while certainly not guaranteed by effective process management alone, is definitely more likely with it. There is absolutely no substitute for a well-designed, actively supported, and professionally managed process. We do not mean that just the various stages in the process are logically arranged, funded, and staffed. A reflective, learning-oriented approach is also needed, so that immediate inquiry about success is taking place. The process is prone to difficulties because of the segmentation of its stages and the number and types of players involved in it. Chapters 4 and 5 contain detailed descriptions of the process and these difficulties.

We found that the process's later stages—the transition and integration stages—are among the least well managed. Post-merger management skills and knowledge are still in their infancy, and there was almost perfect consensus among the executives and professionals we contacted that the time from an agreement's negotiation to the smooth functioning of the two firms is turbulent and full of risk—a time during which an otherwise sound deal can be undone. Both firms must agree about each other's role during this period, and the acquiring or dominant firm must be particularly clear about its role. An overall strategy must be created and executed to guide the transition management process. A model for selecting roles and strategies is offered in Chapter 6. How the transition and integration stages can be effectively managed is explored in Chapters 7 and 8, drawing heavily on the Allied-Bendix and Allied-Signal mergers as models.

Finally, we found that an internal capacity for aiding the process's development and management helps tremendously. We strongly advocate in Chapter 9 the development of that capacity, and we illustrate specific types of interventions that can be made to build it. In Chapter 10, we try to summarize the book's major lessons for key players. Some of these are obvious, some not so obvious. Many of these "golden rules" represent the collective wisdom of some truly impressive professionals, committed to careers in merger work and yet who have never gotten their thoughts down on paper. At the end of the book is an annotated bibliography of the books and articles we found particularly helpful.

A person interested in mergers and acquisitions can easily drown in this topic. It is technically sophisticated and spread across disciplines as diverse as corporate finance, law, marketing strategy, human relations training, and change management practice. The more people who become interested and familiar with these topics and who begin struggling to make them fit, the better the success rate will become. The more this integrated approach is adopted—as, for example, investment bankers become familiar with change management theory, and change management consultants become familiar with the workings of investment banks—the more it will form the basis for increasingly successful merger-acquisition practice.

2

DRIVING
FORCES

Mergers and acquisitions are far from new in American business. There have been several waves of activity over the past 100 years. Each successive wave has been driven by forces both unique to that time and yet persistent over time. An in-depth analysis of the history of merger-acquisition activity is not the focus of this book, but a better appreciation of history helps focus current challenges in managing the process. The unparalleled level of activity since the late 1970s is particularly relevant for several reasons. In this chapter, we first take a brief look at the larger historical patterns and then explore how firms are currently explaining their activity.

Historical Patterns and Driving Forces

As noted in Chapter 1, mergers and acquisitions are simply one of several means for achieving a firm's ends. They are, without question, one of the most powerful instruments available to management. They are capable of improving performance when well executed and of seriously damaging performance when they are not. But historically mergers and acquisitions also have been fundamental to the development and restructuring of entire in-

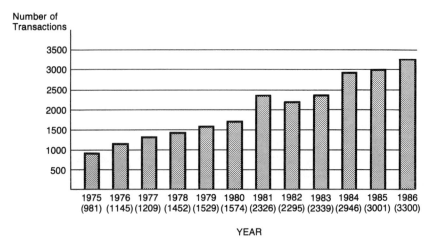

Number of
Transactions

YEAR

Figure 2-1 Merger completion record 1975–1985. (Source: *Mergers & Acquisitions*, 1985.)

dustries—even the entire U.S. economy. They have not yet played an equally great role in reshaping the global economy, but indications are clear that they are beginning to do so.

One danger of ignoring historical patterns and forces is assuming that the present situation is unique. A case in point is Lewis Beman's 1973 *Fortune* article "What We Learned from the Great Merger Frenzy."[1] Beman's article does a fine job putting the past in perspective. Good historians may not be good forecasters, however, since his prediction was that the intense level of conglomerate merger-acquisition activity during the late 60s and early 70s would not be repeated for some time. While slowdowns may have occurred due to economic recessions since Beman's article, the *long-term* trend in mergers and acquisitions definitely has been toward more and larger deals. Figure 2-1 illustrates the overall level of activity from 1975 to 1986.

The Four Waves of Merger-Acquisition Activity

Will this trend continue? Perhaps—particularly when the present driving forces are better understood. The high level of activity over the past decade is best seen as the fourth in a succession of activity waves dating back before the turn of the century. Figure 2-2 from Beman's article illustrates the three previous waves.

There have been very recent attempts to explain these historical patterns of activity, most notably that of Kenneth Davidson in his book, *Mega-Mergers*.[2] Davidson notes that there have been four waves of activity since the late 1800s. We agree with the number but disagree with some of the driving forces he attributes to each of the waves, particularly to the current one.

Each wave was driven by a set of forces whose consequences are now known but were difficult to discern then. Alfred D. Chandler has explained the evolution of business strategy over time; and, again, while we draw upon his historical panorama of American business history to provide a base on which to structure our analysis of merger-acquisition activity, we do not fully agree with his analysis. Chandler's explanations, however, do go a long way in explaining such activity, which closely coincides with his observed corporate strategy shifts.[3]

The three initial waves were horizontal integration, vertical integration, and conglomeration. While Davidson calls the fourth period of activity the "Mega-Merger Wave" because of the large number of very large mergers and acquisitions involved, we believe that more than just numbers characterize this period: It is one of major industry transformation and strategic restructuring.

To some extent the motivations driving each wave overlap because the factors that made horizontal integration attractive 100 years ago still exist, and many mergers and acquisitions are still done for those reasons. For example, Coca-Cola's recent purchases of several of its previously independently owned bottlers are moves towards classic vertical integration motivated by excellent economic reasons. Firm-specific reasons also exist and can be important in explaining merger-acquisition activity. Nonetheless, we feel that much of the merger-acquisition activity makes sense when viewed against larger industry and historical trends.

A Coincidence of Governing Conditions

All four waves can be explained by the coincidence of four sets of conditions or factors. These conditions, working together at

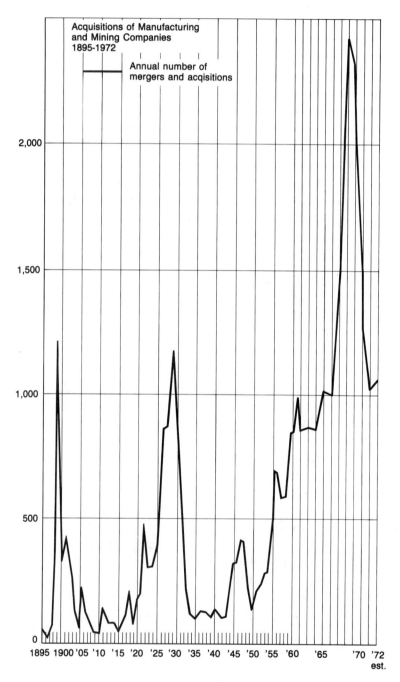

Figure 2-2   Three merger peaks. (Source: Beman, 1973.)

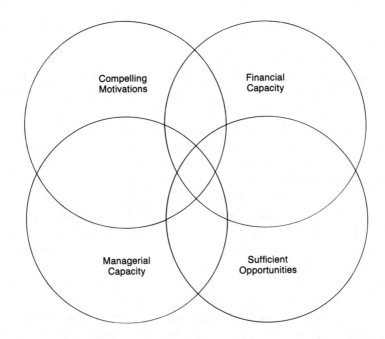

Figure 2-3   A coincidence of governing forces.

any given time, will govern the prevailing level and type of activity. These four conditions are (1) sufficient opportunity, (2) financial capacity, (3) managerial capacity, and (4) compelling motivations at a firm and industry level, perhaps even at a general economy level. Figure 2-3 illustrates the four conditions.

SUFFICIENT OPPORTUNITY.   A sufficiently large number of firms must be willing and able to merge or be acquired. Unwilling firms bid up offering prices and make high premiums difficult to justify and carry, regardless of how attractive the firm is perceived to be. Willingness, as Davidson notes, has not necessarily been a feature of the current merger wave due to the sophistication of hostile takeover strategies and sizable war chests assembled by raiders and acquirers. History may classify hostile takeovers as a passing phenomenon lost against the larger background of friendly merger-acquisition activity. We therefore ignore "greenmail" schemes (in which a premium is paid by the target firm on the shares purchased by the firm attempting the takeover) and "break-ups" (the takeover and sale of the firm's assets).

The availability of excess idle cash reserves is a driving force in this current wave of activity, but higher premiums do help cool activity. The high expense of and negative public response to hostile takeovers also make it even more important that companies join forces voluntarily. Some senior executives, like Ed Hennessy, have simply gone on record saying they will not attempt hostile takeovers because they set the wrong tone for a future relationship.

Other hurdles firms must overcome are constraints on activity. Regulatory and legal constraints have played a strong historical role in dampening activity. Beginning with the Sherman Antitrust Act, a long series of legislation has at first dampened, then redirected activity: Securities Act of 1933, Securities Exchange Act of 1934, Glass-Steagal Act of 1933, Celler-Kefauver Act of 1950, and several current attempts by Congress and several states to prevent hostile takeovers. The relaxed regulatory atmosphere during the Reagan administration certainly affected the current high level of activity. While generally relaxed, antitrust policy still exerts itself in some cases—for example, Coca-Cola's attempted acquisition of Dr. Pepper shortly after PepsiCo's announced plan to buy 7-Up. Nonetheless, a prevailing political climate can be a strong predictor of merger-acquisition activity, and, by any measure, recent policy has certainly been relaxed. However, the courts and SEC are becoming more involved when it comes to hostile takeovers.[4]

FINANCIAL CAPACITY.   Without question, the availability of capital is a major governing condition on how much activity is possible. As the discussion of each wave will illustrate, mergers and acquisitions require fuel, and firms must have sufficient, low-cost capital to sustain activity. Capital can be internally generated and also come from external sources such as the stock and bond markets. Financial capacity is so important that it can stimulate activity when other conditions are less favorable, such as the availability of attractive candidates. This is the "idle cash" argument which postulates that firms make acquisitions to use large amounts of cash they have accumulated and cannot otherwise use productively. As raiders like Victor Posner and T. Boone Pickens have illustrated, any firm sitting on idle cash is also an inviting target. Cash can, of course, be used to repurchase shares, and is being used this way by most of the major oil companies. Dividends were also being increased by these firms until oil prices crashed in early 1986.[5]

Creative investment bankers like Drexel Burnham Lambert, with the massive investment pools they can generate, have added fuel to the activity.[6] The use of so-called "junk bonds" can stretch a firm's financial capacity, and the consequences of hyper-leveraging are beginning to be felt. Turner Broadcasting's acquisition of MGM's film library in March 1986, for example, has resulted in large losses for Turner. Similarly, acquisitions by firms such as Kohlberg, Kravis, Roberts & Co. using leveraged buyouts (LBOs) make sense only as long as the firm's business remains good. A recession can spell disaster when the debt's full weight is felt. In many cases, LBOs become the source of many businesses' divestitures sold to finance the deal, thus adding indirectly to even more acquisition activity.

Our own experience has shown that finding the right deal, not finding the capital, is the major obstacle. There is always capital available to do a deal that makes sense. However, available financial capacity alone is not a compelling argument to justify a merger or acquisition. When financial capacity drives the process, mergers and acquisitions become ends, not means.

MANAGERIAL & ORGANIZATIONAL INNOVATION.   Every successive activity wave has been supported by significant managerial and organizational innovation. Chandler and a number of other management theorists have noted how improvements in the design of organizations, management science, and strategy analysis have provided a foundation for mergers and acquisitions. Some of these are noted soon, but the critical point here is that there must be sufficient managerial and organizational capacity to make successful mergers and acquisitions.

For example, a substantial increase in a firm's size through a merger frequently requires major adjustments and innovations in management control and coordination systems. The failure to produce many hypothesized advantages in merging two firms is often a direct consequence of management's inability to innovate and make the necessary adjustments. We offer several examples in later chapters to support this point.

COMPELLING MOTIVATIONS.   Finally, there must be enough compelling reasons to undertake a merger or acquisition. Frankly, there are good reasons and bad ones, and the history of mergers and acquisitions is full of both. Davidson also summarizes several of these. One is undervalued assets of the candidate firm. A second is that mergers and acquisitions provide a fast way to grow. Third, they offer access to new products and businesses. Fourth, they are an outlet for idle cash. And fifth, they offer a way to respond to change. A sixth reason is that tax and legal benefits are present. We will take a closer look at some of these, and add a few to the list. However, these motivations do not completely explain the activity in the first three waves of the past. A brief look at earlier waves is appropriate to help put more recent motivations in context.

The First Wave: Horizontal Integration

Firms grew by expanding manufacturing capacity in the first wave at the turn of the century. The Industrial Revolution was well underway, large national markets were developing, and U.S. firms were expanding overseas. The firm wanting to grow quickly in this environment would not only build new capacity as fast as possible but also buy other firms in the same industry. Acquisitions also were useful in limiting competition; but as long as the economy was expanding, the need for more capacity, not the elimination of competition, was the driving force. Horizontal integration—the adding of capacity and geographical expansion—thus became the dominant corporate strategy. The strong economy helped finance mergers and acquisitions, and the stock market's parallel growth helped float shares of a relatively new organizational form—the publicly held corporation. Antitrust legislation and a downturn in the economy dampened this activity some between 1910 and 1920. As a result, mergers and acquisitions changed direction. As we pointed out earlier, today's firms still grow through horizontal integration in many industries where concentration is not great. The recent wave of airline mergers, such as Texas Air and Eastern, and food industry mergers, such as R.J. Reynolds and Nabisco Brands, are classic examples of horizontal integration.

The Second Wave: Vertical Integration

The second wave was driven by the desire to create economies of scale through vertical integration: the acquisition of downstream customers or outlets for products and upstream suppliers of raw resources and component parts. Capacity expansion became less of a force and was replaced by the desire to reduce operating costs to maintain profit margins. Some of these efforts were not economically successful. However, as means for internalizing sources of risks which before were outside firms' control, we believe they were more successful than previously thought.

Although antitrust measures were being enacted, some of the largest industrial enterprises in the country were being built during this time. Companies like General Motors, U.S. Steel, Standard Oil, and many chemical and transportation firms became giants through vertical integration. Major organizational and managerial innovations were also occurring during this period. Management was becoming professionalized with better qualified managers running operations and using more advanced methods. Organizational structures were evolving to allow widespread operations to run effectively while freeing top management to plot additional mergers and acquisitions.

The stock market fueled this wave and halted it with its crash in 1929. The financial community's excesses of this period spawned a whole new set of legal and regulatory constraints to prevent recurrences. Given creative minds and large financial stakes, however, merger activity was only rechanneled.

The Third Wave: Conglomeration

The third wave was different from the past in one important respect: Acquisitions and mergers had previously been among essentially related firms, either competitors or those linked by a technology or production process. The third wave, conglomeration, was driven by uniquely different motivations: to get around regulatory constraints, to theoretically stabilize financial perform-

ance by buying diverse firms, and to build earnings almost exclusively via mergers and acquisitions. While some conglomerates such as Textron tried to stay more or less within a set of
specific industries, others such as Gulf & Western were getting
into everything from sugar plantations to movies.

For the first time, an acquisition candidate's financial
attributes dominated marketing and production considerations.
Candidates were screened on their ability to carry greater debt,
and to throw off enough cash to fuel additional acquisitions and
boost stock market performance. The introduction of "creative
accounting" practices, such as "pooling of interests," helped sell
these practices to the public. The "go-go" mutual funds in the
stock market responded by bidding up the stock prices of firms
such as Textron, Gulf & Western, Litton, LTV, and Norton Simon
to levels which generated even more capital for acquisitions.[7]

There have been many reasons offered for unrelated
diversification from traditional core businesses. Chandler, Ansoff, Rumelt, Porter and others have studied diversification efforts and the factors which impact their success.[8] They found
that many of those reasons simply did not hold up under scrutiny. For example, unrelated diversification for risk reduction was
not as viable as once assumed. The idea that countercyclical
acquistions would stabilize earnings was disproven in the deep
economic recession of the early 70s. The faltering financial performance of the conglomerates, coupled with higher interest rates,
soon dried up sources of capital such as the stock market and
cheap long-term debt.

Mergers and acquisitions in subsequent years have been
driven mostly by the need to rationalize this previous unrelated
acquisition binge, and to try to bring more rigorous principles
into merger-acquisition practice. We briefly studied 160 firms
making acquisitions using the *Mergers & Acquisitions'* 1985 Roster,
and found that related-business acquisitions outnumbered non-
related acquisitions by three to one.

Divestitures—whether due to crushing debt or done
voluntarily—increased during the late 70s and picked up speed
in the early 80s. Beatrice, for example, had tried, before its 1986
sale, to streamline more than 400 of its autonomous profit centers.
While Beatrice earned a record $479 million in 1984, $220 million
of that came from selling businesses. The idea is roughly true

that for every divestiture there is a corresponding acquisition. But recent growth in creative alternatives such as leveraged buy-outs—the selling of the business to its own management using heavy doses of debt—and going public with a spun-off business prevents a one-to-one ratio of divestitures to acquisitions.

Nonetheless, the early conglomerates' fine-tuning by divestitures is restoring order to the chaos brought about by their earlier activity. The willingness of corporate raiders like Ichan and Pickens to speed up this process for a firm's management is an added incentive. Firms like W.R. Grace, which are reluctant to dismember what appear to be unwieldy, broadly diversified firms, become the subject of takeover speculation. As Peter Grace said quite simply in a *Manhattan Inc.* article, "We're on every list. . . . We feel the pressure."[9]

Many key players who led the conglomerate movement, such as United Technologies' Harry Gray and the late Charles Bluhdorn at Gulf & Western, also have passed control to others who must dismantle their earlier creations. Occasionally you come across a firm still tenaciously pursuing an unrelated strategy. Textron and W.R. Grace still adhere to such strategies, although their stock market performance suffers for it. Nonetheless, with the recent wave of divestitures, buying and selling major businesses have become routine. It also is very common for a firm to acquire another firm and pay for part of the purchase by selling off some of the acquired firm's businesses. Selling assets can be planned or unplanned. A very active market for sold-off businesses exists in most industries.

A point covered in a later chapter but worth noting here is that the assembling of these very large conglomerates and diversified firms was possible because they used increasingly sophisticated organizational designs. Developments in information technologies and financial control systems, structural design, and of the corporate staff function were major innovations. One of the ways structural design developed was through the refinement of the multidivisional organization design as a device for managing the multibusiness firm. The multidivisional firm's many businesses came to be viewed as a portfolio that could be managed to achieve specific ends, such as generating cash to internalize capital sources and flows, and optimizing return on investment.

Holding companies already had been around for some time, particularly in the second merger wave, and they were still the dominant form for many conglomerates. The multidivisional structure allows closer operating and financial management of diverse businesses than that permitted by a holding company structure. The multidivisional structure is an efficient instrument for executing mergers, acquisitions, and divestitures. It is a quantum improvement in sophistication and capacity over earlier organizational forms. For example, the integration of Bendix within Allied's corporate structure was made easier because both firms had multidivisional structures built around essentially parallel operating and management practices.

It was incomplete mastery and overconfidence in these same innovations, however, that caused many of an acquisition's assumed benefits to vanish. Heavy-handed corporate staff and red tape can smother a newly acquired firm. Nonetheless, using more scientific methods to analyze business performance has vastly increased managerial capability since the turn of the century.

The Fourth Wave: Industry Transformation

We are presently riding the fourth wave, and will likely ride it for some time due to the scale of the forces driving it. While the first two waves built and consolidated industries, the third wave of conglomeration blurred boundaries. We still ride the ripples of the third wave as firms which diversified too broadly begin to follow Peters' and Waterman's dictum of "sticking to the knitting"—that is, staying closer to what you know and do best.[10]

The fourth wave, however, is beginning to radically transform and redefine entire industries. The sheer size of these deals can distort the true underlying pattern of activity. This is explained in a 1981 special issue of *Business Week*, "America's Restructured Economy," which documents the wrenching effects of expensive energy and capital, increasing foreign competition, rapid technological change, and maturation of many industries.[11] As firms begin reacting to rapid technological change, they are looking for new technologies to help reduce costs, improve productivity, and introduce new products into new markets. As our economy also shifts toward services and away from so-called "smokestack" industries, a firm may try to abandon its traditional businesses and enter new ones. History's largest wave of corporate restructuring is still underway, and its full implications still are not clear. They are certainly not all positive, judging from the number of layoffs, closed plants, and deep rifts in the basic commitment of workers and companies to each other.[12]

There is also little question that the globalization of competition in the automotive, chemical, steel, manufacturing, and electronics industries makes mergers and acquisitions an increasingly important instrument for improving competitive footing. Domestic firms are linking up with foreign firms to enter new global markets and protect existing market shares.

Firms such as General Motors, Allied-Signal, and IBM are responding to emerging technologies which can improve their core businesses. GM's $2.5 billion acquisition of EDS, for example, was supposed to be part of a bold strategy for transforming GM. New information technologies were supposed to build its capacity for linking sophisticated new manufacturing systems. However, Roger Smith's and GM's ability to execute this strategy has been increasingly questioned. But the point here is that major acquisitions like Hughes and EDS are part of a transformation strategy.[13]

As linkages grow between computers and communications systems, IBM's acquisition of stakes in Rolm and Intel also creates the possibility of new and extended product lines. Gaining entry to new technologies is a major driving force behind many recent acquisitions by large firms. Conversely, small new technology firms can now raise capital and secure early markets by forming "strategic alliances" with much larger firms like GM. Unlike Davidson's characterization of the fourth wave as one dominated by mega-mergers, like Chevron's $13 billion acquisition of Gulf Oil, we believe the *transformation motivation* is growing even stronger. Jennifer Lindsey, in a March 1985 *Venture* magazine article, noted that 1983's merger-acquisition activity was significant not so much for the size of the deals as for the types of firms that were being acquired. She notes that of the 1881 deals reported by W.T. Grimm for 1983, 1004 were of privately-held firms.[14] As an example, Teknowledge Inc., a small California artificial intelligence company, built an illustrious list of "strategic partners," as Figure 2-4 below illustrates.

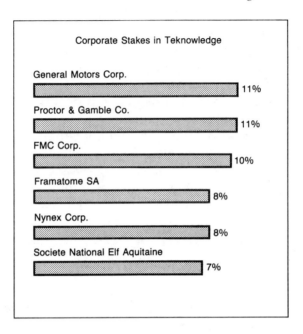

Figure 2-4   Corporate stakes at Teknowledge. (Source: *Wall Street Journal*, December 6, 1985.)

Often such efforts are less than successful or encounter difficulty. IBM and Rolm's relationship is still tenuous, and GM and EDS also are very different companies, making the mixing of their cultures frustrating, to say the least. Gould Inc. also has reportedly found its movement into high technology awkward not only because its traditional management culture turned off smaller, less traditional acquired firms, but also because it created uncertainty about its own culture.[15] While small firms can enjoy many benefits from having larger partners, it is also uncomfortable for them to have these giants breathing down their necks, imposing rules and practices.

Some firms also are lessening their dependence on, and even gradually leaving declining or mature industries such as steel, commodity chemicals, and some extractive industries like mining. Sometimes this is done to keep pace with technological change, but it is also occurring because of increased international competition and regulatory pressure. Ed Hennessy's series of mergers and acquisitions over the past 10 years, most notably those of Bendix and Signal, have successfully moved Allied

Chemical out of the commodity chemical business and into leading-edge technologies. As one manager noted in one of its older
and eventually spun-off chemical businesses, when "Chemical"
was dropped from the name, the page had been turned on the
firm's history. Figure 2-5 dramatically illustrates Allied's transformation in the relative contribution of its different businesses
over time.

Jack Welch also is reducing GE's dependence on mature
products by cutting one-quarter of his work force and moving
even more deeply into plant automation. His most dramatic acquisitions have been into services industries: a $1.1 billion pur-
chase of Employers Reinsurance for GE Credit Corporation, an
80% stake in Kidder Peabody, and the largest non-oil acquisition
to date—RCA. U.S. Steel's purchase of Marathon Oil, its 1985

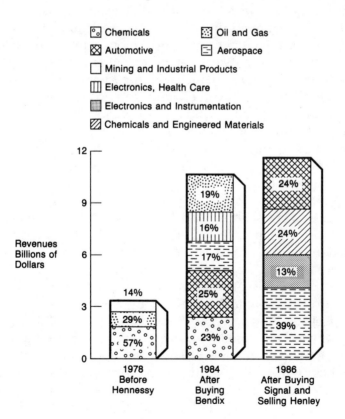

Figure 2-5 The results of Allied's transformation strategy. (Source: *Business
Week*, February 2, 1987.)

acquisition of Texas Oil & Gas, and a name change to USX signals its lessening dependence on steel. In fact, nonsteel business accounted for more than 54% of 1986 revenues.[16] R.J. Reynolds's buying of Nabisco, along with Phillip-Morris's acquisition of General Foods, similarly signals a gradual exiting by these firms from their traditional tobacco businesses. Finally, one of the most visible and dramatic exits from maturing businesses has occurred during Jerry Tsai's transformation of American Can, now called Primerica, from packaging materials to financial services.[17] Figure 2-6 illustrates the impact on American Can's stock price of its exodus via divestitures and acquisitions.

While dramatic and necessary, it is hard to execute a transformation strategy. The clarity of a new vision alone is not adequate. There is, of course, no guarantee that a particular vision is a good one for the firm. For example, U.S. Steel encountered government and community resistance to its oil and gas acquisitions. Congressmen and unions supporting tariff protection against foreign steel helped create artificially high profits for the firm. They now wonder whether they simply helped USX build a nest egg to make oil and gas acquisitions instead of modernizing its plants. Gould also found moving into unfamiliar new high technology businesses a very big step for executives unfamiliar with those businesses. Gould lost key executives in its traditional battery business, and frightened younger executives in the electronics businesses it acquired. Poor morale was also reported in some of GE's traditional businesses and in RCA due to heavy cost cutting and the rapid pace of its transformation.[18] Kidder Peabody's sad encounter with the SEC in a series of insider trading scandals also dampened applause for GE's otherwise brilliant acquisition of that firm.

Entire industries also are being redefined and restructured through deregulation, aided by a more *laissez-faire* regulatory posture. Nowhere has deregulation been felt more acutely than in the airline, banking, transportation, and communications industries. The economies of scale and opportunity to integrate routes has created very real incentives for mergers in the airline industry. The widely publicized battles of Frank Lorenzo for Continental (successful), TWA (unsuccessful), and Eastern (successful) have dramatized activity in this industry. Less dramatic, but also important, are mergers between firms like Northwest

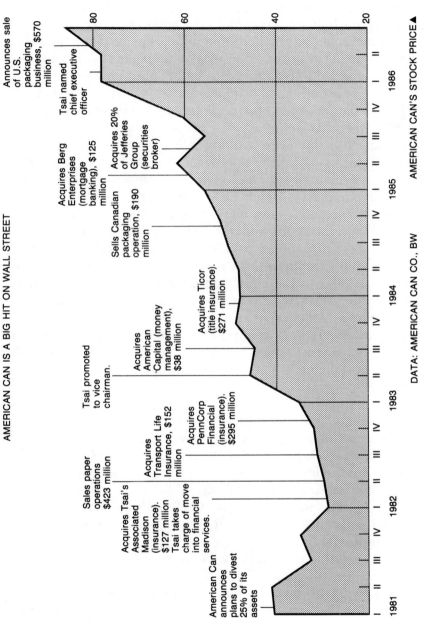

Figure 2-6 American Can's success through acquisitions. (Source: *Business Week*, August 18, 1986.)

Orient and Republic. One has great international routes, and the other has a strong domestic feeder system. Mistakes are being made in this industry, as well. Carl Ichan's takeover of TWA was driven by a plan to break up the airline, but he is now forced to run it intact. Don Burr's "don't-leave-me-behind" acquisitions of Frontier and Britt also proved to be Peoples' undoing.[19]

The traditional banking industry has evolved in less than a decade into the "financial services" industry, as the lines blur between banks, investment firms, and savings and loans.[20] The impact of interstate banking is only now being felt, but in some regions such as the Southeast, merger and acquisition activity has been intense. The North Carolina banks led by NCNB, Wachovia, and First Union have driven other banks in Georgia and Florida into defensive mergers, spawning still other mergers such as Trust Company and Sun Banks, and C&S and Landmark. The prospect of national banking, not just regional banking, is unsettling to executives in this otherwise traditionally secure industry. Adding to the confusion have been moves by Sears to acquire the real estate firm Coldwell-Banker and investment firm Dean Witter. American Express's acquisition of Shearson-Lehman Bros. is another example. Merrill-Lynch's computer technology and financial network have also allowed it to create financial management accounts that compete directly with bank services.

And, of course, there's the break-up of AT&T. The "Baby Bells" have all become acquisitive, some, like Southern Bell, staying close to home in related businesses such as telephone book publishing, while others, like U.S. West and Pacific Telesis, are buying such unrelated businesses as retail computer stores and financial services firms.[21] IBM's buying an interest in MCI also creates the possibility of increased competition for AT&T in its long distance business with a giant, not an undercapitalized entrepreneurial firm.

Firms in these rapidly changing industries are both controlled by and shape the forces driving increased merger-acquisition activity. In the case of airline deregulation, economic and public policy has created the opportunity for airlines to compete and realize operating economies. Mergers and acquisitions become a logical strategy for reducing costs and building routes. In the financial services industry, a relatively small number of

aggressive banks and financial services firms such as American
Express and Merrill-Lynch set in motion a whole round of defensive mergers and acquisitions which redefine the competitive
structure of the industry. Foreign competition in some domestic
manufacturing industries has forced some threatened firms to
combine or leave industries via mergers and acquisitions.

Partly due to changing regulations altering their cost
structure, hospitals have also experienced a fundamental transformation. David Starkweather's *Mergers in the Making* offers a
penetrating study of merger activity in this industry. He quotes
American Hospital Association sources in 1969 as saying that a
merger between two hospitals could expect to produce a 10 percent savings in operating costs.[22] He then demonstrates how
operating costs may not be affected at all. Despite this, very large
multi-hospital systems have been built—most notably Hospital
Corporation of America (HCA) and Humana.

Simply increasing market share in a growing market
had a lot to do with this activity, particularly given very sup-
portive government subsidization. There was also the argument
that for-profit hospitals could be run more efficiently, and the
more hospitals in a system, the more economies of scale that
could be reached in such areas as purchasing, inventory, and
expensive shared technologies. This logic has not held up to
intense financial scrutiny. Hospitals have moved from being profit
centers to cost centers in less than 10 years.

Driving this dramatic shift has been a basic redefinition
of the entire industry. Initially, hospitals were the focal point of
an industry created around illness. As government support diminished and the concern about cost containment and prevention
increased, the industry became concerned with promoting health.
Consequently, the most recent wave of healthcare mergers and
acquisitions have been away from hospitals. Backward and forward integration is now occurring to capture value-added services that previously escaped hospitals. Healthcare firms are
caught in an industry transformation which will continue for
some time.

Overall, the patterns of mergers and acquisitions are
hard to interpret and forecast. Merger-acquisition activity is becoming much more complex and is driven by a greater number
of forces than ever before. As the U.S. economy continues to

mature in some industries, and as new ones emerge, the opportunity to strategically reposition the firm through mergers and acquisitions and respond to industry-wide dynamics is obviously attractive.

Firm-Specific Forces

While we can explain much of the activity at industry and general economic levels, the motivations for merging and acquiring at the individual firm level are more diverse and not always justifiable. There is, again, little argument that some activity is due to firms having no other constructive use for earnings—the so-called "idle cash" motive. It is hard to imagine a CEO taking such a proposal to a board of directors without having his management ability questioned.

Granted, a good staff analysis can do wonders in justifying a proposal, but a proposed acquisition must fit a corporate strategic plan and the firm's vision of the future for it to be successful. Faulty assumptions in the strategic planning process may lead management to the wrong conclusions about what types of candidates may be attractive, and Chapter 4 contains arguments for a strong link between strategic planning and the merger-acquisition process. On the other hand, trying to put excess cash to work as an end may explain why so many mergers and acquisitions go sour.

Including "idle cash," we believe that eight reasons are used to justify mergers and acquisitions. As the discussion below points out, some of these reasons also are shaky foundations for building a multimillion-dollar acquisition. They are as follows:

1. Risk reduction and diversification
2. Competitive reaction
3. Perception of underutilized or undervalued assets
4. Anticipated synergies in markets, finances, operations, or human resources
5. Legal and tax benefits
6. Access to new technologies or processes
7. Ego—emotional or psychological motivations.

Risk Reduction and Diversification

The second wave's push for vertical integration was, in some respects, an effort by firms not only to control their costs but also their sources of supply and markets. In this sense, it was an effort to reduce risks by internalizing potential external sources of disruption. When risk diversification is considered a motivation, the most typical example is found in the third wave of conglomeration. The theory runs something like this: Firms can guarantee investors a certain level of financial performance by acquiring other firms that have countercyclical growth and performance patterns. When one industry is down, the other is up and the two help offset each other.

Stability in earnings, as it turns out, is more desirable from the perspective of the conglomerate itself than that of institutional investors. Investors can just as easily diversify risks in their own portfolios; firms do not need to do it for them. It drags their overall performance down to an average return that can be beat through portfolio management by investors.

Nonetheless, there are occasions when diversifying a portfolio of businesses does make sense from a risk perspective. Consider, for example, the dependence of a firm on one or two key products for a significant portion of its earnings. Diversification through acquisition of another business would be well justified in such a case, particularly when the new products are in their early stages or in other more promising industries with greater growth potential.

The danger, of course, is that two theoretically distinct businesses or industries are, in fact, correlated. As the conglomerates found, when the economy starts seriously sneezing, all their businesses can catch colds. For them, the integral dependencies among their businesses on cash flow and debt-carrying capacity causes overall corporate performance to quickly falter. Still, balancing a portfolio of businesses to stabilize cash flows and reduce dependencies on too few products is reasonable.

Competitive Reaction

One of the most understandable but dangerous motivations for a merger or acquisition is being forced into one for competitive reasons. Ideally, a firm will engage in proactive, not reactive merger-acquisition activity. By *proactive* we mean that the firm has a long-term corporate strategy guiding it, and a merger or acquisition becomes a means for executing it. In the reactive situation, the firm views a merger or acquisition as an end, not a means. It merges or acquires because its management thinks at the time it must, not because it necessarily wants or is prepared to do so. In general, we believe defensive acquisitions are disruptive. They often are made at greater cost and when the acquiring firm is unprepared for it.

As later chapters will illustrate, the case of Allied-Signal is an excellent example of a proactive merger posture. However, some regional bank mergers are being done for defensive reasons. We believe the probability and costs of success will be very different as a result. In the Allied-Signal case, a guiding vision of how the two firms would join forces was present. In some bank mergers, however, a guiding vision was not present. One acquiring bank we studied was as puzzled about what to do next as the bank it acquired. There is a digestive period in both proactive and reactive cases, but one is relatively short and anticipated, while the other may be protracted and unnecessarily disruptive.

As we mentioned in our discussion of the fourth wave, entire industries are being restructured and transformed. Such activity can be very constructive or very destructive. When you are in top management at one of these firms and observe your industry's convulsions, it is extremely difficult to maintain a statesmanlike vision. Managements able to maintain a broad perspective and relative detachment serve their firms well. On the other hand, the momentum that becomes built in an industry can create a "me too" hysteria which is unmanageable. Merging and acquiring firms guided by seasoned professionals will fare better than others.

Restructuring in response to deregulation or major technological change does create very real opportunities for the well-organized, aggressively acquisitive firm. Frank Lorenzo at Texas Air, for example, has successfully parlayed a small Texas carrier into a major airline through acquisitions of Continental and Eastern. Is he done? Likely not, although the time, effort, and expense of salvaging Eastern will keep him occupied for some time. On the other hand, Larry Martin, Frontier Airlines's President and a Peoples Express veteran, noted in a March 31, 1986 *Fortune* article: "We saw the industry shaking down and coalescing.... We felt we had to do something or be left behind." Frontier placed an impossible burden on Peoples, fatally damaging its credibility and survival. Necessary? Most likely they gave a best effort in a rapidly changing industry, but getting caught off-balance in a reactive posture when others are moving proactively definitely is not comfortable nor advisable.

Underutilized and Undervalued Assets

The soft stock market of the early 1980s, coupled with the availability of debt and idle cash reserves, has made this motivation decisive in the hostile takeovers of the past decade. Raiders like Carl Ichan, T. Boone Pickens, Irwin Jacobs, and hostile takeover artists like Ronald Perelman of Pantry Pride recognize a simple fact: Some firms are worth more broken up than whole. They argue that these firms are not serving stockholders and the economy. They are justified in making money on the takeovers of these firms because of the benefit they generate for stockholders. In theory, they do have a point. In practice, we question the means used to accomplish their objectives. Burdening a firm with excessive debt, disrupting communities and suppliers, and a-bruptly displacing thousands of employees is not desirable. It can at least be done more effectively. Since this book is about the constructive and collaborative use of mergers and acquisitions, we will not say much more about hostile takeovers. The excesses, in our opinion, are greater than any purely economic gain, and have begun to make hostile takeovers increasingly difficult.[24]

The Search for Synergy

As a concept, *synergy* is one of the most alluring and potent reasons for mergers and acquisitions. In reality, firms have often found synergy illusive. Assumptions made about synergy frequently have an unpleasant way of being tested in practice only after the merger or acquisition. Synergy is a systems theory concept which, in current merger-acquisition practice, assumes that the collective benefits to be gained by joining forces is greater than the separate existence of the two firms.

The idea that synergies exist between two firms is, in a sense, related to the underutilized-undervalued assets reason above. The assumption is made in the merger-acquisition process that those assets can be better utilized after the two firms join. Selling those assets off in whole or part is not necessarily a requirement. In the Allied-Signal merger, however, the spinning-out of the less attractive, poorer-fitting businesses of both firms into a whole new corporation, Henley Group, became one way of isolating high synergy and low synergy parts of both firms.

Synergies can exist in marketing, finances, operations, and human resources. For example, marketing synergies exist when one sales force can sell both firms' products. However, as Black & Decker initially found out with its acquisition of GE's small appliance division, it may be difficult to quickly merge sales forces. Customers for tools and appliances are different. The requirement that GE's name would be phased out over three years also made a very risky name brand shift necessary. A brand name shift of this magnitude had never before been accomplished. Black & Decker's product redesign and extensive marketing campaign is paying off.[25] On the other hand, Exxon Office Equipment's failure to cross-train the three sales forces that were part of the three firms it acquired made it impossible to create marketing synergies.

Financial synergies also are very attractive. Consider, for example, the aborted 1985 merger of American Hospital Supply and Hospital Corporation of America. HCA was heavily leveraged due to its past hospital acquisitions, while AHS's debt-to-capital ratio was less than half HCA's. The combined firm would have lowered HCA's ratio, thus allowing it to assume even more debt and quicken the pace of its acquisition activity. Financial synergy, even when manufactured through creative accounting, was also the driving force behind conglomeration.

Operational synergies also are possible when one firm's existing plant capacity can be utilized to produce the other firm's products. Another possibility is when technological innovations of one firm can be used to improve the other firm's products, which may have applications in the innovating firm's own operations. The combination of Sperry with Burroughs, which created the computer industry's second largest firm, UNISYS, has left some industry experts trying to figure out what was to be

operationally gained. The two firms are technically and structurally different, yet redundant in other business aspects. Major
changes are necessary to sort out the areas of operational synergy
over the next months.

Human resource synergies are less frequently cited but
are very important in some high technology industries experiencing chronic labor shortages. Consider two firms, each pos-
sessing engineering talent the other needs. They can choose to
raid each other's talent or merge to better pool that talent. In
some industries, such as hazardous waste management, the
availability of technical personnel is a governing factor on growth,
and mergers become one way to continue growing rapidly.

The design of the merger-acquisition process has inherent obstacles built into it, as noted in the next chapter. These
obstacles make it very difficult for the players involved in that
process to validate assumptions they make about synergies. For
example, premature contact with the other firm can bid up its
stock price. Synergy, then, is often something to be discovered
and verified after the firms act. Synergies are not automatic. They
must be nurtured, sometimes at great expense, before they are
realized.

Legal and Tax Benefits

In explaining the benefits of buying another firm because of its
attractive tax-loss carry-forwards, we were once confronted by a
CEO who flatly rejected the idea. His point was perhaps that he
would have to live with the reasons for those losses long after
the tax advantages were used up. Mergers and acquisitions for
legal and tax advantages do occur, however, thanks to the complexity of the tax laws and creativity of financial executives and
accountants. For example, the favorable tax treatments for leveraged buy-outs (LBOs) using employee stock ownership plans
(ESOPs) was a major impetus for this type of buyout.

On the other hand, there also are cases where mergers
and acquisitions were aborted due to legal issues. Some firms
have a simple ground rule that they will not buy any firm in a
regulated industry. Many foreign firms also will quickly shy away
from buying interests in U.S. firms with defense contracts.

While a firm obviously must take advantage of all possible benefits, we are conservative when it comes to mergers and acquisitions done exclusively for those reasons. Consider, for example, the aborted acquisition by Ryder Trucks of Frank B. Hall Insurance. Davidson in *Mega-Mergers* cites this example of how very attractive tax credits for rapid depreciation of trucks and similar equipment could make a deal look attractive. What does insurance have to do with the truck rental business? Not much. How long would the merger last? Likely long enough for the tax credits to be used up.

　　　Such examples illustrate how situational the definition of "success" in a merger or acquisition can be. In general, there should be compelling business reasons related to a business's operations or products and services which make it an attractive candidate. As the SEC, Federal Reserve, and Congress continue to take a close, hard look at mergers and acquisitions, the number of marginal deals done strictly to take advantage of legal and tax benefits will diminish. Restrictions on the use of junk bonds, for example, will make a deal's sound financial rationale even more crucial.

Access to New Technologies and Processes

As we noted in the discussion of the current wave of activity, the pace of technological change for many firms is so great that their internal R&D efforts simply cannot keep up. These firms can gain new technologies quicker by buying them. The acquired firms are frequently small entrepreneurial companies built around a single product or service. In some cases they can be much larger—for example, multibillion dollar firms like Hughes and EDS which GM bought.

　　　Despite the inherent difficulties when two very different cultures meet, buying technology is still one of the best and most compelling reasons for mergers and acquisitions. It can revive mature firms and help others out of declining industries into entirely new ones.

Ego—Emotional and Psychological Reasons

Subsequent chapters will deal with this reason in greater detail, but it is definitely worth noting here that psychological and interpersonal dynamics aspects of mergers and acquisitions have not received enough attention. A CEO's desire to master an industry and create an empire, beat an arch rival to a potential acquisition, and get frequent media attention always are present and, in some cases, are major factors. Two CEOs who leapt before thinking has happened more than once. "Gut feel" and a warm personal interaction between two CEOs definitely are not advocated as the only foundation for a merger or acquisition. Both are useful, even necessary. When feel and friendship prove unjustified, however, the respective staffs and teams are then left to either make a questionable deal work, or confront their respective CEOs, who must then explain to each other why they "can't get together" after all.

Similarly, we also stress the impact of undermanaged emotional and psychological forces active within the core group of internal players guiding the merger-acquisition process. The "thrill of the chase" is powerful and capable of capturing a group. The process's intensity also can quickly create "group think," leading to the group's isolation from other players and staff, many of whom will have to later live with the consequences of the group's work.

A merger or acquisition's excitement is stimulating and can bring out the best in management. We have found that excitement contagious as consultants and researchers. But unchecked and undermanaged emotional and psychological dynamics can distort the process in unconstructive ways. Wanting to buy a company to satisfy egos would be fine if the stakes were often not so high. Too many employees and staff have careers, and investors have money, at risk to approach a merger or acquisition irrationally and unprofessionally.

Chapters 4 and 5 examine the merger-acquisition process in greater detail, including how many of these firm-specific forces come to affect it. The forces driving merger-acquisition activity may change over time and are diverse, but they are compelling. Firms continue to struggle out of their past poorly conceived diversification moves, confront maturing industries and products, and grapple with rapid technological change and new competitive dynamics. New motives may emerge over time, but mergers and acquisitions are a fact of today's business life, and understanding how to make them work is essential.

3

LAYING
THE FOUNDATION:
THE THREE PILLARS
OF SUCCESS

Because the present number of mergers and acquisitions is so high and because they are so important in reshaping firms and entire industries, it is necessary to increase our understanding of what contributes to their success or failure. The amount of empirical research about success and failure factors is growing slowly. Much of this writing is based on single case studies of firms or stories and prescriptive anecdotes having a folklore-like quality—"everyone knows you can't do it like that." The popular business press—*Wall Street Journal, Fortune, Business Week, Forbes,* and so on—and a handful of specialized journals, such as *Mergers & Acquisitions,* give the best running accounts of activity and often do try to draw conclusions and note major trends. The lack of rigorous research likely will resolve itself in the future as considerable interest among business researchers gets translated into published research.

On the other hand, a lot of the folklore does have value, although it often is generalized for too many situations. For example, Peter Drucker's early sayings (see our annotated bibliography) still had merit for at least one executive we met. As president of a small engineering consulting firm, this person said he had managed to violate just about every one of Drucker's admonitions. He unfortunately read them *after* his firm was sold out from under him following his own aborted leveraged buyout effort.

In this chapter we take one of the richest pieces of Wall Street folklore and add substance to it. Some academic researchers also have described aspects of it, yet we turned up similar versions in Salomon Bros. We call this model "The Three Pillars of Success."

The Three Pillars of Success

The three pillars model essentially is a refined version of the old "three-legged stool" argument. A stool is stable and sound when it has at least three legs or pillars. Any fewer, and it becomes unstable and collapses. Similarly, a merger or acquisition's success rests upon its three pillars: financial fit, business fit, and organizational fit. Success is contingent on a good fit in *each* of these areas. Let us state this argument even more strongly:

A weakness in one pillar poses serious, even fatal, consequences for the other two. Weakness in two of these pillars is, with rare exception, unavoidably fatal. All three are necessary, and none is in itself sufficient to make a deal succeed.

There are some obvious soft spots in the model which limit its reliability for explaining success. Indeed, we spend the next two chapters exploring how the quality of the *process*—the way a deal is conceived and executed—is an equally important determinant. Much of this book is dedicated to the idea that process issues are not adequately appreciated and go undermanaged as a result.

The usefulness of the three pillars model also depends on your definition of success. The motives driving a specific deal determine what constitutes success. This is an important point, since much of the empirical research on mergers and acquisitions has relied on financial measures of performance to judge success. While a CEO obviously would prefer a deal with swift, significant financial payoffs, we found many instances of deals cut for other reasons. Financial success was often secondary, at least in the short run.

In this book we use a model case of two firms joining forces to realize a greater value than either could on its own. A raider's hostile takeover is not our concern, as we stated previously. There also are many firms such as Wesray and Metromedia routinely buying and selling companies for profit, with little intention of building them into a lasting, well-integrated giant such as Allied-Signal. Traders like Wesray's Bill Simon and Metromedia's John Kluge use mergers and acquisitions to take control of assets, use them, and sell them off at a profit.[1] A real distinction should therefore be made between deals done to acquire assets and those acquiring and mobilizing human resources to use those assets. As Daryl Conner, an Atlanta change management consultant, said: "Are you buying bodies or souls?"

When only assets such as a new plant or patents are sought, financial fit considerations will dominate a deal more than the other two pillars. Success in these situations is defined as profit on the subsequent resale of the business. Similarly, the success of GM's acquisition of Ross Perot's EDS eventually will be determined by organizational fit considerations, not financial ones. Roger Smith's decision to acquire EDS was partially motivated by his desire to change GM's culture and management style, not just to improve GM's information systems.[2] Price was not as important in this case. Put more directly:

> **One of the three pillars can very well drive the deal; bias can easily exist among the three pillars. A weakness in one pillar may be acceptable in order to take advantage of another strong one. They need not be— and most typically are not—equally important to the acquiring firm.**

Slack also exists in the three pillars' relationship. It may take time before the effects of a weak pillar are felt by the others. Using the foundation analogy, one weak pillar may be placing strain on the other two, but weakness itself is not fatal. Weaknesses can be overcome in some cases, but at high cost and only with time. In other cases, cracks may run so deep that they can never be overcome. Nor does a very strong pillar mean that it can carry the stress of the others. For instance, throwing more money at later problems is a common practice, but more money

BUSINESS FIT

Short-Term Objective — Realize hypothesized synergies within acceptable timeframe and costs.

Long-Term Objective — Strengthen the firm's competitive advantage either within a new or established market, consistent with its strategic plan and leader's vision.

Major Tasks
1. Assess competitive strengths and weaknesses;
2. Define synergies (making explicit assumptions where necessary)
3. Develop tentative plans for realizing synergies within defined time and cost parameters
4. Implement plans

Major Issues
1. Accuracy of assessments
2. Validity of and opportunities to test assumptions
3. Potential for setbacks or failure to realize synergies due to financial and organizational fit reasons

FINANCIAL FIT

Short-Term Objective — Meet financial demands, terms and conditions, while providing sufficient capital for achieving business and organizational fit during transition.

Long-Term Objective — Improve the firm's overall financial performance, including building its capacity for subsequent growth via mergers-acquisitions.

Major Tasks
1. Value the deal (making explicit assumptions where necessary)
2. Secure sufficient capital (including back-up)
3. Negotiate price, terms and conditions that can be met
4. Allocate sufficient transition funds
5. Develop and implement long-term financial plan for improving performance

Major Issues
1. Validity of valuation
2. Ability to negotiate acceptable price, terms/conditions
3. Stability of performance during transition
4. Validity of assumptions made
5. Adequacy of resources devoted to achieving business and organizational fit

ORGANIZATIONAL FIT

Short-Term Objective — Create and deploy sufficient transition management capacity to achieve desired stability while designing integration strategies.

Long-Term Objective — Achieve desired degree of integration to achieve business and financial fit within acceptable timeframe and costs.

Major Tasks
1. Define and negotiate acquiring firm's role
2. Control governing conditions
3. Establish transition structure and processes
4. Develop and implement an integration plan, keeping in mind role and ground rules

Major Issues
1. Clarity and accuracy of acquiring firm's role
2. Ability to control governing conditions
3. Impact of "upstream" assumptions as they become tested
4. Ability to stabilize situation long enough to implement integration strategies
5. Adequacy of resources devoted to transition

Figure 3-1 The three pillars: objectives, tasks, and major issues.

may not cure those ills. Successful firms understand the three pillars' relative strengths in a deal, actively work to strengthen a weak one, and avoid deals with deeply flawed pillars they cannot correct.

In the following pages, each of the pillars is examined in detail and applied to some recent mergers and acquisitions. Figure 3-1 summarizes the objectives, tasks, and major issues associated with each of them.

Financial Fit

In the short term, financial fit is concerned with the price paid, the terms or conditions agreed upon, and the financial capacity of either or both firms that can be devoted to making the deal successful. High fit exists when the price is "affordable"—meaning the firm can service debt from cash flows, the terms and conditions are acceptable to both firms, and there is sufficient financial capacity for initiatives to be attempted during the integration stage.

In the long term, high financial fit means that the combined firms' financial performance meets the expectations of not just management but also external investors. The objective is not to just digest the acquired firm but to see its financial performance improve over historic levels. In the most ideal long-term situation, both firms would be performing better than before.

In reality it may be that one firm's performance is sacrificed to improve the overall performance of the combination. For example, a firm may have been acquired because it was a cash flow generator—a "cash cow" according to Boston Consulting Group. The cash cow would fuel other businesses, even though its own long-term performance eventually could deteriorate.

Poor short-term fit exists when the price paid is so high that the deal seriously damages the viability of one or both firms. It also means the terms and conditions are so restrictive that important advantages and opportunities must be foregone, and financial capacity is so constrained that planned investments can not be made. In the long term, poor fit translates into financial performance below expectations—even the lowered financial performance of the acquiring firm and combination as a whole.

It is beyond the scope of this book to deal with the intricate, even arcane, practice of valuing a merger or acquisition. There are sophisticated methods and models available, and a growing menu of computer software is devoted to the task. Our own observations and readings also confirm that much pricing strategy is not that sophisticated. While "ball park" values can be derived, the popular business press is full of stories of firms that overpriced an acquisition, and of the stock market turning "thumbs-down" on the consequences. Several oil company mergers, like Occidental's 1982 $4 billion acquisition of Cities Service, have resulted in sales of many desirable assets in both firms and layoffs of thousands of Cities Service's employees to service debt.[3] Figure 3-2 illustrates some of this subsequent activity for Occidental and Cities Service.

Incorrect assumptions about future financial performance, and incomplete or incorrect data, often are faulted in costly deals. But we also feel that the psychology of mergers and acquisitions should be blamed, too. Later chapters discuss the "thrill-of-the-chase" syndrome where making the deal at any cost dominates the process. Egos and self-esteem are very real factors—and not just of the acquiring firm's CEO, but also of external players who are supposed to be more objective. Investment bankers, for example, have been increasingly criticized for this, as the next chapter points out.

Good judgment can be colored by the process's powerful psychological dynamics, and a seasoned team and CEO will keep these dynamics in check by setting clear and firm pricing ground rules. The most common one we have encountered is setting a price range and strictly adhering to it. Another rule we like is "It's going to cost more than you think." The idea here is caution by preparing for contingencies which will surely surface. Allied-Signal's Ed Hennessy's rule is to negotiate price and terms, but not so aggressively that it damages future relations. Hennessy stresses knowing what you can afford. There is little room for fantasy, and we want to stress this point:

You must have timely, reliable data, both about the other firm and your own. There should be no assumption so critical to success that it determines success or

Selling Assets to Raise Cash

Occidental Assets Sold

Feb. 1, 1982. An agreement in principle reached to sell Occidental Minerals to Nerco Inc. of Portland, Ore.

Dec. 31, 1982. Best Products, a fertilizer concern, sold to the J. R. Simplot Company, of Boise, Idaho.

Jan. 3, 1983. Zoecon Corp. sold to Sandoz U.S. Ltd.

Jan 20, 1983. A chemical joint venture with ENI, the Italian state energy group, terminated. This raised $176 million cash, but resulted in an $85 million write off in the 1982 fourth quarter.

Cities Service Assets Sold

Sept. 23, 1983. Industrial chemical division, which mines copper, zinc and other industrial chemicals, sold to Tennessee Chemical.

Nov. 13, 1982. Cities Service Gas Company sold to Northwest Energy Company, of Salt Lake City, for $335 million in cash and a transfer of $145 million in debt.

Nov. 16, 1982. Fesco plastics and film division sold to GDI Newco, of Chester N.Y.

Nov. 24, 1982. Tulsa office tower sold to the Boulder Development Corporation.

Nov. 29, 1982. Three supertankers sold to Ceres Hellenic Shipping.

Dec. 2, 1982. Miami Copper sold to Newmont Mining for $75 million in cash.

Dec. 3, 1982. Wyoming Dry Folk coal properties sold to Phillips Petroleum.

Jan. 6, 1983. Texaco-Cities Service Pipeline joint ventures sold a 12-inch oil pipeline, running from Oklahoma to Chicago, to the Williams Pipe Line Company, of Tulsa, Okla.

Figure 3-2 A costly merger for Occidental. (Source: *New York Times*, November 12, 1983.)

49

failure, and any assumptions made need to be tested as quickly as possible.

More will be said about these points in later chapters. While seemingly straightforward, the common sense expressed in such statements is often violated in practice. The potential for a strong business fit will frequently dominate financial considerations, and force the firm to pay more than what is comfortable. Robert Campeau's $4.5 billion acquisition of Allied Stores in October 1986 proved to be so pricey and highly leveraged that several attractive divisions and 35 percent of Campeau's company were sold to handle the deal.[4]

In other cases, an opportunity passes across the screen that simply cannot be passed up, even though from a financial perspective the timing is terrible. The firm may be in the middle of a major capital investment program, and incurring more debt is the last thing it needs. It may also be provoked into an acquisition for defensive reasons. No better example can be found than Peoples Express's ill-fated purchase of Frontier Airlines in 1986. Don Burr's calculus remains a mystery. A financially weak airline buying another financially weak airline does not produce a financially sound airline.[5]

Just as fatal, but slower in damaging success, are the deal's terms and conditions. Three cases illustrate this premise. First, the use of large debt doses to finance a leveraged buyout (LBO) can cause difficulty when the interest on that debt cannot be paid. For example, business downturns in the glass container business in mid-1985 made the LBO of Thatcher Glass from Dart & Kraft precarious—even fatal—in the sense that the company had to be later sold to another company for a third of its LBO value.[6]

Second, Turner Broadcasting's drawn-out, but eventually successful, purchase of MGM-United Artists is a classic study in creative financing. Ted Turner wanted MGM's film library—a nice complement to his television business—and was prepared to sell off other MGM businesses in order to keep that piece. What resulted was a massive "junk bond" debt provided through Drexel Burnham Lambert, and a complex set of terms and conditions which could cost Turner control of his company if business sours. United Artist's Kirk Kerkorian could have gained control if Turner failed to service the debt. As the July 7, 1986 *Fortune* article on the deal describes, new stock is issued to Kerkorian on the following basis:

> ... if the market price of the common stock falls below $15 a share, those dividends of common stock must be enriched with additional shares of preferred. In that circumstance the number of both types of stock could multiply like crazed amoebas. Holders of preferred shares could receive not only common but also more preferred, entitling them to more of both kinds of stock, and so on. The potential dilution is virtually limitless.[7]

Figure 3-3 illustrates the deal's complexity and layers of contingencies used to make it work. How will this specific deal work out? It is hard to say as we finish this book. Turner did recognize the threat, and in 1987 he gave up some control to a pool of investors to restructure the debt and thus kill the amoebas. Whether it works or not is still uncertain. It is educational to watch Turner shrewdly maneuver in tight financial space, to say the least.

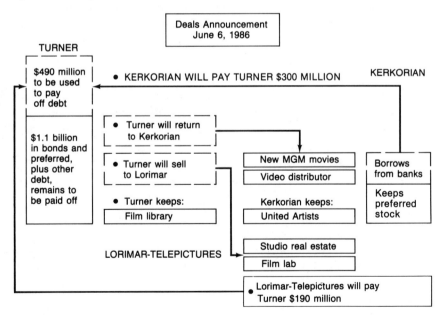

Figure 3-3 How Turner got into and out of the movie business. (Source: *Fortune*, July 7, 1986, p. 30.)

The Turner Broadcasting–MGM-United Artists deal is only one example of many such deals. To Ted Turner's credit, he did get what he wanted, and the creativity involved in assembling it is to be admired like fine art. On the other hand, when the provisions of a deal make its long-term success uncertain, then the concept of financial fit is stretched to the limits. The following stresses this point:

> **High debt levels may mean that additional capital investment cannot occur, other valuable assets must be sold, and rather than help build the acquiring firm's momentum in a dynamic market, an acquisition may actually impede it by overcommitting its resources.**

Finally, as an example of a raider at work, Carl Icahn's acquisition of TWA in a bidding war with Frank Lorenzo provides a nice example of how conditions can haunt you. Icahn, in characteristic raider style, had planned on buying TWA and selling off profitable assets like its reservation system. However, it quickly became clear that the conditions set by lenders and unions would prevent those sales. Carl Icahn was trapped running an airline in serious financial condition.[8]

Financial fit is important because money is the glue that holds a deal together. Financial problems will seriously—most often fatally—affect the quality of business fit and organizational fit. Business fit will be damaged when the synergies or benefits are not allowed to materialize because of underinvestment afterwards. Similarly, organizational fit will be jeopardized when there is insufficient capital to finance the implementation of major changes, or when layoffs of valued employees become necessary to cut costs.

Business Fit

Business fit recently has received more attention from researchers and business media primarily because it raises questions about firms' poor performance resulting from their past diversification efforts. There is a growing realization that just because a deal can be executed financially does not mean that it makes sense to do so. As Morgan Stanley's Managing Director Judson Reis said in a 1982 *Mergers & Acquisitions* article, "We're going to see more 'mergers of equals'—companies getting together for strategic and business fit without premiums involved on either side."[9]

Good short-term business fit exists when both firms can realize relatively swift and cheap tangible benefits as a result of the deal. In many cases, the benefits are skewed toward one firm, particularly in hostile takeovers or "white knight" acquisitions where one firm effectively sells itself to another firm to avoid a more unpleasant takeover.

Short-term business fit really is concerned with the concept of *synergy*. Synergy may exist from either a business or functional perspective. For example, an acquired firm may get access to new markets for existing products, which benefits the acquiring firm through increased overall revenues. Functionally, the acquired firm may get access to new sources of capital or credit while the acquiring firm benefits from access to a better-trained salesforce.

In any case, the combined result is improved performance, which each firm, operating independently, would not have been able to achieve. We want to stress here an important aspect of synergies:

> **Synergies are rarely automatic. They often require sizable resource commitments to make them materialize. To justify the investment, it is essential to be realistic in assessing the potential for synergies. Both firms need accurate, honest appraisals of their respective strengths and weaknesses to best target that investment.**

In the long term, high business fit exists when the combined firm improves its strategic position and competitive advantage in its industry. The issue here is whether short-run synergies are successfully translated into greater value added at the corporate level. That is, an acquisition may be part of a leader's long-term vision for the corporation, and high business fit means that vision becomes more real.

Poor short-term business fit exists when the competitive or functional synergies either fail to materialize, or turn out to be more expensive than expected. For example, not financing the deal quickly by selling off part of the acquired firm's operations can put severe financial stress on the acquiring firm. As another example, an acquired firm's sophisticated technical sales force may have been expected to help the acquiring firm introduce a new product line, but many of its key sales managers may quit to work for a competitor after the deal is announced. Poor long-term business fit occurs when strategic repositioning or operating performance does not result, often because of weaknesses in either of the other two pillars—in financial or organizational fit.

Business fit has become a major concern for firms and business researchers trying to understand how diversification efforts succeed or fail. The trend is toward related diversification, as noted in the last chapter. Of course, exceptions can still be found. Coca-Cola's acquisition of Wine Spectrum was a move into a new industry for Coke, and it failed to meet Coke's expectations because of invalid assumptions made about marketing and distribution synergies. This and many other failed efforts lead us to the following conclusion:

You must know the business well, and assumptions about transferring competitive advantages and management strengths from one industry to another deserve deeper analysis than often given.

Whether Coke can succeed with Columbia Pictures and its other media acquisitions still is not clear. Coke's financial return expectations may mean that financial fit, more than business fit, will determine whether they work.[10]

Overall, the retreat continues from unrelated diversification. Driven by the desire to boost overall financial performance measures—done largely to increase the stock's value on Wall Street—Dart Industries and Kraft Inc. merged in 1980 to form Dart & Kraft. Dart & Kraft now has followed Allied-Signal's lead by spinning off less attractive businesses. One part contains the fastest growing businesses (Kraft) and the other those businesses with poorer fit.[11] Here is a case of a merger initially done because of perceived financial benefits. Short-term financial synergies motivated the deal, but it came apart when longer-term business fit advantages failed to materialize.

As another case, the aborted HCA-American Hospital Supply merger in mid-1985 illustrates how HCA's short-term financial benefits could not overcome clearly perceived negative business fit consequences for American Hospital Supply—primarily the wrath of other major customers competing with HCA.[12]

The opposite result occurred when SantaFe Healthcare, a Florida healthcare organization, acquired from California-based NME, one of the largest HMOs (Health Maintenance Organizations) in the country, AV-MED in Miami. SantaFe's not-for-profit status had a positive and immediate marketing and financial impact on AV-MED, and AV-MED's more liquid asset structure had a positive impact on SantaFe's balance sheet. Just as important, SantaFe also made better business sense as owner of AV-MED, since AV-MED and NME's hospitals were "cannibalizing" each other in the market. They actually had "negative synergy." SantaFe's hospitals did not compete in AV-MED's markets, thus eliminating the problem and boosting performance even further. Financial and business fit was much easier to achieve.

Although there are many other examples of firms which could strategically benefit from buying new technology, some efforts, like Gould's entry into high technology, end up being awkward and uncomfortable. IBM's acquisition of a 30 percent stake in MCI in June 1985 is another such case. MCI immediately benefited by getting access to IBM's resources and talents, but IBM strategically benefited by gaining access to a major related industry.[13] Financial fit was not an issue due to IBM's resources. The stock market immediately bid up both stocks on the announcement, unlike the HCA-American Hospital Supply merger announcement which caused the price of both stocks to immediately fall. Judgment about fit often comes swiftly.

Nonetheless, the IBM-MCI alliance is an excellent example of sound long-term business fit with strategic benefits. However, IBM's sheer size and bureaucratic structure can spell problems for a smaller entrepreneurial firm, and issues of organizational fit therefore are present.

Another deal we particularly like, despite a later unpleasant insider trading scandal, is GE Commercial Credit's 80 percent purchase of Kidder, Peabody, the investment banking firm. Discussing the possibilities with GE, Kidder, Peabody saw

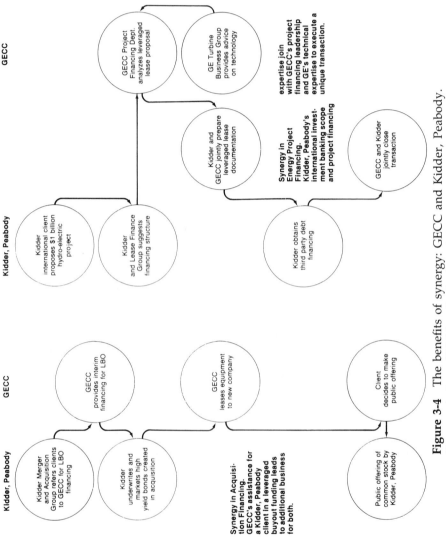

Figure 3-4 The benefits of synergy: GECC and Kidder, Peabody. (By permission of Kidder, Peabody, 1987.)

clear and immediate financial benefits of scale, since Kidder needed access to more capital to do larger deals. However, other strategic benefits were equally real. Figure 3-4 demonstrates what we think are classic qualities of good business fit by using two scenarios to illustrate how the two firms can relate. From personal experience with Kidder-GE for a client, the combination of companies makes sense.

In general, the potential for long-term strategic business fit is the best argument for executing a deal. Fine-tuning and balancing a business portfolio by buying or selling a business, or buying another firm to expand geographical scope remain worthwhile short-term reasons for mergers and acquisitions. However, buying and selling businesses to manipulate financial performance is short-sighted. In those industries undergoing truly fundamental change, short-term performance manipulation via acquisition is perhaps little more than rearranging the deck chairs on the Titanic.

Given the increasing damage of global competition and the need for firms to reposition themselves in mature and declining industries, mergers and acquisitions serving a firm's long-term vision make the most sense. Major mergers and acquisitions driven by truly strategic motivations may stretch the firm financially. Firms in declining industries often are not the most financially sound. Organizational fit issues may also be created because the firms may be entering alien industries and businesses. These are not reasons to avoid mergers and acquisitions—they are reasons to better manage them.

Organizational Fit

Business fit has received much attention lately, but the attention given to organizational fit issues has been overwhelming. Martin Sikora, Editor of *Mergers & Acquisitions*, recently said in a presentation that

> The risks associated with mismatches in business styles and cultures are high, and those risks increase when companies make acquisitions in new business areas; a classic example being when a company in a basic industry with low to

moderate levels of technology takes over a high technology firm.

Jim Allwin, the Managing Director of Mergers and Acquisitions for Morgan Stanley, said when we asked about the three pillars model in an interview,

> With few exceptions, all three corners (pillars) of that analytical triangle have to be in place. The most unsuccessful mergers are ones that don't pay attention to the management issues . . . (T)here is no substitute for really getting to know the people who run the organizations and understanding the human issues involved in managing the new organization.

Organizational fit is how well the two firms can be integrated to optimize their financial and business fit. Fit in those areas are most likely only hypothetical at the deal's closing. They will stay that way without organizational fit. Either the "management issues" that Allwin talks about are minimal, or, if they are substantial, they must be actively managed and overcome in the transition and integration stages of the process.

Specific areas between firms in which sufficient organizational fit is needed include their (1) structural designs, (2) major processes and operating systems, (3) human resources (managerial and line), and (4) cultures. How much organizational integration is needed varies as the financial and business characteristics of the respective firms vary. We want to stress this point:

Initiatives to build organizational fit should go only to the point where the desired level of integration is achieved to realize financial and business fit potential. Going beyond that point is not only unnecessary, but possibly damaging.

As a general rule, the greater the differences between the two firms in the areas just mentioned, the greater the difficulty encountered in achieving the desired level of integration. The greater the differences, the more difficult it will be to realize business synergies which ultimately show up in financial performance. It takes time, tremendous resources and effort, and perhaps most of all, careful thought to overcome big differences. Chapter 8 focuses exclusively upon integration issues and strategies.

From a short-term perspective, differences should ideally not be so great that they jeopardize the transition stage. If differences are so great that the transition stage is damaged, longer-term integration issues can become moot. A botched transition can severely damage potential long-term success. For example, key managers could leave and business performance deteriorate to a point that it never recovers. The two firms' cultures could be so different that open communication and mutual trust and understanding between the involved managers is prevented in the transition process. They must be able to quickly create a shared appreciation of the issues and choices confronting them, and they must build a process for solving problems in an orderly way. Common ground needs to be quickly established to bridge the two firms—the creation of a temporary organizational structure, in a sense. Chapter 7 contains a discussion of this temporary structure concept as an aid in managing the transition.

THE IMPACT OF SIZE AND STRUCTURAL DIFFERENCES.   Differences in the two firms' overall sizes have been found to be strongly related to merger and acquisition failure rates. Size differences are, of course, only indicative of other factors like management style differences which cause communication and coordination difficulties. However, as an indicator the results are telling. For example, one study found that 84 percent of the "failures" involved situations in which the acquired firm's sales volume was less than 2 percent of the parent firm's sales at the acquisition.[14]

Case studies abound. Schlumberger's acquisition of Fairchild Camera & Instrument quickly submerged Fairchild and sparked an exodus of top management. Former Fairchild managers went on to spawn a host of other successful, entrepreneurial Silicon Valley start-ups. Similarly, Exxon's foray into office systems through the acquisition of three small firms resulted in "squashing" the three small firms, and very visible failure of its office systems group in 1984.[15] Reliance Electric was eventually bought from Exxon by its management in early 1987.

On the other hand, "lighter touches" can lead to success, despite size differences. Kraft's acquisition of tiny Celestial Seasoning, the herbal tea maker based in Boulder, Colorado provides an example. Kraft apparently understands that the acquired company's independence will be a key element in its continued success and is prepared to keep its distance.[16] Time will tell. In general, we want to stress the following:

> **The greater the size difference between firms, the lighter the touch needed by the larger firm. It is all too easy to smother and squash the very thing you sought.**

The big-small difference is being recognized as an issue by corporate development staff. As Jack Roberts, vice president-corporate development for BellSouth, told us, the company has to be careful not to burden small acquisitions and start-ups with procedures that evolved in a different environment. Some human resources and accounting practices, for example, were developed in response to close government scrutiny and rate-of-return regulation and may not be appropriate for smaller companies without regulatory oversight. Nurturing and protecting new acquisitions typically has not been part of a corporate development manager's job description. But BellSouth is quick to recognize that its success in executing a deal means little if it fails later.

Structural design differences also are a source of poor organizational fit. The two companies' respective structural configurations in numbers of management levels, patterns of reporting relationships, and relative size of their administrative staffs are specific factors which must be considered in advance. In general, big differences demand much study to explore potential consequences. Smaller differences require less study. For example, Allied's merger with Bendix was comparatively easy due to the basic similarity of their structures. Both had multidivisional designs, although Bendix's corporate staff was considerably larger than Allied's. On the other hand, Signal Corporation used a holding company structure, meaning that it had a small corporate staff with tremendous delegation down to the managers of its operating businesses. Signal's management orientation was much different than Bendix's, and their cultures also were notably different. The transition team in the Allied-Signal merger had to pay much closer attention to structural differences than the Allied-Bendix transition team did.

Another example of a merger eased by structural similarities is that of Nabisco and R.J. Reynolds in 1985. Both firms had prepared for a merger by selling off less attractive businesses in advance and by studying other firms for similarities which could be used to both firms' benefit.[17] The issue of structural compatibility leads us to conclude as follows:

> **If a firm is pursuing an aggressive acquisition strategy, it should create and maintain a structure which facilitates both integration and, conversely, shedding of its acquired and divested businesses.**

Discussing all relative merits of alternative structures is beyond the scope of this book. But it is clear that the multidivisional group structure used by firms such as RJR and Allied-Signal makes a lot of sense. Individual businesses are placed within divisions, the divisions are organized into groups, and a small but efficient corporate staff is maintained to monitor critical variables like financial performance, planning, resource allocations, and reward-incentive systems. A pure holding company structure is not as attractive since it can lack the facility to coordinate and control critical interdependencies between businesses.

PROCESS AND OPERATING SYSTEM DIFFERENCES. Structural differences inevitably mean differences in the systems and management processes used by both firms. Here again, the extent to which the two firms need to be integrated is a fundamental issue which determines just how significant the differences in systems and processes may be. Greater structural differences can be tolerated with greater autonomy between the firms. However, even if left autonomous, some minimal degree of system uniformity will be necessary for coordination and control reasons. Specifically, differences can be expected in operating or production technologies, information systems, human resource systems, and control and decision making processes.

Differences in production and operating technologies are inevitable. Even with very similar businesses, the backroom operations of two merged banks, for example, can vary dramatically in how items are processed, float is controlled, adjustments are made, and transportation networks between branches are managed. Standards also will differ in critical areas such as quality control and productivity management.

As discussed later in Chapter 8, the integration issues encountered by Bob Kirk when he arrived at Allied-Signal from LTV Aerospace proved formidable. His task of integrating Garrett and Bendix Aerospace at the appropriate technology level in each division's business could have a direct impact on the advantages of the two firms in their fiercely competitive markets.

Small emerging firms with batch or craft technologies also may find the continuous process orientation of a larger acquiring firm uncomfortable. For example, the acquisition by a large laboratory, with a highly standardized analysis process, of a small R&D-oriented laboratory recently resulted in severe conflict about how work was to be scheduled and overhead allocations made. The issues were important since using the large lab's allocation methods resulted in the R&D lab's showing losses when it had a long history of profits before the acquisition.

Differences in large firms' information systems can be particularly costly. For example, when Dome Petroleum acquired Hudson Bay Oil and Gas in 1982, the two firms' information systems differed in hardware, software, and information system design. With millions of dollars and retraining of several hundred staff at stake, the decision about which system should prevail was highly charged.[18] The designs of their information systems possibly should be different, depending upon their information needs. One firm may require on-line, real time access to a "global" or organization wide data base while the other firm requires only periodic (weekly or monthly) access to "local" data bases within each division or function. Sharing information across firms for control and planning purposes will be awkward until the two firms can agree upon system design.

Less tangible, and often more slowly recognized, are differences in management control and decision-making systems. In decision making, the degree of differences can be seen in the amount of participation encouraged and delegated by top management, and the timeliness and formality of decision making. Using a Black & Decker example, Black & Decker managers were described as using the backs of envelopes to make decisions while

GE managers would come into the same session with multicolor slides and three-piece suits. Perhaps exaggerated, but the story is an illustration of how two groups can differ in decision-making style.

Some of the most notable cases of control system misfit concern financial reporting and control systems. Exxon Office Systems, the now defunct office system venture described earlier, reportedly was performing fairly well as long as the Office Systems managers had direct access to senior Exxon management. When this access was blocked by an intervening level of Exxon planners and staff, things reportedly started to fall apart. Exxon's large company reporting and control systems eventually overwhelmed the much smaller new venture.

BellSouth had to adjust some long-established ideas in order to ensure that its expectations of new ventures and acquisitions were realistic. Rather than calling for immediate profitability, Jack Roberts adopted an alternative "three-stage performance model." In Stage 1, the new acquisition was to be evaluated by how well it achieved specific milestones such as the building of a management team or development of a business plan. In Stage 2, the firm would be evaluated in terms of its market performance, such as market penetration and share, without immediate measurement of profits. Only in Stage 3 was the firm to be held accountable for its financial performance.

Other structural design factors may shape decision making. One firm may utilize groups or teams extensively, particularly for strategic planning, while the other firm may expect an individual manager to perform the same tasks. These differences can have significant consequences. Getting left out of decisions can be demoralizing when a manager is used to playing an active role. As one manager said, "Decisions appear to fall like rain from above."

Similarly—and very importantly—strategic planning and budgeting processes also will need to be examined and then integrated. In a decentralized structure, each business can plan and set its own resource needs, but a new and powerful overseeing role played by a distant corporate staff can immobilize an acquired firm's management used to its freedom. Because these issues are always present and will always take time to sort out, we believe as follows:

Create temporary, perhaps alternate processes and systems when possible, rather than prematurely adopting one or the other firm's. Keep radical change down until organizational fit issues are better understood.

HUMAN RESOURCE DIFFERENCES.   Perhaps the most difficult differences to overcome may be in each firm's human resource systems. These issues are potentially so important that they can determine success or failure in themselves. Egon Zehnder International, the Zurich-based executive search and management consulting firm, reported, in a study with the London Business School, survey results from British executives about factors which affected the success of their acquisitions.[19] Figure 3-5 is excerpted from their study.

The results speak eloquently about organizational fit. "People problems" head the list, while issues that should be addressed in the process, a topic of the next chapter, are in the next three slots. Only 7 percent of those surveyed in their study listed poor business fit an issue. This same study also showed that 75 percent of the surveyed executives felt that the acquired firm's management was not "utilized to best advantage." Recommendations for preventing such problems are summarized in Chapters 7, 8, and 9. We offer this advice here:

People problems (problems with management, human relations, and corporate culture clash)	33%
Lack of understanding of acquired company	25%
Lack of clear purpose or plan for acquisition	14%
Inadequate financial analysis	11%
Companies not compatible; lack of synergy	7%

Figure 3-5 The five most commonly cited reasons why mergers fail. (Source: Egon Zehnder International USA, 1987.)

More than any other issue, how you handle employees in the first three to six months will set the tone for future relations between the two firms.

We have found that human resource problems, whether at the highest or lowest management levels, can be traced to differences in many of the systems used to manage those resources. Without question, pure and simple personality clashes can and do occur. Values, beliefs, and engrained patterns of behavior can differ and lead to so-called culture clashes. However, the major contributors to "people problems" are differences in the performance appraisal, career planning and development, succession planning, and reward-compensation systems used. For example, in Bendix, company cars were available to managers at a lower relative level than in Allied. Should the Bendix managers get to keep their cars or not? Even more pronounced were differences in IBM's and Rolm's management compensation packages. To IBM's credit, the stock options and sabbatical leaves traditionally offered Rolm managers were retained by IBM after it acquired most of Rolm.[20]

A merger also can open up new career paths for managers in both firms or block current ones. The historical orientation of the Black & Decker sales force fit poorly with that of the small appliance force of GE, and a great many questions were being asked by both sales forces about compensation and career paths. A year into the acquisition, the two sales forces were still operating as independent entities for several marketing reasons. Black & Decker's long-term competitive strategy may or may not require greater integration of its two sales forces. However, there is great impact on productivity, morale, and turnover for all employees in a merger or acquisition, but it is deadly for sales forces.[21]

The very composition and demographics of the two work forces can vary. For example, it soon became clear in one merger that the firm which had essentially been acquired had a superior corporate staff in terms of skills, experience, and general energy level. To fully utilize this staff, all of the corporate staff positions in the combined firm were declared open, the result being that the best of both staffs were retained, with a large representation from the acquired firm.

Whether a firm is union or nonunion also has a direct impact on employee compensation and work rules. For example, unionized construction firms are acquiring nonunion firms in the South and West to lower overall wage levels and create greater job flexibility. The union issue today is perhaps greatest in the airlines. Texas Air's ability to win wage concessions from Eastern employees will be a major factor in Frank Lorenzo's success in turning around Eastern's financial performance.

CULTURAL DIFFERENCES.   Concern about cultural differences between firms is justified, but there can be tremendous difficulties in overcoming any differences. Culture, from our perspective, is a function of the firm's values, beliefs, and symbols. These things are expressed in the organization's patterns of behavior and design. Culture is expressed and reinforced by structure, process and system design, and human resource systems. As noted in Chapters 7 and 8, cultural change takes time, is often costly, and may be unneeded. Our position is summarized by the following:

While significant to understand, cultural differences between firms can best be overcome by changing structure, processes and systems, and human resource systems.

In summary, organizational differences are inevitable. Negative consequences can be anticipated and overcome, but some effects are revealed only over time. Their impact can have serious effects unless a constructive climate and an ongoing process for resolving them are in place. Some interventions and methods for clarifying and resolving differences are presented in later chapters.

On the other hand, organizational differences can be very beneficial. New perspectives and methods can be examined and adopted by both firms, and a synthesis found which produces benefits and economies not found without the merger or acquisition. We used the example of GM's acquisition of EDS in the last chapter to illustrate Roger Smith's espoused theory for changing GM's culture by introducing the more free-wheeling style of EDS's managers into his firm. The infusion of GE's small appliance management into Black & Decker's tradition-bound structure also is creating a new culture. While there also should be compelling business fit reasons for a merger or acquisition, the desire to capitalize upon organizational fit differences to forge a new culture makes equally good sense for many organizations.

The effective integration of two firms is not without discomfort and it is often accompanied by frustration and conflict. If not managed well, it will lead to the loss of valued managers in both firms. Organizational cultures are strong and not very amenable to change in the short term. As O.D. Resources's Daryl Conner said, "Whenever there is a contest between change and culture, culture will win most of the time."

We want to demystify the concept of culture by emphasizing how cultural change can be greatly eased by changing structural design, as well as operating and human resource systems. For example, reducing the number of management levels between senior management and the acquired firm's managers can improve communication and increase their participation in key decisions. Similarly, extensive and carefully designed executive development programs can over time build a common knowledge and skill base, build teamwork and communication, and build a shared identity and sense of common fate. However, cultural change requires deep interventions that require changing the values, beliefs, assumptions, and symbols that may have contributed to both firms' success before their joining.[21] As a general rule for helping manage organizational fit, we offer the following advice:

> **Change and be prepared to be changed. The objective is to seek the very best structure, systems and processes, human resources and culture; and that may only be achieved by adopting the other firm's or creating something totally new to them both.**

Summarizing the Three Pillars

We have tried to provide a model for thinking about factors essential to success. Our argument is a simple one in concept, but as many of our examples demonstrate, difficult to put into practice. The successful firms we studied use in one form or another the three pillars model to help them articulate their motivations for a deal and define areas of concern for study and active management.

We want to again stress that all three pillars must carry the weight of a deal, and weaknesses in one create serious problems for the others. Weakness in itself is not necessarily fatal but certainly a cause for great concern. Poor business fit most often is fatal, and perhaps overcome only with additional capital to create synergies where none may exist. If there is weak financial fit, then there are no odds for success. Similarly, weak organizational fit can undermine business fit and cost a great deal to overcome. The three pillars depend on each other and are integrally related. The ideal merger and acquisition will show strength in all three, and management will want to create a well-planned strategy for overcoming any weaknesses diluting that ideal.

4

ACTIVELY
MANAGING
PROCESS STAGES

Process management and questions about business, financial, and organizational fit cannot be separated. Early process stages help articulate business and financial fit issues, and later process stages are devoted to building organizational fit. These tasks are so critical that we believe that effective management of the merger-acquisition process is the second major determinant of success. The process is much more than simply identifying an attractive candidate and negotiating a deal. Indeed, it is only after the deal is negotiated that the hard work begins.

While good luck and intuition may occasionally help, consistently successful merger-acquisition practice springs only from a solid understanding and active management of the process. If mergers and acquisitions are part of a firm's long-term strategy for growth and change, then luck and intuition are far from sufficient. Successful firms develop a deep appreciation of the process, master it through the development of relevant expertise, and devote whatever resources are required to actively manage it.

As several key managers involved in Allied-Signal's past mergers and acquisitions are quick to point out, the inherent complexity and difficulty of the process make each deal different. Successful firms like Allied-Signal have over time created a resident expertise and capacity to make their efforts as routine as possible. Yet they still acknowledge that the process is full of surprises, and they stay flexible enough to accommodate each deal's uniqueness. They have built their odds for success by becoming excellent process facilitators and managers. This point needs to be emphasized:

> **Thinking too far ahead to the successful end of a deal without active management of process issues encountered along the way is a recipe for failure.**

For the firm doing only one or two acquisitions, or merging only once in its life, deep experience and capacity will never be built to the level of the actively acquisitive firm. The potential for difficulties, even failure, is much greater for the less active firm. This fact obviously also holds for firms being acquired. The entrepreneur-founder who wants to sell to a larger firm does not have the luxury of becoming a merger-acquisition expert. For corporate staff who have also not had much previous involvement in their firm's acquisitions, the learning curve can be steep.

Learning from experience can be costly, even fatal. *Business Week* and *Fortune* typically average a story every other issue about some merger or acquisition that is encountering trouble. Our annotated bibliography lists several articles about why difficulties occur, and most of these articles offer prescriptions. We were less interested in what does not work when we began our own study. Instead, we wanted to understand how the successful process managers like Allied-Signal, Browning-Ferris, Citibank, Gannett, and many smaller firms, like IT Corporation, routinely buy (and sell) businesses with success. These firms are notable for their *lack* of negative press in the business press.

A deep appreciation of the merger-acquisition process is a key factor in success. As one researcher, James Young, noted, "After detailing the case studies and reviewing the available body of knowledge, one finds the lack of expertise and competence in coordinating the acquisition most obvious, actually glaring.[1]" There is no substitute for a well-articulated, rehearsed model for guiding the process. The model offered shortly is simplistic compared to some of the very detailed models, action plans, and flow charts in use. It does, however, provide insight about the most critical phases of the process that do need active management. The model also helps introduce the many players in the process and their roles.

Again, our basic premise is that the odds of a successful merger or acquisition will be increased when the issues present in each stage of the model are understood and actively managed. For the active firm with a successful model in place, our discussion in this chapter can perhaps serve as a basis for internal discussion, comparison, and training. Less active firms need to pay even closer attention to this chapter for even more compelling reasons: They have fewer opportunities to get it right.

The Seven-Stage Merger-Acquisition Model

The merger-acquisition process has been flowcharted and described by writers for some time.[2] Figure 4-1 is a composite of several general models. We want to stress, as some of the research about merger-acquisition decision making has revealed, that the stages are not as discrete as the model suggests; they can overlap and be very dependent on each other.[3] Chapter 5 contains greater detail about how the process is prone to difficulties, but our purpose here is to describe a general model and how its stages relate to each other and to the players involved.

Figure 4-2 summarizes the major objectives, tasks, and major issues associated with each of the stages in this model. Appendix A consists of a list of questions we have used with clients in helping them think through process management issues. They are the kinds of questions that need to be asked and answered before committing the firm to an acquisition strategy.

Strategic Planning as a Prerequisite

We cannot overstate the importance of a well-articulated concept of the firm's desired future—its vision of itself—for guiding the process. This vision is best cultivated and manifested through the firm's strategic planning activity. For example, it was Ed Hennessy's vision of Allied Chemical Co. as a leading-edge high technology firm that moved the firm in less than 10 years out of its maturing, commodity-like businesses through several well-

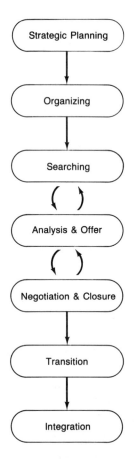

Figure 4-1   The merger-acquisition process: a seven-stage model.

executed mergers. Today, as one of Allied-Signal's early adver-
tisements pointed out, only GE, IBM, and AT&T hold more
patents.

Similarly, Laurence Farley's vision of a "globalized"
and diversified Black & Decker led to, among other actions, the
$300 million acquisition of GE's small appliance division. A big
gamble, conceded Farley at the time, but the largest name brand
transfer in history is working, due to a very effective advertising
campaign and extensive product redesign. Black & Decker's ability to compete against Japanese firms is increasing as it builds a
strong position in a new business.

STRATEGIC PLANNING

Objective   Create a corporate development-oriented planning process
which directly supports merger-acquisition activity,
including articulation of the leader's vision for the firm.

Major Tasks 1. Refine planning process, whether portfolio or vision-driven
approach
2. Assure development of support systems (human resource, control,
structural)

Major Issues 1. Clarity and validity of vision
2. Ability of planning process to support merger-acquisition
activity
3. Capacity of firm to actually engage in merger-acquisition
activity
4. Adequacy of support systems to reinforce planning and
merger-acquisition activity

ORGANIZING

Objective   Create an effective management capacity within the firm
with sufficient authority (influence) and resources to actively
manage the merger-acquisition process, including management
of relations among all key players.

Major Tasks 1. Organize and fund the merger-acquisition function consistent
with the desired level of activity (ad hoc group, team, formal
corporate development unit and staff)
2. Define roles/responsibilities of all key players
3. Assure access to and active involvement of senior management and CEO as needed
4. Build relations among key players, particularly those external
to the firm
5. Build the skills/knowledge of key players and sophistication
of the techniques used
6. Develop protocols (step, flows, linkages, and timing)
7. Assure close integration of planning process

Major Issues 1. Capacity and sophistication of function relative to
demands placed on it
2. Role/responsibility clarity of key players, particularly
concerning the timing and depth of their involvement
3. Ability to manage key external players
4. Process management skills, particularly during transition
stages
5. Authority/influence of function and staff to manage process effectively

SEARCHING

Objective   Identify most attractive candidates, track, and develop
sufficient data about them to allow subsequent analysis in
preparation for an offer.

Major Tasks 1. Create a systematic process for scanning potential
candidates
2. Articulate attractiveness/hurdle criteria to screen candidates
3. Build profiles and background data
4. Input results to senior management for action

Figure 4-2 The merger-acquisition process: objectives, tasks, and
major issues.

Major Issues 1. Ability of process to quickly respond to unique opportunities
  2. Influence of process in moderating the personal or psychological biases of senior management
  3. Depth and breadth of search
  4. Timing of involvement of senior management

ANALYSIS & OFFER

Objective Develop sufficient data (including articulation of critical assumptions) to allow evaluation of business, financial and organizational fit, which allows valuation and presentation of an offer.

Major Tasks 1. Apply sufficiently sophisticated analytic techniques to allow valuation
  2. Articulate the most critical assumptions, including how these will be validated
  3. Set value range and terms/conditions parameters
  4. Develop at least an initial strategy for later transition stages
  5. Agree on an approach for presentation of the offer

Major Issues 1. Sophistication of analytic techniques
  2. Commitment of senior management, particularly the CEO
  3. Time and competitive pressure to execute the deal
  4. Importance and number of assumptions that must be made, including how and when these may be tested
  5. Quality of data and input of key players into the analysis

NEGOTIATION & CLOSURE

Objective Reach agreement with candidate about an acceptable price, terms and conditions, ideally on as mutually an attractive basis as possible.

Major Tasks 1. Approach the candidate firm in such a way to create a positive climate for negotiation
  2. Assure sufficient secrecy of negotiation to control price
  3. Quickly and efficiently evaluate counter-offers
  4. Reach agreement about terms and conditions governing price
  5. Test as many assumptions as possible during due diligence activity
  6. Disclose deal and its rationale
  7. Outline and communicate the transition time-frame and most immediate action steps, being sensitive to the symbolic content of all communications

Major Issues 1. The approach and its impact upon the subsequent climate for negotiation
  2. Level of involvement of the CEO and senior management
  3. Adherence to valuation range and terms/conditions parameters
  4. Ability to quickly evaluate and respond to counter offers
  5. Exposure of negotiations and the pressure to conclude
  6. Ability to test critical assumptions early on
  7. Disclosure and acceptance of the rationale
  8. Initial symbolic acts and their impact

Figure 4-2 Continued

TRANSITION

Objective   Swift, effective control of situation through the
                 design and implementation of a transition management process.

Major Tasks   1. Assess situation
                 2. Apply transition ground rules

Major Issues   1. Ability to stabilize situation
                 2. Commitment of key managers in both firms to stay
                 3. Effectiveness of transition management process that
                    is created
                 4. Acceptance and accuracy of acquiring firm's role
                 5. Adequacy of resources provided to effort

INTEGRATION

Objective   Implement integration strategies that were developed
                 in the implementation stage.

Major Tasks   1. Design ways to test any remaining assumptions
                    about fit
                 2. Define specific action priorities
                 3. Allocate sufficient resources to implementation efforts
                 4. Monitor and control implementation

Major Issues   1. Effectiveness of implementation stage
                 2. Accuracy of fit assumptions made early on
                 3. Appropriateness of acquiring firm's role given
                    initial results

Figure 4-2   Continued

Smaller firms have also proved the importance of vision in guiding a merger-acquisition program. Within 10 years, Murray Hutchison and Bill King's vision of a full-service hazardous waste treatment and disposal firm created IT Corporation—a Wall Street star with over $200 million in 1986 sales. Not bad for a company that started as a small, family-owned California marine and industrial cleaning firm with $10 million in sales. IT Corporation's carefully executed acquisitions of small, independent firms has quickly made it a major player in a rapidly growing industry.

The SantaFe Healthcare–AV-MED deal mentioned in the last chapter also provides an excellent example of how a unifying vision can facilitate the transition and integration stages. Ed Peddie, SantaFe's CEO, has for several years expressed commitment to the not-for-profit concept in the intensely competitive healthcare industry. This concept was not only consistently and actively communicated to AV-MED management and staff during the transition, but it served as a frame of reference for evaluating areas for business and organizational fit. This concept was an expression of human, not just corporate, values, and was manifested in services and products. AV-MED was culturally and organizationally converted to the not-for-profit concept. With another local HMO implicated in a scandal during the transition period, AV-MED's adoption of the not-for-profit service concept could not have been better timed competitively.

In each of these cases, mergers and acquisitions have played a key role in making a vision manifest. The vision itself also builds commitment to the firm and becomes an organizing principle binding the firm together both before and after a merger or acquisition. Obviously, not all acquisitions have a dramatic, strategic impact on a firm's vision. A great many deals may simply broaden geographical presence, or add a new product line or manufacturing capacity. The difference is whether an acquisition has corporate or simply business level impact. The point here is that mergers and acquisitions are most effective when guided by a larger vision or concept of the firm. We stress this point as follows:

Mergers and acquisitions are means, never ends. They are instruments for actualizing the firm's vision. If that vision is ambiguous or impossible, then its mergers and acquisitions will likely become failures.

The strategic planning process is the best vehicle for operationalizing the leader's vision. Vision, expressed either in a formal mission statement or verbally communicated through a CEO's interactions with key managers, provides a rationale and focus for mergers and acquisitions. Vision also provides a unifying identity for both firms once they are merged or acquired. The mission statement, as a reflection of this vision, expresses ideals, values, and direction. IT Corporation's mission statement also includes a brief statement about the role of acquisitions in the firm's plans:

We seek acquisitions that reduce time and/or risks in the pursuit of desirable new markets, services, and technologies. We will also seek purchases that add clients for existing

Corporate Strategy	Type of Merger-Acquisition
Concentration in Core Business	Divestitute of Unrelated Business or Marginal Units (e.g., Gulf & Western)
Horizontal Integration	Merger of two firms with competing or overlapping businesses (e.g., Northwest Orient and Republic)
Vertical Integration	Acquisition of sources of supply or major customers to lower costs and increase value added to a product or service (e.g., Coca Cola acquiring its independent bottlers)
Diversification into Unrelated Businesses	Movement from a mature industry such as retailing into other industries such as financial services (e.g., Sears and Dean Witter)

Figure 4-3   Corporate strategy and merger-acquisition activity.

services provided the revenue benefit clearly exceeds absorption costs.

Each new acquisition should have special transition care during its early months, to assure smooth management and cultural assimilation, and conformance to initial business plans.[4]

Several strategic planning activities generate tangible outcomes which can be directly factored into the merger-acquisition process. For example, a strategic self-assessment of corporate and business-level strengths and weaknesses, opportunities, and threats will generate data that can be translated into acquisition screening criteria. Specific strategies flowing from such an analysis can be expressed through mergers or acquisitions. Figure 4-3 above summarizes various corporate strategies and how these relate to mergers and acquisitions.

If, for example, below average R&D expenditures have resulted in a largely mature business with few new products in the pipeline, then an acquisition of another firm with newer products or a history of extensive and productive R&D could be considered to overcome this weakness. Paying a premium for an acquired firm may still be cheaper and quicker than spending the money on new R&D. Along these lines, Northwest Orient's merger with Republic Airlines makes sense, given Northwest's weak domestic feeder system for its international flights. In today's rapidly changing industries, firms do not have time to build large new businesses.

The strategic planning process in the firm wanting to grow or change through acquisitions must therefore provide information to help answer questions that must later be asked in the merger-acquisition process.[5] For example, what is the opportunity cost associated with building the firm's own internal capacity in a particular business versus buying a firm already in that business? Does the start-up cost exceed the premium to be paid for this firm? This type of question is typical in an organized acquisition screening process, and the strategic planning process should be prepared to facilitate such analyses. Actively acquisitive firms build strategic planning processes with strong biases toward acquisitions. Indeed, a corporate planner may report to the corporate development manager—a merger-acquisition specialist.

Geonex Corporation, a small high technology firm based in St. Petersburg, Florida, had a typical problem in this respect. It had just gone public a few months earlier and was trying to put the money gained to best use. Acquisitions were an obvious way. As Harold Flynn, Geonex's CEO, put it, "Everything looks good, but is it what we should be doing?" Lots of investment bankers were offering advice, and opportunities were constantly being presented. A coherent sense of priorities and needs built around a strategic gameplan was absent. After an assessment of Geonex's strategic goals, an acquisition program was created. The heart of this program was designed to secure Geonex's already strong competitive position within its core business, while taking advantage of some unique, closely related diversification opportunities. This program depended on a strategic assessment of the firm.

Poor strategic planning, driven by an ambiguous vision, can seriously undermine the merger-acquisition process. As a case in point, there is little question that part of the merger and

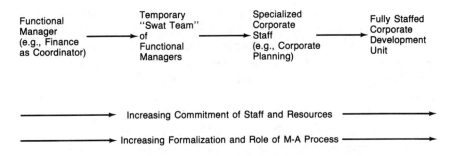

Figure 4-4   A range of organizing options. (Source: M. Feldman, 1985.)

acquisition activity in regional banking is now motivated by the panic reactions of some banks to the acquisitions of their neighbor banks by "outsiders." While many deals do certainly have a sound strategic logic to them—NCNB's moves into Florida and South Carolina and the Sun Bank-Trust Company merger are nice examples—other deals are motivated by fear of "being left out of the party." As a consequence, there is often a long period of sorting, sifting, and unnecessary confusion and anxiety following a poorly thought-out, defensive acquisition. As one bank executive recently said, "They (the acquired bank's management) are looking to us for direction. This thing has created so much confusion inside our own operation that we are in no position to be giving direction to anyone right now." In summary,

> **Long-term success comes from well-articulated strategic thinking operationally linked to a strategic planning process that directly supports the merger-acquisition process.**

Organizing

Given the choice by senior management to pursue mergers and acquisitions as part of the strategic plan, a core question becomes how to organize to do so. Figure 4-4 illustrates a range of organizing choices.

At its simplest, one functional manager, as part of other primary duties, would also be responsible for managing the process. Additional support from other managers and staff would be provided as requested. The danger here is that critical issues can be overlooked and key managers and staff not included when most needed. Tacking process management responsibilities onto an already busy manager will reduce the priority the process deserves.

The firm can also use what Mark Feldman of Hay Management Consultants calls the "SWAT Team Approach"—the ad hoc formation of a team of staff and functional managers: with representatives from marketing, finance, human resources, and strategic planning as minimally sufficient.[6] Prospects, proposals, options, and alternatives are screened by this team, which also manages post-acquisition integration.

At the other extreme, a highly trained, full-time professional staff could exist to handle many of these tasks, involving other staff, senior management, and functional managers only at critical points in a highly structured, even routine process. As well as the task of managing the involvement of many internal players, this staff would have responsibility for working with many external players. Both internal and external players need their entries and exits in the process coordinated and their assigned tasks and completed work evaluated. Hence the desirability of a specialized function to assure coordination.

While ad hoc groups can play meaningful roles, the importance of good strategic planning to successful mergers and acquisitions is best expressed in the way formal corporate development functions have become organized in larger firms. The Conference Board's 1980 study of corporate development functions in 177 firms clearly reveals the close, natural relationship between strategic planning and merger-acquisition activity.[7] In that study, 80 percent of the participating corporate development managers indicated planning as a primary responsibility, while 90 percent said they also were responsible for some aspect of merger-acquisition activity. The corporate development directors or vice presidents in a great many of these firms report directly to their CEOs or Presidents, and have broad academic and work backgrounds, frequently with line management experience. They are, in other words, very often key players with expertise, resources, and access to power and authority—all absolute necessities, given the importance of their activities to the firm. They are the primary internal facilitators and gatekeepers. We stress this point as follows:

The wise response by senior management is to provide a focal point within the firm that is vested with primary responsibility for process management.

These units need not be large, just effective. Corporate development units do tend to have small core staffs. Over half of those surveyed in the Conference Board study had two or fewer full-time professionals in addition to the unit head, but they were able to draw extensively on other functions for staff to execute specific tasks. They had ready access to the CEO and senior management, and the authority and influence to manage the participation of other corporate staff, line managers, and many independent-thinking external players such as investment bankers.

Jim Balloun, head of McKinsey's Atlanta office, says that these individuals may well also serve as "beachmasters" during the post-acquisition period, focusing their full energies on the integration task. In other firms, these individuals may primarily be responsible only for packaging a deal, turning their attention immediately to another prospect once one has been completed, and making a "baton pass" off to the senior line manager under whom the newly acquired firm will operate. In all cases, they need skills, experience, and interpersonal abilities not often found in corporate staff.

The importance of an organized approach for acquisitions is illustrated by the structure of BellSouth's corporate development organization shown in Figure 4-5. By being located in BellSouth Enterprises, the company that manages the unregulated BellSouth companies, the group is well positioned to ensure that each acquisition or start-up will be a good strategic fit. In addition, the president of BellSouth Enterprises reports to the chairman of the board of BellSouth, ensuring a close coordination with the holding company and the other major subsidiaries.[8]

At least four conditions should be met at this stage to avoid later problems. First, process management responsibility, along with commensurate authority, should be explicitly fixed to an individual or unit. The other internal players must also have

BELLSOUTH ENTERPRISES CORPORATION

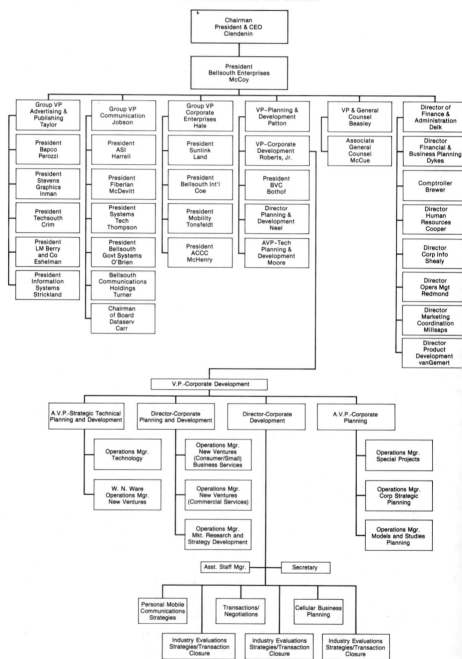

Figure 4-5 BellSouth corporate development unit. (Source: Bell-South Corp., 1987.)

their roles and responsibilities explicitly defined in relation to this individual or unit, including expectations for the type of involvement they will have, the extent of time and effort that may be required, and the quality of work to be produced.

Second, the specific steps in the merger-acquisition process should be flowcharted to define acceptable action timeframes and the entry and exit points of all key players. Taking a prospective deal to the CEO and Board too early can be a waste of time that also diminishes the credibility of staff. The flowcharting of the process also becomes a good way of identifying gaps and trouble spots—a "fatal flaws" analysis. Deviations from the path are, of course, inevitable, but the flowchart can at least be a recognized point of departure.

Third, relationships with external players need to be built in advance. Getting to know each other's strengths and weaknesses during the middle of an acquisition or merger is unnecessarily risky. Experienced merger/acquisition staff typically come with established ties with many of these external players, and a broader network can also be built to offer alternatives to these established relationships. Advance interviews with several management consulting firms, for example, can identify those which may best be used at different points in the process—some being better at analyzing businesses while other may be better working with staffing issues. In the Allied-Signal merger, for example, Booz-Allen was brought in to explore the fit between the two firm's different businesses while McKinsey was used to explore issues around the integration of the two corporate staffs. Keeping such firms available on a retainer basis may be necessary to have them available when needed. Organizing, from this perspective, means building both internal and external players into a flexible, but effective team.

The sole objective at this stage is to build a capacity that can be brought quickly and decisively into play. As a fourth condition, training programs are available and can be developed, and off-site "dry-runs" to model the steps in the flowcharted process are useful to give assurance of that capacity when needed. Our major point in discussing what needs to be done can be summarized as follows:

Invest willingly in the development of capacity. Resources required for hiring skilled staff, training management, and building relationships with external players are trivial compared to the gain from an attractive acquisition.

Searching

The searching stage is concerned with how prospective merger and acquisition candidates become known to the firm and studied in preparation for contact. This stage has received an incredible amount of attention, and is rapidly evolving in sophistication, thanks to new analytical techniques and information accessing technologies. We do not need to go into detail about this stage, and the annotated bibliography can be used as a reference. A useful framework for thinking about this stage here, however, is provided by Jerold Freier.[9] He classifies search activities in three ways: opportunistic, research, and combination approaches.

The opportunistic approach relies upon broadly defined screening criteria that do not target a specific firm. Instead, the acquiring firm will rely on a network of professionals such as investment bankers or the personal relationships of the CEO or other managers to generate candidates. Finder's fees and the opportunity to execute the deal and generate additional fees have made this activity a favorite one on Wall Street. Indeed, the early neutrality of the investment banks has given way to active "beating of the bushes," sometimes with ethical implications, according to some recent accounts.[10] Often these candidates are being sold by other firms as part of a restructuring effort—some of the businesses of Revlon, Gulf & Western, or Beatrice are examples— or need to be saved in a "White Knight" move (Fluor Corporation's acquisition of St. Joe Minerals, for example).

The opportunistic approach can be likened to a radar screen on which blips appear, or to a trout facing upstream, waiting for food to come to it with the current. As Harvard professor Jay Lorsch said in an October 1, 1984 *Wall Street Journal* article, "The popular imagination is that managers are very analytic and very systematic. I think a lot more decisions are made on serendipity than people think. Things come across their radar screens and they jump at them." It is not a particularly proactive or aggressive approach, but does not require a lot of effort either.

What may be most troubling about this approach, however, is the potential it brings for the CEO's impromptu initiation of a merger or acquisition in lieu of careful staff analysis. The ill-fated Hospital Corporation of America and American Hospital Supply merger, for example, was reportedly the result of too casual an analysis of its repercussions. GAF's purchase of a classical radio station, Gould's purchase of a polo club, and Gulf & Western's acquisitions under Charles Bluhdorn can all be questioned from the perspective of CEO "whim" versus wisdom.[11] More than one deal has been agreed upon in a matter of hours or days—not weeks or months—of study, because two CEOs got along well and sold each other on the idea of "getting together."

The research approach is more proactive and is very often aggressive. It does require time, effort, and resources. Strict screening criteria are set based upon needs defined through strategic planning and are used to target specific candidates. Well-defined criteria, based on financial theory and intimate experience with previous acquisitions, is applied religiously by many firms. Gannett, the world's largest newspaper chain, has pursued an aggressive acquisition strategy that many industry analysts question, for example, but can be defended because acquisitions have been measured against strict financial criteria.[12] Gordon White of England's Hanson Trust PLC places so much emphasis upon his yardstick measures that he reportedly boasts of never having entered the offices or plants of the firms Hanson has acquired.[13] This is extreme, in our opinion, but illustrates the extent to which criteria can be used.

On-line computerized databases such as Compustat and databases managed by firms such as ADP Services for *Mergers & Acquisitions* can be remote accessed, and pertinent data can be extracted based on predetermined criteria and stored in micro-computer databases using commercially available software.[14] A lot of the research burden can be reduced. However, there still remains a need for deep research as specific candidates make the "hit list" of top 10 to 20 most attractive firms. Corporate development units with strong merger and acquisition orientations routinely update files of firms on their lists. The key point here is that the acquiring firm knows what it wants and actively seeks candidates out; there is nothing passive about this approach. It is becoming a sophisticated, almost routine technology.

The third approach—a combination of the opportunistic and research approaches—is what a great many firms use. While an active research effort is underway, the firm is also adaptive enough to take advantage of situations as they present themselves. The acquisition of Bendix by Allied is an excellent example. What may have appeared as serendipity was not. Allied had previously identified Bendix as an attractive candidate and was maintaining a file, although it was admittedly not adequate enough to provide the deep research needed to allow as rapid action as was eventually needed. When Allied entered the Bendix-Martin Marietta situation as "White Knight" for Bendix, it was moving with some confidence.

The key tasks in the searching stage are therefore to be clear and consistent about the screening criteria to be used, and to apply these in as proactive a fashion as possible, while preserving enough flexibility and rapid response capacity to take advantage of opportunities that present themselves. The criteria should have enough legitimacy to withstand emotional and impromptu initiatives by top executives. It is easy to let interpersonal dynamics and personal motivations short circuit the search process. We do believe, however, as follows:

> **Intuition and "gut feel" can play a useful and important role, and for this reason should never be ignored, only balanced with an ongoing, systematic search and screening process.**

Analysis and Offer

The initial analysis and presentation of an offer to merge or acquire is a critical point in the process. A price range must first be agreed upon which sets the upper and lower limits the acquiring firm can and wants to afford. Who makes the contact is also important; is it staff, the CEO, or a third party intermediary?

Whether the offer is solicited or unsolicited will also set the climate for subsequent negotiations. In general, this stage is characterized by rapidly increasing emotional and psychological commitment and personal stakes in the outcome. It can be compromised and far from rational due to many inherent obstacles.

Because it is a technically complicated stage, deal structuring has been the primary domain of financial and legal staff. External players such as law firms and investment bankers also play an active role, particularly if a tender offer for traded stock is involved and large amounts of financing must be locked in. The intricacies of deal structuring are best recounted in books such as those cited in the annotated bibliography.

In terms of setting a price range, a number of analytical approaches are in use, the Alcar Model being common for publicly traded firms.[15] Without delving deep into these models and valuation models, suffice it to say that they are useful in setting a broad price range that must be based on many critical assumptions. Some of these assumptions may be accurate, others much less so. For example, an assumption that an acquired business will produce profits at a certain level for a certain time period may or may not be accurate. However, these profits are part of the net present value calculation used to fix a price for the acquisition. Fluor Corporation's acquisition of St. Joe Minerals in 1981 in a "White Knight" move was predicated on two assumptions: metals prices would be stable, if not rising, and the metals business was countercyclical to construction. Not so. Metals prices plummeted, and high interest rates killed both industries at once. Fluor has since had to sell, among other things, its stunning Irvine, California headquarters to Trammell-Crow to service the $724 million in debt it incurred.[16] The Fluor story has a happier ending, however, because St. Joe's positive culture has helped change Fluor's historically less aggressive and competitive culture; a long but positive mending process is underway.

For privately held firms—about 75 percent of all deals in 1984—the valuation of the firm gets even trickier. If the candidate is run by an entrepreneur-founder, count on widely differing perceptions of the firm's worth. Individuals who create a firm will place a higher value on it than a "rational man;" the premium over book value becomes the focus for negotiation. High premium acquisitions force the acquiring firm to swallow hard and hope that the factors which motivated the deal in the first place hold true.

We found one aspect of the initial valuation effort to be particularly uncomfortable for acquiring firms. While making initial assumptions is understandably risky, there are few opportunities for low-risk testing at this stage. For example, a strong sense of secrecy and time pressure prevail, whether the offer is solicited or not. If news leaks to the investment community or to the target firm, count on the opening price going up. Insider trading has become a major problem, and acquiring firms pay dearly for leaks as they watch the target's stock get bid up. Nor is it wise to have a team enter the other firm's operations at this stage to try and substantiate assumptions. Employees may react without knowing the full details, and negotiations become disrupted by the need to deal with rumors. Rumor control procedures should, we add, be established very early as part of the organizing stage. As a general rule,

Make all assumptions explicit, try to avoid making any that are so critical that they will determine success if invalid, and create opportunities to test any assumptions as early as possible.

Perhaps as important an issue as valuation is the question of how contact is established and who establishes it between the two firms. One consultant in Atlanta told us the story of how one of Europe's largest distillers lost a very desirable acquisition in the U.S. because the European firm's president delegated early contacts to lower, although still senior, managers. The U.S. firm's president was put off by the apparent lack of respect shown him and the seemingly low priority assigned to the deal by the European firm.

In general, the level of difficulty in resolving the issues associated with initial contact depend on whether the first contact has been solicited or not. If the candidate is "in play"—meaning it is being actively sought by other firms and is soliciting offers—then a favorable contact climate can be created. A firm that is the target of an unsolicited tender offer may also find another friendly offer attractive. We want to stress this point:

Friendly offers lay the foundation for the building of trust, open communication, and later collaboration.

Indeed, these ingredients are so important that many actively acquiring firms will not make hostile offers; they are simply not worth the grief later on, as one group of executives put it. Unfriendly offers and prolonged "scorched earth" moves to resist can be damaging.

Initial contact is the CEO's responsibility if the merger or acquisition is truly important to the firm. A third-party intermediary can be used to introduce the idea of a meeting, but the CEO must demonstrate the importance of the two firms' possible combination by getting personally involved. If the candidate is a business being spun off in a divestiture, then lower-level managers and corporate staff can perhaps take the lead.

The contact and offer is the result of a process that may have involved a lot of work and management involvement. The CEO and Board have typically been "brought on board." Personal stakes in the outcome are being built, and the staff's credibility and CEO's reputation for making deals may even be at risk. If the candidate is well known and the investment community and media are following its pursuit by other firms, then an air of excitement and expectation may also prevail. The air becomes charged with an electricity that is both addictive and draining. The "thrill of the chase" begins to create a momentum which is difficult to control. For Texaco in its push to acquire Getty Oil, mistakes were made. It interfered at the contact and offer stage with Pennzoil, and rather than face a multibillion dollar damage judgment, declared bankruptcy.[17]

In a 1981 *Fortune* article about DuPont's acquisition of Conoco, Lee Smith also vividly illustrates the importance of effective communications to clarify intentions.[18] Misinterpretations regarding each other's willingness to do a deal led Ralph Bailey, then Chairman of Conoco, and John Gallagher, Dome Petroleum's Chairman, to very different conclusions. Gallagher's launching of a tender offer put Conoco "in play" and caused the eventual loss of Conoco to DuPont in an apparently unnecessary bidding war. The first contact and offer stage, in this case, was not managed well and resulted in a very different outcome than Dome had anticipated.

Firms that routinely do acquisitions and mergers make a serious effort to control the climate and conditions within each stage, particularly once contact is established with the other firm. A sense of "calm professionalism"—at least on the exterior—is demanded. For those experiencing this stage, however, it is never boring.

Negotiation and Closure

An offer can either be rejected or accepted for consideration. If rejected, the search process begins again or the offering firm can bide its time waiting for events to change its target's mind. Some acquirers have been known to wait for years. Assuming an initial offer is accepted for consideration, then the negotiation stage begins, ideally culminating in a tentative agreement about price and conditions, but perhaps also again resulting in rejection. Figure 4-6 summarizes a quick study of 70 "cancellations" of deals that had been announced in 1982 and 1983. The majority of cancellations occurred in the negotiation stage due to inadequate bids or the inability to come up with sufficient financing to meet the candidate's terms. Estimates are that one in ten fails at this point, with 191 of 277 cancellations in 1984 due to these same reasons.[19]

The negotiation stage has also received considerable attention, but it is worth noting a few key points here. First, it is in this stage that some initial assumptions can begin to be tested, assuming a collaborative climate exists between the two firms. For example, tours of facilities and an opening of the books to the acquiring firm's staff can occur. SantaFe Healthcare was already doing management assessments and reviewing detailed aspects of AV-MED's operations two months before an ageement was even reached, for example.

Much more likely, however, is the need to put an audit team together to do "due diligence" work to validate the accuracy of some details. When third-party intermediaries such as business brokers are involved, an arm's-length negotiating style can prevail. It is essential, however, that the two principals, preferably the CEOs of both firms, quickly establish personal rapport if the offer is going to be seriously considered. John Duncan, Chairman of St. Joe Minerals, tells the story of how Edgar Bronfman's

Top Cancellations
1982-1983

Reason for Cancellation	Outbid	Key Information Missing	Government Intervention	Repurchase of Shares by Target	Change in Market Conditions	Insufficient Number of Shares Tendered	Insufficient Financing	Deficient Bid	Other	Totals
Number of Cancellations	16	3	4	5	3	2	5	19	13	70
Percent Cancellations	22.9%	4.3%	5.7%	7.1%	4.3%	2.9%	7.1%	27.1%	18.6%	100%

Figure 4-6 Sources of acquisition negotiation failure. (Source: *Mergers & Acquisitions Almanac*, 1983, 1984, 1985.)

93

seeming rudeness in letting him personally know about Seagram's public tender offer put him off the deal, despite Bronfman's later explanation of his actual attempts to do so.[20]

Second, there is an absolute premium placed on clear communication between all players in this stage. Semantics can vary from organization to organization, and unwritten norms and expectations can complicate communication and understanding. What is or is not part of the deal, when and how actions are to occur, and the contingency plans for overcoming inevitable setbacks and resolving disagreements—all of these issues need careful consideration and mutual agreement. Trust and good faith certainly help, but thoughtful, accurate communication is also needed to make a deal successful.

> **Negotiations need to be clean, crisp, and decisive. The conditions under which negotiations must take place put an absolute premium on effective communication.**

Third, promises get made at this stage, and these can come back to haunt both buyer and seller in later stages. Promises can be expectations that may be unstated or parts of a written letter of agreement. Sometimes promises get made and cannot be kept. For example, a promise to maintain current levels of R&D may make sense, but the pressure to service the debt incurred to make the deal can force the acquiring firm to renege on its agreement. Perhaps such situations cannot be avoided. They definitely should be minimized. This point should be stressed:

> **Promises have downstream consequences, and these consequences must be understood and anticipated in advance. Never break a promise publicly made. It will cost you later. Count on it.**

Fourth, mergers and acquisitions are like any negotiation in which a buyer is strongly motivated. An established price range for the deal needs to be adhered to. The buyer must know what it can and cannot afford and must expect to spend a lot more than anticipated to successfully integrate the two firms. On the other hand, trying to drive a hard bargain can also create unnecessary ill will. It may be better to give a little on price to make life afterwards easier for everyone.

Too many acquisitions do get into later trouble due to the "thrill of the chase" when the consequences of a high price become reality. There are many case studies to demonstrate this point: Chevron's expensive acquisition of Gulf, Champion's acquisition of St. Regis, United Airlines' purchase of Hilton International, and Ted Turner's drawn-out junk bond purchase of MGM/UA. When you want something a great deal, price becomes secondary, and more than one executive has been able to gloat about an expensive deal that later paid for itself. However, leverage is one thing, but crushing debt which later ruins the deal is another. Now that SEC rules on the use of junk bonds and other restrictions are making cash tender offers more of a necessity, discipline may be easier to find. Still, we offer simple advice:

There is, very simply, no substitute for discipline during negotiations.

Finally—and very importantly—the ground rules established for negotiation and afterwards play a critical role in setting the climate and expectations for later collaboration. They establish the tone and norms which can govern interactions and set precedents for years to come. Ed Hennessy of Allied very successfully set several important examples in the Bendix and Signal acquisitions. For example, he never called the Bendix deal an acquisition—it was a merger. All of the Allied staff very much expressed this point of view. This rule meant there would be a joining of equals—a point of great importance for Bendix because it came so suddenly for Bendix management. There would be no conquering hordes descending on Southfield, Michigan headquarters. The best of both organizations would be identified and merged. Top performers in Bendix could be assured a place in the new scheme, even though much was still uncertain.

In addition, no expense was to be spared to facilitate integration of the firms. As our later descriptions of the Allied transitions point out, no one in Allied to this day has an accurate idea how much the integration efforts actually cost, and these costs were considerable. As Dennis Signorovitch, Allied's head of Public Affairs, playfully responded, "If you have to ask what it costs, you shouldn't being doing these."

A common element of several acquisitions was good communication. Full disclosure was the norm. "Communicate, communicate, communicate" was not only a motto, it was adhered to in disclosing the negotiations and in selling the idea to all players—particularly employees. This precedent, we stress, is one *every successful merger or acquisition we looked at had in common.* For example, Don Revelle, head of Human Resources at Black & Decker and an experienced former TRW merger and acquisition player, says it is best to err on the side of too much communication, not too little.

With these ground rules clearly articulated during negotiations, one can clearly see if the two firms will be able to share a future together. Price is important because it can control what can and cannot later be done by both firms, and the deal has to be sold to stockholders and a number of other players, but the norms and promises set during negotiations can have equally important consequences. Put another way,

Intangibles count but are more subtle than price. The acquiring firms need to think carefully about the signals and messages it wants to communicate. Every bit of information will be gleaned for meaning and value.

At least in broad brushstrokes, several issues must be negotiated beyond price. In many ways, price becomes secondary. Some discussion should occur about which identity will dominate or survive. John Robson, now Dean of the School of Business at Emory University and formerly CEO of G.D. Searle when it was sold to Monsanto, believes in what he calls "the dominant gene" theory about which firm will eventually dominate. Despite explicit discussions about which firm will lead the way, or how both will be equals, he asserts that one firm's culture will inevitably come to dominate the other's. Perhaps so, but the initial expression of which, or whether, one will dominate is symbolically important and nonetheless needs to be discussed. A related balance of power issue is the question of who shall lead the firm, at least during the transition period, and how those who do not and will leave shall be compensated.

The major themes, "drivers," or emphases for the future should also be discussed. This discussion can perhaps be framed in terms of how the firm's competitive advantage will be enhanced or changed—for example, "We will be the low-cost producer in our industry." Specifically, some discussion must occur about which businesses are kept and which are to be dropped. Specific action and funding priorities may also be identified. For example, the relative commitments to R&D or marketing can be discussed. An action timeframe, while certainly dependent on a closer study of issues during the transition stage, should also be a part of the discussion. Finally, there definitely must be some discussion about what will be communicated to employees and to a great many external players. The rationale for joining forces, and statements about the issues just raised will need to be communicated unambiguously and consistently—a job for the Public Affairs group if one exists. We have more to say about this task in Chapter 6.

Transition and Integration

Assuming an agreement is reached, the merger or acquisition must now be implemented. The transition stage is different from the following integration stage in several respects. The deal must be ratified by stockholders in both firms and examined perhaps by regulatory agencies, financing firmed up, and an initial although temporary structure created for helping guide subsequent change. It is a period of maximum uncertainty and anxiety to employees, even for suppliers and customers, as they try to make sense out of the news. It is a time when a deal constructed by the inner core of players must be sold to other less informed players. To summarize,

> **The primary objective of the transition stage is to stabilize the situation enough to assure satisfactory ongoing performance while establishing a climate receptive to change.**

In the integration stage, action plans created in the transition stage are executed to help build organizational fit. The two stages will overlap due to the uneven pace of change. Our point in differentiating them here is that too little attention is given to effective transition management. It is not simply a period of discomforting uncertainty that must be endured. Indeed, it is a unique time with greater opportunities for change than perhaps at any other period in a firm's life other than a major leadership change. It is also a time when tremendous damage can be done to future success if it is not managed well.

The duration of the transition stage varies from case to case. During it, the deal solidifies and its implications for the two firms' operations become clearer. It can be a hiatus—a dead period—or a time which can be very effectively used. It can last six weeks or six months—perhaps more; hopefully, never more.

Chapters 6, 7, and 8 include much more detail about both of these stages, but one of their most important features is worth noting here. The Wharton School's Tom Gilmore notes a curious, almost paradoxical, feature about such situations. He points out that uncertainty, and a resulting potential for anxiety and stress, is greatest when the structures for controlling it are weakest. The weakest point in the two firms' life is right after the deal is agreed upon because new roles, responsibilities, procedures, and operating systems are typically underspecified. Yet it is during this time that the greatest demands for certainty are being made.

As a result, every action and word communicated about the deal is being screened for its implications about the new order that will emerge. What is not said is as important as what is said. Realistically it may not be possible to say much about how life will be in the future. It is here that all the early assumptions and unresolved questions have their greatest impact; they will lengthen the integration period and prolong uncertainty. The potential for damaging a deal during integration is very real if an effective temporary transition structure and process is not rapidly introduced.

The integration stage ends once recommended changes have been initiated and a coherent, effective pattern of relations between the two firms develops. This stage can be long, as some business units get spun out and others merged. Two to three years is not uncommon. To illustrate this long timeframe, an early retreat of Allied executives with their new Signal counterparts was a notable event for one observable reason. It was apparently the first time Bendix executives were seen to be so casually and freely interspersed among Allied executives. All of the Allied and Bendix managers were on the same side of the room and the newcomers from Signal were on the other. It was only after three years that the seating arrangement finally reflected the Allied-Bendix merger.

Summary

Our position is a simple one. The odds of success are vastly improved when an explicit model like the seven-stage model we have introduced is used. Sufficient time and resources must be devoted to actively managing this process to assure its effectiveness. Effective process management counts!

The various stages of the model are not nice, neat, and discrete. They overlap, and ideally they will have feedback loops built into them so the process is constantly being improved with knowledge gained further "downstream." Unfortunately, the process is inherently plagued by difficulties that make its mastery difficult. We turn in the next chapter to the players and how they interact, including a discussion of how they contribute to these difficulties.

5

THE PLAYERS
AND
THEIR DYNAMICS

One of the most important yet difficult aspects to manage during the merger-acquisition process is the sheer number and variety of involved players. In this chapter, we first define the players most active in the process, and then illustrate how their dynamics can lead to setbacks and difficulties. Specific recommendations are offered for better managing their roles and dynamics.

Much has been written about each player's role.[1] Our purpose here is to briefly identify how they become involved in the process. We then identify the nature of their involvement and the most critical issues surrounding that involvement. The matrix offered in Figure 5-1 divides the players into four groups: internal or external to the firm, and central or peripheral to the process. However, their influence is dynamic and situational. For example, while the unions may be more peripheral, there are several cases of deals that were very significantly shaped by the role the unions chose to play. Therefore, Figure 5-1 is a general model.

Internal Players

There is a clear division between core internal players and the more peripheral players within the firm. Very often there is a

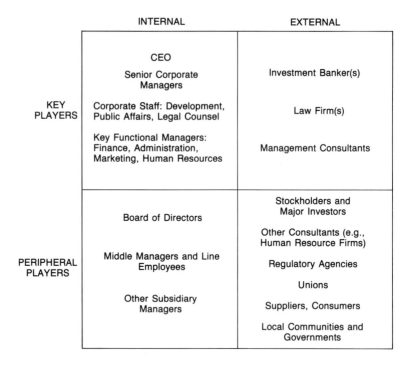

Figure 5-1 Process players in terms of location and level of involvement in the merger-acquisition process.

clear consensus about who is or is not part of the core group of insiders directing the firm's merger-acquisition activity. The boundary between the core group and other members of the firm is often very rigid, with the tendency being to make the core group smaller and tighter than is healthy. Some membership is episodic in that someone may be asked for advice and input early in the process, but not be involved again until the integration stage. There are reasons for limiting membership. Secrecy is often needed to prevent premature disclosure of a deal, and the pace of events can quicken so fast that a smaller group can often function more effectively than a large one. Nonetheless, the dynamics within this core group are a serious issue.

Key Internal Players

The key internal players typically consist of the CEO; a few senior corporate executives representing either their respective areas or acting as members of an executive team; key corporate staff; and, to varying degrees over time, key functional managers from marketing, finance, and human resources. Depending on how important mergers and acquisitions are to the firm, this core management group will vary greatly in terms of its sophistication and skill level. In the actively acquisitive firm, it may be officially known as the "merger-acquisition team," and will meet regularly to review possible acquisitions, evaluate the progress of negotiations underway, plot strategy, and oversee the performance of any operating transition teams. In less active firms, it may meet irregularly and only when needed, literally disbanding in the interim.

THE CEO'S ROLE.   The role of the CEO in this core group deserves close scrutiny. The extent and timing of the CEO's involvement is perhaps the greatest issue in managing the process. At one extreme, a large firm's CEO can delegate to an executive or a team all but the final decisions—even the final closing of a deal—and remain detached from the team's day-to-day functioning. There also are many instances of CEOs essentially delivering a deal already negotiated in principle to the team for execution, not evaluation.

At the other extreme, a CEO may be an active, regular participant in the group, with decisions emerging from active discussion and consensus. In general, the less experienced the CEO is with mergers and acquisitions, the greater the team's influence should be. In cases where the CEO is very experienced, the group's role may be more consultative and implementation oriented. For example, Bill King at IT Corp. brought several years of merger-acquisition experience at McKinsey & Co. to his job at IT, enabling him to use his staff in a different way than would a less-experienced executive. Ed Hennessy's leadership in defining a vision for Allied, his careful organization of the merger and acquisition group, and his personal involvement with both Bill Agee in Bendix and Forrest Shumway in Signal, were decisive factors in Allied's success. The CEO's role therefore needs clarification:

> **Unless the CEO is a tried and proven dealmaker, there is greater risk in assuming a detached role from the**

**team than a more interactive ongoing role. It is better
to err on the side of more rather than less involvement.**

The timing of the CEO's involvement is an equally
important issue. Prematurely bringing a deal to the CEO can
waste time, while involvement too late can cost an otherwise
attractive acquisition. While entry timing is important, so is exit
timing. There is a tendency for CEOs to withdraw too soon in
the process by overdelegating implementation and integration
responsibilities to lower-level managers. For very large deals such
as Signal, which required senior management changes and a
major restructuring of businesses through spin-outs, Hennessy's
continued involvement was essential. For the president of a small
firm acquired by a large firm, having prematurely limited access
to the larger firm's CEO can be personally humbling and an-
noying. Being sensitive to the feelings and sensibilities of the
acquired firm's managers is important during the transition and
integration stages.

Clearly deciding when the CEO should or should not
be directly involved in a deal is an important organizing stage
task. In general, the CEO's role in the early stages should be to
(1) decide on screening criteria, (2) narrow choices from a select
few candidate firms to a single target, (3) agree upon price and
terms parameters for structuring an initial offer, (4) making initial
contact if the deal is very important to the firm, and (5) actively
working to negotiate a tentative agreement. Over time, the CEO's
involvement can diminish, and Figure 5-2 illustrates this transfer
of responsibility from one player to others. Transfer can be premature or prolonged beyond what is necessary, depending upon
a specific deal's needs.

SENIOR MANAGEMENT AND STAFF'S ROLE. Senior managers such
as a President or Executive Vice President are often given the
leadership role of the team and may be actively involved in the
organizing, contact-offer, and implementation stages. The core
group's leadership from an operational perspective is most frequently determined by member rank and experience. With few
exceptions, we found these groups to be dominated by managers
with very strong financial backgrounds. Chief Financial Officers
(CFOs) or Corporate Development staffs reporting to senior man-

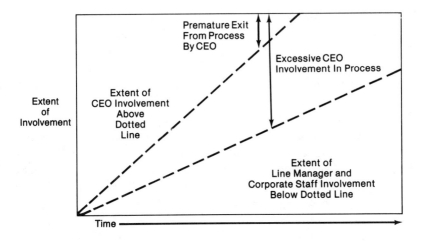

Figure 5-2 Shifting levels of CEO involvement in the process over time.

agers will frequently lead the team if a President or Executive Vice President does not. BellSouth's corporate structure—illustrated in the last chapter—provides a good example. In the firm where an experienced CEO does play an active role, the Corporate Development staff will report directly to the CEO.

Corporate-level staff in Corporate Development, Legal Affairs, Public Affairs, and Corporate Information Services may be the most actively involved players early in the process. Corporate Development typically is responsible for managing the overall process—particularly the organizing, search, analysis and offer, and negotiation stages. This person or unit also is responsible for coordinating the external players' involvement, and plays a critical facilitating and coordinating role in the transition stage.

Legal Affairs staff oversees the work of an external counsel, and explores an offer's implications for the firm. Given the growing use of defensive strategies for protecting a firm from takeovers, an internal legal counsel's role can be important. Insurance liability, tax, and regulatory issues also need evaluation and pre-planning to avoid implementation difficulties.

Public Affairs and Corporate Information Services may be most active during the negotiation and transition stages. This unit is responsible for controlling information—including leaks and rumors—and selling the deal to the media, other external players, and employees. In some firms this responsibility is given to a functional manager, often Human Resources. The Public Affairs role is an important one explored further in the next chapter.

Key functional managers from Finance, Marketing, and Human Resources also play critical roles, but may or may not be deeply involved in the early stages. Depending on the industry, additional functional managers from Operations or Engineering may be involved. For example, managers from R&D may be brought into the team to evaluate the quality and usefulness of a candidate's R&D activity. They also would be involved in the search stage, helping generate specific criteria for screening candidates. They may not be involved again until negotiations are well underway and direct contact is needed with their counterparts in the other firm. They would generate specific questions to be asked during negotiations, evaluate responses, and work with external players such as management consultants. A key task for functional managers prior to a deal's closing is to develop from their functional perspectives detailed strategies for maximizing the benefits of the merger or acquisition.

Peripheral Internal Players

THE BOARD'S ROLE. The Board of Directors' role varies tremendously from firm to firm, depending on factors like the number of outside directors on it, their skills, and the extent to which they are controlled by the CEO and senior management. In a great many cases, they are brought in primarily to give "go–no-go" advice on a specific candidate, and to approve price and conditions for a deal already negotiated by the CEO. Board members may not have the skill levels or the abilities to participate actively, and for these reasons many CEOs prefer to keep a tight rein on their directors.

Not all board members are excluded from the internal core group. Their role can be important in heading off bad ideas or shaping outcomes—but sometimes with mixed success. The Bendix Board's inability to slow Bill Agee's assault on Martin-Marietta, for example, resulted in several members resigning in protest. TWA's Board played a decisive role in accepting Carl

Ichan's bid over Frank Lorenzo's. Perhaps one of the most vivid examples of a Board's effective role is in CBS, where the Board sided with Laurence Tisch over Thomas Wyman, thus giving Tisch control of the firm, even though he held only 24.9% of CBS's stock. Wyman had ironically invited Tisch to buy the stock earlier in 1986 as a means of preventing an unwanted takeover.[2]

In general, however, the board's role is too weak for many observers. The board's legal liability can be great in merger-acquisition negotiations. This liability may not be understood, plus, a strong CEO may be unwilling to let the board play an active role. Because of this situation, we believe the following:

> **Serious questions exist about the capacity of boards to play meaningful roles in mergers and acquisitions. Their capacity should either be built or the board's composition changed to bring the necessary knowledge and skills into it.**

MIDDLE MANAGEMENT'S ROLE.   Without question, one of the most affected groups within the firm is middle management. In Chapter 1 we noted the extent of the impact on this group, and we focused on it again in the last chapter through interventions that can minimize negative consequences. In general, middle managers are asked to live with the consequences of a deal—whether positive or negative—and with little, if any, prior participation possible.

This lack of input is paradoxical in one respect: The active commitment of these managers to a merger or acquisition is often critical for its success, yet they have so little a role prior to its execution. For example, if high-demand scientific personnel within an industry do not like a deal, they will walk out the door. Yet their continued presence in the acquired firm may be essential to the deal's success. Their staying's importance is obvious, yet many acquisitions of smaller high technology firms by larger firms have turned out badly precisely because such managers were ignored. As one consulting firm president once said about acquisitions in his industry, "There's no such thing as a hostile takeover in the consulting business. The assets get up and leave." His own firm was subsequently gutted by several resignations of key, hard-to-replace scientists when it was sold.

The usual strategy for assuring these players' continued commitment is by actively "selling" them on the acquisition after it is completed. A well-prepared "roadshow" featuring the CEOs of both firms and senior managers travels to all facilities to personally present the positive benefits of the deal. In the Allied-Signal merger, for example, a film was prepared which had been shown to several thousand employees in both firms by the time the merger was finally approved. The importance of middle management is worth stressing:

> **One of the earliest and most important tasks of management is to think through how a deal will impact employees and to carefully plan how it can best be communicated, with its merits and risks accurately presented.**

Benefits and salaries, career paths, and security figure most prominently in their thinking. Even the most dedicated employees will tend to think about what the deal means for them first and their company second. In many cases, "reductions in force" are required, and handling these very disruptive changes without jeopardizing the success of a deal is a major transition management task. We offer specific suggestions for presenting the deal to employees in Chapters 6 and 7.

Less directly, more than one executive in a subsidiary has seen an acquisition made in another part of the firm have an impact on his or her subsidiary. For example, cash flow from the subsidiary's business may be drained to service the debt that is incurred. Our personal experience has shown, for example, that the performance criteria and bonus systems of all other division and subsidiary managers will need to be examined to make sure that acquisitions do not strain the pool of funds available. Acquisitions will not be supported if other divisions or subsidiaries are asked to pay for them indirectly through lowered capital budgets and bonuses, unless their contributions are recognized in some way.

External Players

A whole industry has emerged to service mergers and acquisitions, and this industry is no small contributor in generating activity when none may otherwise exist. Without doubt, much of the attention on mergers and acquisitions has been focused on the external players, particularly the investment bankers. The three types of key external players we focus on are investment bankers, law firms, and a limited number of the most prestigious consulting firms.

Key External Players

THE BANKER'S ROLE.   The glamour and money involved in "megadollar" deals is considerable, but recent. Ten years ago, for example, investment banking was far from being the hot career for graduating Harvard, Wharton, or Tuck MBAs. The firms were conservative and staff had to judge their career progress over a lifetime, not just months.[3] The same pattern applied for Wall Street law firms. The volume of merger-acquisition activity, the complexity and size of the deals, and a stronger marketing orientation among these firms changed all this. Our own contacts with investment bankers still confirm the reality of the incredible stress and pressure they experience, punctuated by periods of deadening boredom.

Statistics noting the relative size and success of the investment banking firms are readily available in major business publications, and books such as Ken Auletta's *Greed and Glory on Wall Street: The Rise and Fall of The House of Lehman* certainly provide some insight into this world. The January 1983 *Fortune* article on dealmakers at eight firms also adds glamour and perspective, with First Boston's Bruce Wasserstein generating $31 million in four 1982 mergers as one striking example. The success of firms such as Drexel Burnham Lambert and Salomon Brothers has been spectacular. Drexel, for example, grew from 3,000 employees in 1979 to 6,200 in 1984. *Forbes* estimated a twenty-fold increase in earnings for Drexel during this period.[4] The "junk bond," as one innovation, gets an "A+" grade.

What is so curious about the role of investment bankers is the contrast between how they and how others see their role. Large acquisitive firms such as Allied see the investment bankers as necessary only for giving a third-party opinion about a deal's legitimacy and for helping resolve any differences of opinion during negotiations. Allied could otherwise execute the deal with its own internal staff. On the other hand, staff at the largest firms contend that they play an essential role in bringing clients together, valuing and structuring a deal, and rounding up enough financing to make a deal happen. It is an impartial role, from their perspective. The size of their fees (several million dollars, in some cases), growing interfirm competition, and insider trading scandals are challenging this arm's-length image.[5]

There is little question that investment bankers have become aggressive and creative in recent years, but their basic role of legitimizer, intermediary, and funds finder is established and important. They play their most active roles in the search, analysis and offer, and negotiation stages. Our conversations with some of these key players confirm that they see little or no role in later stages, yet their actions have profound consequences for downstream success. One role they do play in the integration stage is helping sell off unwanted businesses and assets. They also may be brought back in to help restructure debt and find additional capital if the deal begins to drain financial resources.

Along with investment banks are other financial institutions who obviously play a critical role in helping finance deals. Typically, the long-established ties of a firm to its bank will dictate who is or is not involved. As lines blur the boundaries between firms competing in the financial services industry, banks have become more active players, particularly in financing leveraged buyouts. The financiers and bankers play their greatest role in arranging and maintaining financing during the analysis and offer and negotiation stages.

THE LAWYER'S ROLE. Tales of Wall Street law firms are also legend these days, primarily due to the early raiders such as Boone Pickens and Carl Ichan. Boards of directors had to be creative to repel hostile offers, and law firms turned their imaginations to this end. They became, for many firms, the prime strategists in the attack and defense, accumulating large fees along the way. For example, Joseph Flom of Skadden, Arps, Slate, Meagher & Flom has created many strategies for both takeovers and defenses. His firm has grown from 40 lawyers in 1970 to 274 lawyers by 1982.[6]

Not surprisingly, both attacking and defending firms often feel they are caught in an unwanted, costly cross-fire benefiting no one but these law firms. Mounting and then being forced to "ride a dragon" is a popular pastime on Wall Street these days. The complexity of many deals from a tax perspective has also taken the contributions of the law firms to a high art form. But the lawyers also see their role as a relatively limited one without any significant responsibility for its impact downstream.

THE CONSULTANT'S ROLE.   Major consulting firms such as Booz-Allen, Boston Consulting Group, McKinsey, Hay Associates; executive search firms like Egon Zehnder; and "Big Eight" accounting firms are also active players. The "due diligence" requirement assures their involvement in confirming accounting practices and account balances. Their involvement tends to be in the analysis and offer and integration stages, and is confined to very specific tasks.

There is a strong desire, as we have observed, for the acquiring firm to try to limit the involvement of consulting firms to specific tasks, with little if any responsibility in the overall process. One consulting firm may be asked to develop background information and perform an analysis of a candidate's competitive position in a key market. Another consulting firm may be asked to evaluate that candidate's top management strengths and weaknesses. The acquiring firm often has established relationships from previous work with such firms, and they continue to use them. Each firm has its strengths and weaknesses, although all have been developing expertise in mergers and acquisitions over the past few years. Integrating the work done by different, sometimes competing, consulting firms becomes a significant issue in some cases. With the large number of powerful external players involved, we want to emphasize the following:

> **Ownership and control of the process must remain in the hands of the key internal players. When control shifts to external players with lesser stakes in the long-term consequences, there is less of a guarantee about what those consequences may be.**

Peripheral External Players

In addition to the management consulting firms, there is a host of peripheral players such as public relations firms, consultants who identify candidates for a finder's fee, and others who assemble blocks of stock in tender offers. Others may track stock market activity for firms wary of hostile tender offers. Still others do outplacement for displaced executives and counseling for employees dealing with the stress of an acquisition. Consulting in all these areas is big business, requiring a high level of sophistication and competence.

Aside from the core external players, there is a host of more peripheral players. These include stockholders and major investors who must tender stock and later approve the deal. For the most part, stockholders play a role late in the process by voting on a deal which has already become virtually a *fait accompli*. In more than one deal, stockholders have found their interests not well-protected by boards and management. For example, there is the questionable management practice of buying out a firm to take it private and then later reaping even greater profits by taking it public or breaking it up and selling the parts. T. Boone Pickens' somewhat self-serving attempt to organize a stockholders' association is a needed step in challenging practices such as the use of "poison pills" that restrict stockholder rights.[7]

Arbitrageurs, whose interventions can either help or hurt negotiations, and other interested firms who may want to buy spun-off businesses from the acquired or merged firm, are added to the set of very interested, but peripheral players.[8] Arbitrageurs like Ivan Boesky were influential in bidding up a stock's price and thus raising the acquiring firm's costs. On the other hand, there are a great many firms wanting to buy divisions that are spun off in a deal, and they play a useful role by lowering a deal's total cost.

There are other players such as the media, whose coverage can play a critical role in a deal by prematurely disclosing or distorting information, perhaps leading to stock price changes. How a deal is reported and viewed by commentators also can shape the reactions of stockholders and regulatory agencies. Smart firms will have well-prepared rumor control procedures and media campaigns in place to put the best light possible on a desired merger. Allied's merger with Signal, for example, was uniformly and enthusiastically reported by the media. Allied's Corporate Information Services staff very effectively produced a steady stream of news releases, visual aids and videos about the merger to assure a positive climate.

The regulatory agencies are major players in some industries. The SEC can halt a deal, and approvals by other regulatory agencies can slow up closure or force the sale of portions of a business. The experience of Frank Lorenzo in buying Eastern is a good example. The 1986 and 1987 scandals concerning insider information in mergers and acquisitions also has generated increased surveillance by the SEC. Congress's concern about hostile takeovers and the impact of mergers on communities has also made it an interested party, if not an active player.[9]

Outside the airline industry, labor unions have been largely silent about mergers and acquisitions.[10] There are occasional cases where a union protests, primarily due to plant closures or conflicting wage rates and bargaining agreements, but the overall pattern has been one of relative restraint. As Markley Roberts, an AFL-CIO economist in Washington, D.C., noted in an interview with us, the AFL-CIO wants to protect workers and their communities, but there is not a clear consensus about how or what to do.

In a few cases there has even been active support for a merger when the acquired firm was failing. TWA's unions, other than the flight attendants', supported Carl Ichan over Frank Lorenzo thinking that Ichan would be easier to live with than Lorenzo.[11] In another airline industry case, the inability of United Airlines to negotiate an agreement with its unions killed its 1986 purchase of troubled Frontier Airlines from Peoples Express. The union effectively sealed Peoples Express's financial fate in the process.[12]

There has also been indirect union resistance to a deal. To help cover the $300 million "greenmail" paid in the attempted takeover of Disney in 1985, Disney management reportedly tried to get concessions from the unions. The attempt resulted in the first strike in 25 years against Disney, and the union successfully "beat back the worst of the concessions.[13]" In other cases, unions have forced management to discuss the effects of a proposed leveraged buyout on workers.[14]

Suppliers and customers also can be active players and they are certainly affected by a merger or acquisition.[15] The collective wail of hospitals who were customers of American Hospital Supply, and of other suppliers to Hospital Corporation of America was certainly a factor in casting a cloud over the unfortunate American Hospital Supply-HCA proposed merger. Saatchi & Saatchi, in its attempt to become the world's largest advertising firm, made a critical assumption that the clients of the advertising firms it acquired would come along, too. Not so. Many clients like Colgate-Palmolive not only did not want a "mega-agency" representing them, but also found it unpalatable that one of their major competitors was also represented by another part of agency.[16]

Finally, there are the cities and communities where firms operate. They typically have little influence in a deal, although they can be profoundly affected by the closing of a plant or use of a firm's funds to diversify away from traditional industries.[17] Whether they will remain on the sidelines is difficult to say, but states such as Indiana and Washington are taking action in some takeovers.

The reactions of these more peripheral players must be evaluated and anticipated because they can be significant. An active campaign to inform these peripheral players and to gain their support is essential during the transition stage. Very active firms have well-developed strategies and procedures for working with most peripheral players to either channel their reactions or gain their support. The sheer number of players, as we noted when we began this chapter, places a premium upon active management of the process.

Their Dynamics and Consequences

In Chapter 3 we stressed the importance of good fit among the "three pillars:" financial fit, business fit, and organizational fit. That chapter's basic premise was that weakness in one of these pillars will undermine the others and the deal's eventual success.

Because of the number and variety of involved players, we are trying to make a case for effective process management in this chapter. The process is inherently prone to difficulties because of the high level of interdependence between stages. The outcome quality from one stage poses serious consequences for the outcome quality from other stages. Add to this already complex process the episodic, uneven, and very substantial roles played by the large number of actors. Not only are a great many of these players external, but several of them wield considerable power with differing degrees of commitment to the process. We stress this point by the following:

> **The timing of player entries and exits, the effective integration of their contributions, and the quality control of those contributions become major process management tasks. Indeed, this may well be the most important process management task!**

The interaction of process stages and players generates a complex dynamic which

1. Encourages *process fragmentation*—poor integration among process stages, leading to uneven quality
2. Promotes a heavy *front-ending* of the process—a bias toward earlier stages and undermanagement of implementation and integration stages
3. *Escalates commitment*—makes it difficult to abort the process when necessary
4. Allows a *susceptibility to surprise*—an inability to buffer the process from unanticipated events

A few researchers have begun focusing on the process management aspects of mergers and acquisitions, and we found the coincidence of their findings helped validate own observations.[18] The early work of Dave Jemison and Sim Sitkin has been particularly useful in framing some of the concepts, and we have adapted an early model of theirs in Figure 5-3 to illustrate the complexity of the process when various players are integrated within it.[19]

Process Fragmentation

An obvious feature of Figure 5-3 is the episodic involvement of the process's key players. Perhaps only with the exception of Corporate Development staff, no single player has continuous

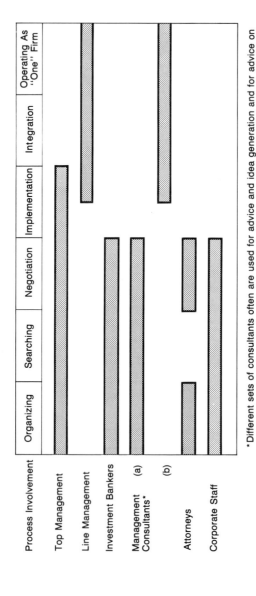

Figure 5-3 Involvement of key actors at different stages of the merger-acquisition process. (Source: Adapted from D. Jemison and S. Sitkin, "Corporate Acquisitions: A Process Perspective," Working Paper. Graduate School of Business, Stanford University, Stanford Ca, 1984.)

*Different sets of consultants often are used for advice and idea generation and for advice on integration activity.

involvement over the entire process. Even Corporate Development phases out its involvement as line operating managers assume responsibility for integrating the two firms to the desired level. We used the example of BellSouth's Corporate Development unit as an example of a group that played a positive role by prolonging its involvement. But even its staff eventually had to turn to other deals and reduce contact with previous acquisitions.

Process fragmentation, or "activity segmentation" as Jemison and Sitkin call it, is therefore a function of the necessary division of labor required to manage a complex, drawn-out process. The process is complicated when each player has specialized knowledge, often divergent interests, and different vocabularies. The world of investment bankers and Wall Street law firms is very different than that of a vice president of human resources. Each has essential knowledge that must be brought to bear, and making sure that this knowledge is folded into the process is an important process management task.

The players' divergent interests are also easy to appreciate. Involvement in an acquisition may absorb only a small portion of a human resources manager's time and effort, but 100 percent of the director of corporate development's time and effort. Keeping involvement a high priority for all players is therefore another important task, and a tricky one. The investment bankers, for example, may have as many as 10 to 20 major deals in various stages of completion, with some demanding much more attention than others. Unless a deal has particular attraction for an investment bank, its attention span can be very limited. Nor do investment bankers necessarily see their role extending beyond a very limited scope of activity. As one senior partner at one of the largest and most successful Wall Street firms confided, what happens after the completion of a deal is "not in our sphere of influence and (is a matter) to which we are rightly indifferent."

A major process management task is to assure a uniformly high quality of the various players' contributions. Responsibility for quality control rests with the team leader and ultimately with the CEO. Quality control becomes important in doing the studies of candidate firms and is essential later when very in-depth reviews of businesses and functional areas are performed. The "Big Eight" accounting firms doing "due diligence" work have refined and standardized their output, and relatively few deals go sour afterwards due to their faulty work. However, exceptions can be found. The practice of making a banker or auditor's fee contingent upon the execution of a deal is definitely suspect. In general, actively acquisitive firms have well-developed formats and procedures for analyzing other firms and getting the information they need. We have encountered detailed routines in areas such as accounting, public affairs, and human resources. There is always the lurking doubt, of course, that the "right" information may escape a rigidly structured process.

In summary, process fragmentation is a serious negative consequence arising from the need to perform process tasks using different players, all interacting unevenly and episodically throughout the process's stages. Some of them—primarily the investment bankers and law firms, but also unions—are very powerful and independent. Effective process management therefore demands sufficient integration and quality control of their contributions. We stress these ideas by adding the following:

> **The responsibility for assuring integration and quality control must rest with an individual or unit, most typically corporate development. The knowledge, skills, and influence of staff in this unit must be critically evaluated and built before needed.**

Process Front-Ending

One issue not previously studied by other researchers is the tendency to place too much emphasis on the stages before the deal's closing and not enough emphasis on the crucial transition period encompassed by the implementation and integration stages. Process "front-ending" is not surprising, given the key players involved in those early stages. The size of fees earned by the law firms and investment bankers—several million dollars in many cases—demand management's full attention to their work.

The importance of setting a price and structuring terms and conditions, establishing a compatible and comfortable rapport between managements, and even perhaps having to bid against other firms in a media-charged climate obviously makes the early stages critical to success.

Less appreciated until recently have been the consequences of undermanaged transition and integration efforts—"post-merger management" as it has been called.[20] Front-ending is characterized by disportionately larger amounts of management attention and resources being devoted "upstream" compared to the later "downstream" stages. To illustrate the importance of providing adequate resources for transition management, we can use a non-merger example of a newly elected governor's transition into office one of us worked on a few years ago. After spending massive amounts of money in the election, the new governor discovered the stark reality that less than $100,000 could be found in the entire state budget to assist his transition. Historically, much of that money had been used to remodel the new governor's offices. Given the importance of maintaining momentum and quickly mobilizing his new change agenda, he found himself seriously handicapped in the transition. He went on to have a very successful term, even becoming a presidential candidate later, but he admits that he lost about three to four months' work because his transition process had been inhibited.

As another example, a successful merger-acquisition team arrived at its transition stage totally exhausted physically and mentally. In doing so it created about a two-week hiatus where very little happened. Precious momentum was lost and unnecessary uncertainty created. The team simply had not planned on the process being so demanding, and that so much of its energy would be expended up front without having a plan for dealing with the period afterwards.

In general, the actively acquisitive firms like Allied-Signal have "open tab" policies about resource allocations for transition periods. Whatever resources are needed to succeed will, within reason, be provided. If this means, as in the Allied-Bendix merger, keeping a corporate jet "with engines running" to ferry transition team members between Morristown, New Jersey and Southfield, Michigan, so be it. This policy, while sounding extravagant, at least produces consistently good results. This is an important point worth stressing:

With so much at stake, putting constraints on what can and cannot be afforded is near-sighted. Spend and do what is necessary to be successful. The middle of an important deal is not the time to count change.

Process front-ending also is characterized by not appreciating how the terms and conditions so readily agreed upon upstream have unanticipated downstream consequences that may jeopardize transition period success. In the "three pillars" chapter we stressed how pricing and terms negotiated early in a deal can later compromise business and organizational fit. It is best to remember that saying "no" later, when "yes" was agreed upon earlier, has very real monetary and nonmonetary costs. The anxiety and uncertainty inherent in the transition period will mean that every action and statement by the acquiring firm's management will be scrutinized for its value in signaling intentions and direction. Trust is particularly fragile during this period, as we point out in the next chapters, and backing out of agreements reached earlier is definitely one way of destroying trust. Team members and other players involved early in the process need to recognize the impact of even casual statements.

To prevent excessive front-ending, clear commitments are needed of management time for later stages. Realistic budgets for transition period tasks and events also need to be developed and agreed upon as early as possible, unless the "open tab" policy is adopted. Balancing top management attention and making sure that sufficient resources are available to optimize the transition period thus are critical process management tasks. The early stages are exciting and fun. For younger staff, they are also the domain of the "heavy hitters" and are great opportunities to learn from skilled specialists. Later stages are much less exciting. Extremely long hours must be spent in implementing an acquisition. Work sessions can be full of conflict and difficult, particularly if major reductions in workforce or a plant closing is needed. We stress again, however, that it is the execution of a deal—not just its negotiation—that causes many fatal mistakes to be made.

Escalating Commitment

Jemison and Sitkin believe "The forces that stimulate momentum in the acquisition process are stronger than those forces that retard its momentum.[21]" These authors say that there are great dangers in moving too quickly. For example, setting a number of committed players into motion, particularly those working for large contingency fees, can take events out of a CEO's control. Similarly, the desire to maintain secrecy necessitates fast action, and overconfidence in the acquiring firm's ability to manage a large deal can lead to undesirable escalation. Regulatory and legal obstacles can slow the pace—but often for only short periods. The airline industry is a classic case of how relaxed regulatory supervision of mergers created waves of mergers, and even when questions were raised by regulators, as in the Eastern-Texas Air merger, the deal was slowed, not aborted.

We certainly accept the idea that there is a tendency toward escalating momentum, but we differentiate between momentum and commitment. *Momentum* refers to the pace of events, which we have already stated as something needing constant monitoring. *Commitment* refers to the tendency for CEOs and merger-acquisition teams to deepen commitment, to "up the ante," and even rationalize bad news in order to negotiate a deal. Assumptions made later and later in a deal that is encountering difficulties have a way of getting more and more suspect. The "bearer of bad tidings" in a hotly pursued deal has a chance of being executed. The willingness to overlook or rationalize bad news is an unhealthy aspect within the process. Investment bankers and other consultants can help keep the process objective. For example, Roger Miller, Director of Salomon Bros.'s Merger-Acquisition Division, has counseled clients that "some of the best deals are the ones you don't make." We want to stress this idea:

The ability to abandon a bad deal needs to be valued as highly as that for executing a good one.

The CEO needs to cultivate a climate within the team that allows potentially negative data to surface and be factored into decision-making. As Chapter 7 will illustrate, there is a very real need within the core group of players to create healthy, constructive norms governing their interactions. A willingness to share information, question assumptions, and debate pros and cons is invaluable. Sometimes the contrary norm prevails. A team or group is dominated by a CEO who has already formed strong opinions about a deal and offers it for execution, not debate. To the extent possible, clearly defined criteria are used to guide decisions about increasing commitment and stakes over the process. Preserving options and choices as long as possible is a generally accepted groundrule.

Being able to maintain perspective and remain somewhat detached from the process is another valuable skill. Strong emotional and ego stakes do get built over time, so it is easier to call for detachment than achieve it. After putting several weeks of work into a detailed evaluation of an attractive acquisition candidate, watching it sink becomes a painful experience, as one of us personally found out not long ago.

Susceptibility to Surprise

The sheer number of players and distinct tasks involved is so high that breakdowns and "surprises" are inevitable. Process fragmentation breeds surprise: the unanticipated event which disrupts an otherwise smooth process. Finding out, for example, that a candidate's new products—an initial attractive feature of the deal—flopped in market tests can be a nasty surprise. Similarly, making assumptions that can only be tested well into negotiations, perhaps only even in the implementation stage, is a natural set-up for surprise. Assumptions about cash flow, key managers staying, and major clients remaining after a deal closes can all prove unfounded. Clearly, it is better to encounter surprises earlier rather than later in the process. How the acquiring firm manages surprises thus becomes a critical process management issue. To put it simply,

Count on surprises. Knowing they will occur means developing the ability to move quickly and decisively to deal with them as they occur. There is, nonetheless,

no substitute for doing your homework to minimize their number and impact.

Executives and staff at the firms where we interviewed readily admit that no two deals are the same. The overall process may be comparable across deals, but the pacing of events, difficulties encountered, and responses to those difficulties have a unique quality. Over a sufficiently long time, however, a repertoire of strategies and responses helps them jump the hurdles a bit easier each time.

There is definite merit in a well-structured, well-paced process, but there must also be a resident capacity and sufficient slack to deal with the unexpected. The process can otherwise bog down and lose momentum. Managing the pace and flow of process tasks, and maintaining an ongoing "what if" contingency planning dialogue among the key players can help maintain momentum.

The pace and flow can be easily disrupted when sufficient resources and effort are not devoted to the process. During one acquisition, key staff were pulled from the team because of a major project that encountered trouble. The loss of the staff slowed the analysis of the candidate firm, prolonged the offer stage, and resulted in a higher price because the candidate firm's business experienced a quick upturn in profits before the deal could be negotiated.

Another sure way to disrupt the process is to overload it by simultaneously pursuing more than one acquisition at a time. A small, rapidly growing firm we studied wanted to diversify through acquisitions, but repeatedly had deals break down in the negotiation stage because they were pursuing three or four at the same time. A setback in one deal could snowball and jeopardize the other deals. Such activity is not for the smaller, less-experienced firm. There are simply too many pieces floating about at once, and a setback in one deal would not be overcome quickly enough to prevent failure.

A major merger or acquisition, as so many executives told us, is all-absorbing. There is no substitute for full attention and maximum allocation of resources to prevent surprises from derailing the process. The pacing of stages and events through active monitoring and management can help prevent some surprises.

Summary

Like the last chapter, this chapter has demonstrated the complexity and dynamic quality of the merger-acquisition process. The dynamic generated by the interaction of players across process stages becomes a major source of process failure. Added to the potential for poor financial, business, and organizational fit, it really is not too surprising why so many mergers and acquisitions fail.

Nonetheless, many do succeed. Careful, highly professional scrutiny of fit among the "three pillars" does occur. So does very effective, skilled process management to prevent, or at least minimize, the sources of setback and difficulty just discussed. Perhaps the weakest aspect of process management is in transition management. The next chapters focus upon this critical, but undermanaged, aspect of merger-acquisition practice.

6

DEFINING
A ROLE

The "make or break" stage in the merger-acquisition process is the time from a negotiated agreement up to the implementation of the most critical changes and the establishment of new routines. This is the transition stage in our model presented in Chapter 4. As noted in that chapter, it is a particularly vulnerable time because it combines maximum uncertainty with minimum clarity about new operating responsibilities, roles, and systems. The transition stage varies in duration. It may be three months or a year long, but generally accepted sources state that the first 100 days are most critical; the potential for assuring or preventing success is greatest in this period. (The integration stage may require many additional months, and is our focus in Chapter 8.)

The transition stage is a natural opportunity for introducing change that may not be as easily introduced at any other time in an organization's life, except perhaps during a major leadership succession.[1] However, there are many factors during the transition period which determine its success. Some are within management's control while others are not. Because these factors are so important, we explore them in two chapters. This chapter focuses on the acquiring or initiating firm's fundamental need to define and articulate both a sound short- and long-term strategy for managing the acquisition. This strategy is expressed as a posture or role the firm will initially adopt, at least until the discovery of another more appropriate one. The costs of changing these roles can be high, and it pays to get it right the first time. The senior managements of both firms must acknowledge that a specific role is being played and adhere to it.

The next chapter focuses on the actual operational management of the transition process. In it, we define five conditions which must be met for effectiveness. Using transition management teams and task forces to manage this period is strongly advocated, and several suggestions for their use are offered in that chapter. A case study of the effective Allied-Bendix transition management task force, with some comparisons to the more recent Allied-Signal task force, illustrate these key concepts. We conclude with a look at long-term integration issues and strategies, particularly the issues associated with cultural change.

We begin with one worthy caveat stressed in the "three pillars" and process design chapters: Don't forget how greatly earlier "upstream" decisions and choices affect later "downstream" stages. Flaws in financial or business fit, for example, may not easily repaired by assuring an even better organizational fit. Assessing and developing all three types of fit are the primary objectives of the transition stage. Executing those strategies is the objective of the integration stage.

An acquisition that is either too expensive or too dependent on what nonexistent synergies surface can seriously damage management's later ability to implement the deal. Peoples Express's acquisition of Frontier was a financially bad idea— one which helped drain the company so much that it was impossible to ever effectively integrate Frontier. We must assume in this chapter that both financial and business fit pillars are basically sound, although much may still be uncertain about just how sound they are at the time an agreement is negotiated.

One more caveat also is appropriate. We assume that the joining of forces accomplishes sound business objectives, not the complete dismembering and break-up of the acquired organization. We assume the acquiring firm wants more than simply assets. People are an essential element in an effective transition process, and the desire to retain the most valuable people, along with key businesses, is paramount.

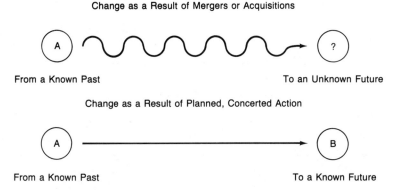

Figure 6-1   Two views about change.

The Fundamental Tasks of Transition Management

Figure 6-1 illustrates the basic difference between most change management efforts and merger or acquisition changes. Planned change efforts involve taking an organization from a known past to a known—or at least planned—future. The change induced by a merger or acquisition means moving from a known past to an essentially unknown future. Detailed plans may be incomplete or nonexistent at the time of agreement.

The futures of the merging organizations may be fairly clear to the key players actively involved in the process, and hopefully well known to the CEO who initiated the merger. However, few others in the acquiring firm may know of future plans, and the future may be a complete mystery to the acquired firm. Therefore, the first and most basic task of transition management is clearly defining and actively communicating its vision of a desirable future for all those inside and outside with stakes in the success of both organizations. The two firms need to define the roles they will play in creating this future. Simply put, the task is to clarify what role is to be played and communicate it clearly and unequivocally.

Second, the following transition questions must be answered during transition and integration to help employees adapt to the change they will confront in living with this new, still uncertain future:

1. Why change? What are the legitimate reasons and purpose for changing?
2. Where are we going? What will it be like there (for me)?
3. How are we going to get there? What actions and resources are needed to get there?
4. Can we get there? Do we have the capacity to do what is asked?
5. When will we get there? What is the timeframe and significant milestones?
6. Who will lead us there?

Obviously, complete answers to these questions are impossible—even undesirable—this early in the new relationship. Initially, only broad, nonspecific answers may be possible. As James Brian Quinn noted in discussing when and how to communicate strategic goals, there are situations when ambiguous goals are most appropriate.[2] Quinn contends, among other outcomes, ambiguous goals can allow greater "buy-in" and can prevent unwanted centralization. In its first moments, the transition is a time for symbolic action and broad definitions of direction. Symbolic acts and broad statements can be extremely powerful. For example, Laurence Tisch, in taking control of CBS from Thomas Wyman in September 1986, made it very clear that quality programming, not cost cutting, would be his goal. Coupled with William Paley's rejoining CBS, this symbolic act and Tisch's statement created an initially positive climate for subsequent change without prematurely limiting choices.[3] While some cost-cutting was expected, his initial cuts proved so large that his first statements unfortunately later lost much of their impact.

In the ideal situation, the two firms will collaborate to answer the above questions. In the least desirable situation, they will be answered by one firm for both. So what conditions determine whether collaboration or mandate is the most appropriate approach? To best answer that, the transition period should be viewed from a change management perspective. A considerable amount of valuable theory exists in change management literature and some of it applies here.

A Change Theory Perspective

As a change management effort, the transition management process is subject to what Zaltman and Duncan call "pitfalls.[4]" They note that change efforts can be overly rational because those efforts require rational thought and action by those involved. When their careers, livelihoods, self-concepts, and business success are greatly affected by a merger or acquisition, managers and employees are not necessarily rational.

Change goals may also be poorly defined, Zaltman and Duncan note. Ambiguous goals may lead to conflicting actions, and problems identified in the process also can be poorly defined. As a consequence, effort, considerable time and resources can be wasted on the wrong root problem.

Another serious pitfall is the lack of attention spent on the implementation of change versus that given to the formation of change goals. A major premise of this book is, of course, that too little attention, resources, and time are devoted to the transition and integration stages of a merger or acquisition.

Finally, Zaltman and Duncan note that many change efforts overfocus on change at the individual level, while not enough attention is paid to larger changes at group and organizational levels. We have found just the opposite to be true when it comes to mergers and acquisitions. Changes in the purposes and goals of major units, performance expectations, reporting relationships, and changes in major systems such as decision making and planning are initiated, but often there is not much change initiated from the individual perspective. While employees in some businesses and work units may exit the organization as a consequence, those remaining are primarily asked to simply go along with these changes. A merger or acquisition is done *to* them, not *by* them.

The highest level of change in a merger or acquisition is in the individual manager or employee, who will ideally internalize the values, beliefs, and assumptions—that is, the "culture"—of the acquiring organization. We should add, of course, that a true integration of both firms would ideally result in a mixing of the best features of both firms' cultures. We have much more to say about cultures shortly, but Figure 6-2 does illustrate the possible levels of support for change. Daryl Conner of At-

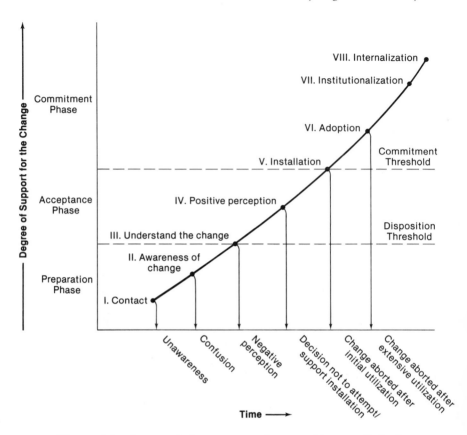

Figure 6-2 Stages of change commitment. (Source: O.D. Resources, Inc., all rights reserved, 1986. Used with permission of O.D. Resources.)

lanta's O.D. Resources, Inc. stressed in an interview that this figure emphasizes how the simple adoption of change does not necessarily mean that true internalization of the change occurs. Adoption may mean compliance while internalization yields commitment. With compliance you gain "bodies;" with commitment you gain "souls," according to Conner.

Corporate staffs and senior managements will initially be most directly impacted, and the commitment required below these levels can rapidly decline depending, of course, on the extent of necessary change. Even when a major business is sold because it does not fit the plans of the merging firms, life frequently goes on as before for that business's line managers and workers. Indeed, some businesses have reportedly been sold so many times that their employees have psychologically and operationally buffered themselves against such frequent disruptions.

Sources of Resistance to Change

If not well planned, change efforts can encounter what has come to be called "resistance to change." This is an interesting concept because the phrase has a negative connotation—resisters are "bad," while those seeking change are "good." As the Wharton School's Tom Gilmore used to point out to clients, resisting change that threatens important and sound values is not only good, but essential. As well, Jim Rosenzweig, formerly a professor at Seattle's University of Washington, was fond of saying, "No organization is so screwed up that someone doesn't like it as it is." Those initiating change in a merger or acquisition would do well to keep those ideas in mind.

> **There is a burden on the initiators of change to demonstrate that what they offer is better than what already exists.**

It is essential to understand the sources of difficulties and obstacles in change implementation. There are typically many good, as well as bad, reasons for resistance, and knowing these can help to effectively overcome them. Zaltman and Duncan again provide insight by classifying these sources in terms of individual, group, and organizational factors. Figure 6-3 summarizes several of these.

Depth of Intervention

Structuring these sources by individual, group, and organizational factors emphasizes a critical concept introduced by Roger Harrison—the "depth of intervention" attempted in a change effort.[5] In some ways, it is easiest to implement changes at an organizational level. These changes tend to be in basic systems and structures, plus other areas mentioned above: purposes and goals, performance standards, and relationships between divi-

Individual Factors	Group Factors	Organizational Factors
1. The perceptions about what is being done	1. Change violates group norms	1. Lack of top management support to change
2. The desire to conform with others	2. Change evokes conflict that threatens group continuity	2. Change threatens established power and influence patterns
3. Amount of change overwhelms them and they "hunker down" to wait it out	3. They fear rejection by others	3. Organizational structure does not support changes
4. Personalities are incompatible with what is expected	4. They lack insight and understanding of what is required	4. Negative change climate; closed to change
5. They lack knowledge and skills to do what is asked		5. Basic technology of organizaton not compatible with changes
6. Basic values and beliefs are threatened		6. Cultural "ethnocentrism" may prevail—an attitude of "We are the best" already exists

Figure 6-3   Sources of resistance to change. (Adapted from Zaltman and Duncan.)

sions. Group level changes in these same areas are more difficult, but still feasible. However, interpersonal relationships within a group—a department or business unit—tend to be stronger than those across an entire organization. The reason is size. Thus, a poor introduction of change within groups tends to have more severe consequences. It takes time to build effective team relations within a corporate staff.

Changes at the level of individual manager and employee are even more difficult, since these may entail not only the introduction of new concepts, knowledge, and skills, but also basic changes in beliefs and values—even an alteration of the individual's self-concept and identity. The simplest levels of individual change call for the reluctant and passive acceptance of change, while at higher levels the active acceptance and complete identification of the individual with the change are possible. Paul Tillich views this dynamic tension between individual change and continuity as a choice between self-identification and self-alteration.[6] The result is some level of transformation.

From the perspective of mergers and acquisitions, Tillich's dynamic implies that the acquiring firm should appreciate and value the culture of the acquired firm because of its importance to the firm's employees. Grafting an alien culture onto this firm is risky, as so much of the recent literature on mergers and acquisitions has noted.[7] Again, the joining of Peoples Express with Frontier Airlines presents an example. The two firms were built around very different concepts—one nonunion and highly decentralized, even "free form," while the other was unionized and more classically structured. The legitimate need to maintain Peoples' identity, (self-identification), versus the need to effectively integrate Frontier, (self-alteration), would either result in a profitable joining of forces, or a deterioration of the Peoples Express concept and culture. Neither has occurred, of course, due to the eventual sale of Peoples to Texas Air.

Therefore, Harrison's depth of intervention concept is important because it emphasizes that those managing the transition process must recognize the need for change at all three levels: organizational, group, and individual. What will be attempted at all three levels, and the impact of change at one level upon other levels, needs to be understood.

Timing of Intervention

Another concept with great significance is the timing of change. To act now versus later in a merger or acquisition depends on several factors, and arguments to defend either can be made. For example, a simple trade-off exists between seizing the ripest opportunity for change, and acting prematurely without adequate information to guide the change. How quickly to attempt change depends on the condition of the acquired firm and the speed necessary to realize opportunities or synergies.

Selecting a Transition Role

The acquiring firm must define the role it will play in its relationship with the acquired firm. The roles are situational, driven by the nature of the business unit's needs. We offer two models to help a firm select an appropriate role.

The McKinsey Role Model

As Jim Balloun, Managing Director of McKinsey's Atlanta office, states, "In post-acquisition management, business unit needs are defined by the value creation opportunities in the acquisition; consequently, corporate actions are driven primarily by the management levers that must be exercised to achieve the opportunities.[8]"

He outlines the potential roles management can select in Figure 6-4.

Examples of these roles include the acquisition of a small capital-constrained business with excellent management which would suggest a "financier" role. By contrast, a "restructurer" approach would be best for a failing business with inadequate management. And healthy businesses acquired to capture available synergies would call for corporate management to assume an "architect" role. "Over time, as the potential source of value changes, so should corporate management's role. For example, one shift might be from restructurer to monitor-coach, as an organizational change program progresses," Balloun feels.

The Intervention Depth and Timing Role Matrix

While the McKinsey role typology is useful for defining tasks, it is possible to tie the selection of an appropriate role directly back to our depth of intervention and timing criteria. Figure 6-5 illustrates how the two criteria can be expressed as two dimensions in a matrix.

In this transition role matrix, a "shallow" intervention depth refers to changes that would be made to build business fit, and relatively easy and selectively made changes in (1) staff and top management, (2) individual and unit reporting relationships, (3) processes such as decision-making and planning, and (4) control and information systems. Financial fit may not be an immediate concern since the performance of both firms is fundamentally healthy, although opportunities for improvement are assumed to exist. Indeed, the acquiring firm would possibly make significant investments in the acquired firm to develop its long-

Levers for realizing value

Financial ——→ | Functional ——→ | Strategic ——→

Management role	Financier	Skills exploiter	Restructurer	Architect
Basic approach	Create value through changes in financial strategy	Create value by transferring general management systems, functional skills, resources, or assets to acquired BU	Create value by integrating acquired BUs with existing BUs	Create value by changing industry competitive dynamics
Potential management actions	Leave basic management structure/plans/goals in place Remove capital and/or operating funding constraints to growth Capture available financial benefits — Operational (e.g., ITCs, tax losses, overfunded pensions) — Balance sheet (e.g., sale/leaseback, leverage) Sell off or refinance independent stand-alone business units	Functional improvements — Change focus of business system elements (e.g., start off-shore sourcing) — Take control of selected key functional activities (e.g., R&D, sales) General management — Replace some or all top managers — Set financial improvement targets and nonfinancial operating targets — Provide project management for high-impact programs	Consolidate staff/corporate functions for greater efficiency Typically, fully integrate acquiree's structure and operations with existing business units Develop new strategy, organization, and values for acquired BUs and existing BUs	Work with top management to initiate joint ventures, strategic partnerships, and/or selective acquisitions Pursue horizontal and vertical integration opportunities

Figure 6-4 McKinsey role matrix. (Source: Jim Balloun, McKinsey & Co., 1987.)

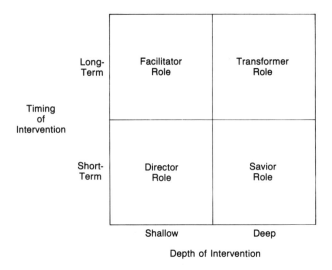

Figure 6-5   The transition role matrix.

term performance. Cultural change is not attempted in shallow interventions due to a perceived compatibility of their cultures or willingness to keep the two firms separate.

In the short term, a shallow intervention requires the acquiring firm to exercise control to quickly induce change. The combination of shallow depth and short-term timing leads to what we call the "director" role. The acquiring firm asserts its leadership and, working with information and assistance from the acquired firm, defines specific changes that need to be made within the transition stage itself, typically within three to six months. The acquired firm may be left relatively autonomous within the acquiring firm's larger structure. When a long-term perspective is taken, shallow interventions lead to what we call the "facilitator" role. The acquiring firm works with the acquired firm to define desired changes. It is a developmental orientation designed to work with management personnel, systems, and structure. The effort can take several months, if not years. Active coordination between the two firms is the norm, and the acquired firm may function autonomously under this role.

Deep interventions are necessary when the acquired firm is seriously troubled financially and damage control is required. They are also necessary when both firms need to significantly improve or change their strategic competitive performance within major businesses.

Deep interventions made in the short term lead to what we and McKinsey call the "savior" role. The savior role is very directive. It requires the fullest exercise of power over the acquired firm and leads to prompt, deep cuts in leadership and staffing, structure, processes, and systems. The culture of the acquired firm is seen as a "non-issue" or even as an obstacle to change. The savior role focuses upon financial performance and fit issues, undertaking whatever business and organizational changes are necessary to turn the acquired firm's performance around. Typically, business units are either folded or broken up and merged. Wells Fargo's acquisition of Crocker Bank is an excellent example of an effectively played savior role.

When deep interventions can best be made over a longer time, a "transformer" role can be played. Active collaboration between the two firms is the norm. The objective of the two firms is to merge their identities and businesses to create something new. Their interactions are complex and ongoing. The leadership reflects management from both firms, and, in this respect, the transformer role becomes shared between them. Allied's joining with both Bendix and Signal reflects Ed Hennessy's adoption of a transformer role. A key point here is role flexibility. Management must respond situationally to the needs of the acquired firm, as McKinsey's Jim Balloun suggests.

Approaching each new acquisition with the same role or change strategy can put the acquiring firm out of touch with the requirements and possibilities of a new situation.

One strategy or role may be appropriate in one case while another strategy is appropriate in another. It is important to be able to judge a situation and be flexible in matching role strategies with situations.

Every firm we encountered had a bias toward a particular role strategy. For example, Bill King, President of International Technology (IT) Corporation, said his preference was to wait as long as possible before intervening but always to preserve the ability to act first and before having to. His decision to intervene is not just based on quantitative performance indicators, but qualitative ones as well. One qualitative indicator he uses is to see whether the acquired firm is "networking" or beginning to voluntarily integrate activities and resources with other parts of IT Corporation. King adds that he will change telephone protocols and make sure that blue and white IT buttons are placed in a large bowl in the lobby, but meddling with successful operations is taboo.

Importantly, Bill King does not make acquisitions of firms requiring fast turnarounds. Other firms we studied also limit their acquisitions to fundamentally healthy organizations that give them time to study and plan their change efforts. Whatever the rule of thumb, a major transition management task is to accurately judge the situation, and to bring to it the appropriate effort and resources needed to intervene at the appropriate depth and speed.

Change and Be Prepared to Be Changed

In addition to the criteria suggested by the McKinsey model, we have also suggested that there is another criterion for selecting a role. The willingness of the acquiring firm to change must also be considered, as well as the condition of the acquired firm. This willingness to change is driven by the vision of the firm's future, and a merger or acquisition is a means for helping realize that vision. The acquiring firm can become compulsive about changing the acquired firm's culture and systems. Such a compulsion can have little to do with the acquired firm's financial condition, or needs. Instead, it has more to do with the attitudes of senior management and their satisfaction with the acquiring firm's own culture and systems. We believe the following:

The acquiring firm must be prepared to be changed— not just to change the other firm—for long-term success.

Placed in this larger context, a process of *mutual* adjustment may well begin with the agreement to join forces. Figure 6-6 illustrates how an acquisition can result in four major outcomes: (1) relatively autonomous operations for both firms, (2)

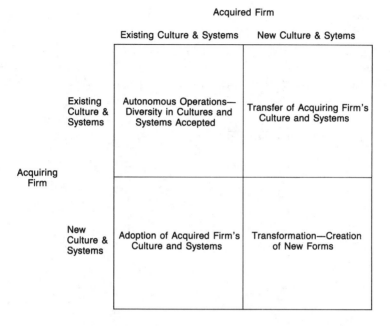

Acquired Firm

Existing Culture & Systems   New Culture & Sytems

	Existing Culture & Systems	New Culture & Sytems
Existing Culture & Systems	Autonomous Operations— Diversity in Cultures and Systems Accepted	Transfer of Acquiring Firm's Culture and Systems
New Culture & Systems	Adoption of Acquired Firm's Culture and Systems	Transformation—Creation of New Forms

Acquiring Firm

Figure 6-6   Change options for both firms.

the changing of the acquired firm's culture and systems, (3) an adoption of the acquired firm's culture and systems by the acquiring firm, and (4) the search and adoption of a new culture and systems for both firms.

Daryl Conner of O.D. Resources calls autonomous operations "coexistence," and notes that diversity between the two firms may even be encouraged.[9] This situation is rare, but exists due to regulatory constraints, geographical distance, or the wise recognition that the two firms are indeed very different and could never be totally merged. On the other hand, Conner calls the changing of the acquired firm's culture and systems "assimilation" because the dominant firm imposes its own on the other. Assimilation can work in reverse when the acquired firm's culture and systems come to dominate and supplant those of the acquiring firm. While unusual, attempts like those of Roger Smith at GM to change GM's culture through the EDS acquisition are increasingly common.

There can also be a willingness of two firms to join and transform, creating a synthesis of their two cultures and systems in the process. Allied's merger with Signal made good business sense because it reinforced Hennessy's vision of Allied as a leading-edge high technology firm. But Signal's more relaxed culture also had its attractions, as Signal found out about Allied in terms of its management systems and style. The result is the "transformation," as Conner would call it, of the two firms into something new. There is, as we noted in Chapter 2, an increasing trend toward transformations via mergers and acquisitions.

7

MANAGING
THE TRANSITION
STAGE

The cornerstone of effective merger-acquisition implementation is sound transition management. Unless the transition stage is viewed as a special project requiring substantial capital expenditures and the best efforts of the firm's finest managers, the merger results are likely to be disappointing. John Robson, former CEO of G.D. Searle Pharmaceutical Company echoes this view. "I am a real believer in gold-plated transitions, whether in government or the private sector. The importance of a carefully planned, well-executed transition effort, one that is done with sensitivity and an eye for detail, cannot be overemphasized." Robson has been the architect of numerous merger-acquisitions and governmental reorganizations, and his experience has led him to conclusions similar to those of other experienced leaders who have transformed a number of different institutions. Unfortunately their wisdom is often not put to use. Transition management is the most neglected part of the merger-acquisition process.

There are two broad reasons many transition and integration efforts fail. The first is that the very foundations of the merger-acquisition are weak. Those involved have failed to take into account all issues related to business fit, financial fit, and organizational fit. The second major cause of failure is the lack of good transition management. Even if the strategic planning is flawless, the transition process is perilous by nature. Organizations, like individuals, resist change. Yet companies pay large sums to acquire other firms and then don't follow through with the necessary involvement, assuming the predicted changes will occur. As one merger-acquisition consultant remarked, "You can't believe the number of companies I see that pay huge premiums to buy another company and then they do nothing with it—they assume that synergies will magically occur and generate torrents of cash flow!"

Unless the acquisition plan calls for the parent company to function simply as a holding company, enriching only its assets portfolio without actively managing them, there must be some form of active intervention. The reason? Organizations do not successfully merge because their employees suddenly meld, instantly syncronizing all their activities. Instead, a prolonged process ensues in which the acquiring company deals with layers of resistance before achieving change and integration. The predictable causes of such resistance are well known and can be clearly summarized. They are

1. Habit that creates inertia
2. Anxiety that produces rigid or "conservative" responses
3. Previous commitments—often unwritten—supporting the continuation of past practices; included in this is the tug of old allegiances and the general regressive pull of the past
4. Commitments based on sunk costs—people fail to accept that returns from past practices are diminishing, so, because of a need to justify past courses of action, people adhere to them, vainly hoping they'll finally pay off
5. Threats to existing power and influence bases
6. Resource limitations
7. Pressure of conformity to norms
8. Lack of a climate supporting change[1]

These predictable forces of resistance call for vigorous transition management. We have found that such transition efforts can be managed either by the original architects of the

merger-acquisition plan or by a special transition task force established by top management. Successful transition management
requires extraordinary effort from established groups and organizational structures, plus the creation of new roles and structures.

**Successful merger-acquisition outcomes are achieved
through vigorous transition management programs that
implement strategic visions and overcome organizational resistances.**

Establishing a Climate for Change

Senior management's most important task during the transition
period is to ensure a climate is created that nurtures change and
innovation. They must do this while preserving stability and
operating continuity. Senior management also must seek a delicate balance between achieving current goals, and creating momentum for change and innovation. Whether the transition time
is stagnant or chaotic depends on how well it is actively planned
and managed. Senior management's most basic task is to prevent
the anarchy of total revolution *and* the inertia of conservation.
Figure 7-1 illustrates the relationship between the amount of
disruption accompanying change and the corresponding degrees
of management necessary.

Here, low amounts of unmanaged change show up as
"noise," and may have little significance. But high amounts of
unmanaged change can lead to anarchy. Anarchy in a transition
process appears as widespread perceptions of confusion and drift,
false or unintentional signals, undesirable losses of many managers, attempts by external players (for example, investors) to
control the process, and avoidable conflict that embitters and
damages working relationships. Anarchy typically results from
intervening too deeply, too soon without a clear strategy or role.
Some disruption is, nonetheless, desirable.

**When managed well, the disruption associated with
change can serve as a constructive precondition for positive transformation.**

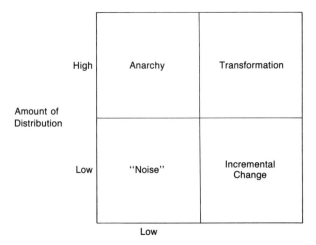

Figure 7-1 The relationship between disruption and its management.

Preconditions Determining Transition Success

The transition management process needs to address six major areas as a precondition for success. These are (1) governing assumptions and ground rules that set the climate for change; (2) extent to which communication channels are managed; (3) availability of accurate, timely information about events and climate; (4) access to sufficient resources to complete the process; (5) effectiveness of the structure created to manage the process; and (6) extent to which dysfunctional psychological and social dynamics are managed.

Governing Assumptions

Acquiring firms make both implicit and explicit assumptions about the "critical success factors" needed to achieve positive results. For example, they make a number of crucial assumptions about how they will add value to their investment and thereby increase the financial returns on their expenditures. We have stressed in previous chapters why these fundamental assumptions must be consciously made and clearly articulated.

When explicitly stated, the acquired company can readily respond to these assumptions, and the acquiring company can then create early opportunities to test its presuppositions and make corrections.

Establishing Communication Channels

Establishing communication channels upward and downward is an essential feature of the successful merger-acquisition effort. We have observed many situations where an organization's merger-acquisition efforts were damaged either because of isolation at the top or because of insufficient information at lower levels. In one healthcare takeover, some key managers were ready to leave the organization because they assumed that a new management team was being sent in to replace them. In fact, the new team was meant to help them carry out the extra duties created by the reorganization, and this team of helpers was instructed to move to another facility after six months. The current managers did not know this, and the executives in the home office, who were unaware of this communication problem, did nothing to correct it until they heard that one of their most valuable directors was about to resign.

Establishing effective two-way communication systems early in the merger-acquisition process is of paramount importance.

The CEO of a firm involved in one of 1985's largest takeovers observes,

Communication is crucial, somebody has to be aware of every detail. If the location of the drinking fountains is important to employees, someone has to be prepared to deal with that issue. If information like that isn't communicated, you can't be sensitive to the subtle and symbolic concerns that can make or break you during the transition process.

Don Revelle, Black & Decker's Senior Vice President for Human Resources, says his experience has taught him to have a communications specialist involved early and deeply in the process. In some cases, this has even been the Human Resources person because so many transition issues involve questions of staffing, benefits, and compensation. A plant may also have to be closed or moved. In most cases, however, a Corporate Relations or Public Affairs person will assume responsibility for communications.

As the Allied-Bendix and Allied-Signal cases illustrate, an effective public affairs staff can play an active, key role. Among other activities, they screen, edit, and prepare public and internal statements using mediums such as news releases, internal newsletters, special announcements, touring presentations by senior management, and, most recently, videotapes. A fifteen-minute videotape outlining the positive reasons for the Allied-Signal acquisition was professionally prepared and shown to several thousand Allied and Signal line employees. These communications were coordinated with personal visits by the CEOs and senior managers of both firms, who made personal presentations and answered questions.

Accurate, Timely Information

If the screening stage is effective and sophisticated, then much useful information will be available to guide later stages. The offer and negotiation stages will generate more information for the acquiring firm, and the task is to make sure that this information can easily be made available during the transition. The transition stage is also a period of discovery and an opportunity to test previous assumptions and proposals.

A plan for gathering and assembling information must be developed by the transition management team. Outside consultants may be necessary in this effort. Such consultants often are retained to gather specific types of information. In fact, accounting firms conducting "due diligence" studies will be asked to attest to the accuracy of that information. In other cases, management audits will help determine the capacity of key managers and current systems. Outside consultants can be useful because many of them may be already well known to one or both firms, and they can quickly field a large staff for an efficient study.

The objective in gathering information is to develop the capacity to collect and collate data and quickly fill informational gaps. The Corporate Development staff or the transition team typically does this. Quality control becomes essential to assure the work is well coordinated.

We strongly suggest the creation of a running record or history of events, decisions, and actions to facilitate later evaluation of the merger-acquisition effort.

A ground rule during the information gathering process should be that the "bearer of bad tidings"—a person with negative or bad news—is immune and, therefore able to place such news before management. At this stage it is easy for the deal's momentum to cause bad news to be buried, rather than presented before a potentially wrathful CEO.

Access to Resources

"Inadequate resources" looms large on the list of classic, avoidable errors. A merger-acquisition will consume about 50 percent more time and money than originally projected. Less experienced players often are surprised to learn that small deals can consume vast amounts of capital and senior management time. Underfunded transition efforts endanger the new venture's success in tangible and intangible ways. Increased needs for staff, information, equipment, and support services must be met for an effective transition program. The tendency to economize after already large acquisition expenditures can be counterproductive, damaging tangibles such as productivity, and intangibles such as morale and corporate image.

Creating Transition Structures

Firms manage the transition stage in different ways. In no case is a single individual or unit made responsible for the entire effort. An individual or unit may be responsible for guiding or coordinating the process, but they are dependent on a larger cast of players for assistance. This lead role is what McKinsey & Company calls a "beachmaster"—a coordinator with considerable influence who reports directly to the CEO of the acquiring firm.[2] In some cases this person is the head of Corporate Development. In other firms, this person is a senior operating manager such as an executive vice president. In either case, the beachmaster plays the role of an orchestrator who brings other players together and lets temporary leadership of the process shift to the individual or group most significant at any given time, but who always brings the focus back to the larger task and timetable for action.

We have found that the most common practice is what we call the creation of a parallel structure. That is, a temporary organization (transition team, task force, or steering committee) that bridges the two organizations is created to handle the transition process, while both line operating structures remain essentially intact until changed by the temporary organization. In most cases the CEO personally selects and announces the composition of the transition task force and defines the scope of its work. Its typical task is to study, identify issues, and make recommendations.

Task force recommendations are actually implemented either by subgroups related to the issue, functional area, or business unit involved, or to line managers of the units affected. For example, an issue that might surface is the incompatibility of computer hardware. Either a subgroup of the larger task force can be formed or an MIS task force composed of staff from both organizations can be created to study the issue. Recommendations are then made to the larger task force and referred to appropriate senior management, and any decisions are implemented by the MIS groups during the integration stage.

The task force must be large enough to carry the burden of a major transition effort. We have found that the best design strategy is to mirror the actual functional and business structures with senior managers and staff from both firms. This design may mean a group with 30 to 40 people, but they may rarely meet all at once. There also would be permanent and ad hoc members. Standing members frequently are from major functional groups such as marketing, finance, and human resources, and from staff units such as strategic planning. Subgroups can be formed and a reporting process organized to coordinate their work and to communicate its results. In some instances, we found task forces too small to effectively represent all interests and carry the workload, which stalled the process.

The role of finance and human resources deserves particular mention. These two groups often serve as "shock troops." They are the first to enter the acquired firm. The finance team is charged with effectively gaining control of cash, other liquid assets and the financial reporting system. The second group on the scene is the human resources team, which must tackle the immediate personnel issues of job security, pay, benefits, and seniority.

First National Bank of Atlanta has made several acquisitions over the past few years, and its Vice President for Human Resources has developed a very effective entry process. Becky Ellenburg listens closely to the concerns of the acquired firm's employees, responding promptly and empathically. Her work stabilizes the situation until the transition process can handle subsequent details. The "damage control" effort has reaped many benefits. Ellenburg's sensitive management style helps establish a positive relationship with the newly acquired bank, and it allows the new management team to gather important information about the acquired firm, its employees, and their needs. Ellenburg trains her staff to make graceful entries into the new firms, communicating the proper tone for a positive transition process.

The most successful transition teams we observed seldom used outside consultants. There are several reasons for this. Thanks to prior experience, the most seasoned firms do not need external consultants. These firms had a clear strategy, so their implementation efforts were based on their own successful past experience and were managed internally.

Internal management of the transition process is the optimal choice. But there is great value in an outside perspective gained from feedback on the transition team's efforts. An external consultant can provide the team with insight into its own dynamics and help it avoid negative group processes. One transition team became involved with an organization rife with internal conflict and territorial battles. The team unconsciously mirrored the conditions they were asked to correct, setting up competing fiefdoms and waging war. When the striking parallels between the acquired organization and the transition team were pointed out at a team meeting, there was a moment of stunned silence, followed by a collective sigh of relief. "All the madness suddenly made sense, and the moment it did, it started to go away," said one group spokesperson. The conflicts in the group became resolvable once the overlay of unconscious strife was removed.

Transition teams are heir to previous patterns of conflict within their organizations, and while a certain amount of repetition is inevitable, reliving the old scripts is unprofitable and unnecessary. A detached, skilled observer—preferably a skilled process facilitator—can be invaluable during a difficult transition. Such an observer must participate in a general transition-monitoring system that tracks the unfolding transition's effect on the organization. This helps insure that people are being properly treated and that plans are being correctly implemented.

A transition team should have a clearly defined deadline. Setting a realistic completion date creates constructive pressure and reinforces the planned time limits. Such planning must allow for deadline renegotiation, but it must make those deadlines credible and meaningful. Deadlines should serve as incentives, rather than embarrassing traps. The firms' operating structure can take comfort in knowing that the transition team will be phased out.

Finally, the transition team should be well recognized and rewarded. The most frequently suggested reward proposed by transition managers was, not surprisingly, a few days off.

Managing Dysfunctional Psychological and Social Dynamics

There are numerous psychological and social threats to successful transition management. Because of their importance, many articles in the annotated bibliography focus on those threats. These threats include the following:

1. Perceived job insecurity, anxiety, and high turnover, with the loss of management and technical capacity
2. Decline in morale, commitment and loyalty
3. Increased absenteeism, illness, substance abuse problems, and other stress symptoms
4. Mourning, depression, and impaired performance
5. Anomie and "postmerger drift[3]"

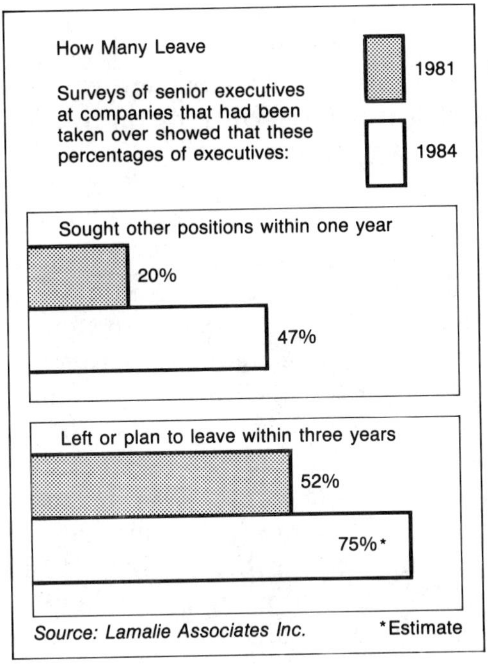

Figure 7-2 The increasing trend toward management turnover. (Source: Lamalie Associates Inc.)

All these contribute to one of the most serious transition problems: unwanted employee turnover. Key managers, scientists, and skilled technicians are the most likely to leave—and are the most difficult to replace. According to a survey by Lamalie Associates, an executive recruiting firm, almost half the senior executives at acquired companies begin searching for new positions within one year. This appears to be a growing trend, since a similar study in 1981 found that only 20 percent of acquired company executives left in the first year.[4] Figure 7-2 contrasts these trends.

These findings are corroborated by Mitchell & Company, a management consulting firm specializing in post-merger restructuring. According to their research, 30 percent of the key people in acquired companies left after the acquisition. Managing Director, Don Mitchell, says many companies lose up to 70 percent of their people during the first five years of the acquisition.

"Since the first to go are the senior general managers, you have a major problem with continuity," he says.

Some turnover is inevitable and is even encouraged in many cases, but it can reach very disruptive levels if not well managed. Indeed, as another consultant observed about the Wells-Fargo–Crocker Bank acquisition in which Wells-Fargo played an aggressive turnaround role, the task was not getting some Crocker managers to leave, but getting desired ones to stay. Preventing unplanned turnover and maintaining continuity amid change are two major transition management tasks. It remains one of mergers' and acquisitions' major paradoxes that people are part of an acquisition's value, yet often so little is done to retain them.

Apart from losing valuable skills and knowledge, losing valued employees negatively affects remaining employees, who can feel that only losers stay with the firm. This secondary turnover effect can be very damaging to morale and productivity. Turnover also disrupts established teams and functional groups that require staffing continuity and rebuilding time. Some of the departing employees also take with them parts of the firm's history and culture.

Profitability requires high performance employees with a strong sense of commitment—even loyalty. An unwritten psychological contract bonds them in time to the firm, and it must be renegotiated during periods of transition and uncertainty. Positive, well-managed transitions can work to build this bond's strength. Poorly managed transitions can break the contract without leading to turnover—a "psychological quit" where employees are physically present, but are no longer actively contributing.[5]

The degree of an organization's employee commitment is related to how well employees are informed about the basic conditions of their employment. As CEO of G.D. Searle when it was acquired by Monsanto, John Robson wanted to make certain that people had a prompt, clear answer to their central questions. And he learned that these questions included the following: What is going to happen to my job? Will I have to move? What is going to happen to my benefits? How do I do my job—the old way or some new way? And what is going to happen to our bosses? Answering these questions alleviates this psychological stress. Clarity and structure is a helpful antidote to uncertainty and distress. Most of the corporate leaders we talked with agreed that in a transition environment, the only thing worse than bad news is uncertainty.

Providing even minimal clarification allows people to begin redefining their roles and resuming their activities.

As an example, researchers evaluating stress levels of Indianapolis 500 drivers found that the highest levels of measurable stress recorded occurred during pit stops when drivers had to turn control of the car over to others. Being in control, even at over 200 mph, appears preferable to losing even temporary control over one's work life. Helping people have active control over the workplace, and the changes affecting it, especially during merger-acquisitions, is an important part of stress management.

The Role of the CEO and Top Executives

Many of the essentials for managing post-merger–acquisition complexities are outlined by Beckhard and Harris, in *Organizational Transitions*. In their view, steering an organization through a transitional period requires the following:

1. A clear destination
2. Landmarks, or *intermediate checkpoints*
3. Accurate, detailed maps, or *scenarios*
4. A clear knowledge of the condition and capacity of the . . . organization
5. The ability to get the best performance out of the . . . organization[6]

It is critical that senior management determines that each of these conditions are met. Regardless of the transition methods, senior managers, and the CEO in particular, must stay involved in the entire transition process. The reasons for this may be obvious, but bear stating.

1. The CEO must reinvoke the original vision that set the entire process in motion. Otherwise, the vision fades, and the guiding sense of purpose is lost.

2. The CEO must actively serve as the role model, defining new forms of leadership and establishing new cultural norms.

3. The CEO must reinforce constructive, new political alliances to make the necessary changes occur in both the formal and informal organizations.

4. The CEO must continue to publicly and symbolically express commitment and enthusiasm for the new organization so employees will be motivated and inspired.

5. The CEO's active involvement at a time of great stress and uncertainty provides visible structure and clarity. Top management also can provide the necessary vision of a future state. That action can have a catalytic effect on restoring purposeful, goal-directed activity in the corporation.

6. The CEO can help alleviate anxieties and minimize organizational drift by helping people understand the inevitability of turbulence associated with change.

7. The CEO's continued involvement provides continuity and the strategic perspective needed to implement necessary changes on the managerial and operational levels.[7]

Success is built through the continued active involvement of the CEO and senior management.

Leadership is one of the key ingredients in a successful merger-acquisition effort. The tasks of understanding the current corporate realities, identifying the core mission, envisioning a future, defining intermediate future states, and establishing the values and norms of the new organization all must be done by senior management.[8] Delegating these particular tasks can lead to dramatic and visible failure. In one such situation we met with the top executives of an acquired firm who had asked us for guidance. In response to our opening question, "Why were you acquired," glances were cast about the room until someone spoke up in response. "Yeah Pete, why *were* we acquired?" It was not long before the acquiring firm's senior management found it necessary to reinvolve themselves in managing the transition process.

In contrast, some organizations go through an exhaustive process to give employees a "personalized" understanding of what the changes mean for the company and for themselves. We have observed varied approaches to this process. They include videotaped presentations by top executives, skits performed by theatre groups in "town hall" meetings, one-on-one sessions between subordinates and executives and focus groups. All of these mechanisms were designed to give each person a sense of what was involved in creating the new organization. One middle manager we interviewed, who had experienced a number of these transition meetings, commented, "By the time we got through, we all pretty much knew what was happening, why, and what the new direction would be. Even if you didn't totally agree with it, you found yourself getting caught up in it and participating. The spirit of togetherness outweighed some of the negatives we experienced during the transition."

There are four communication activities critical for the CEO or managing executive. As we have emphasized before, one task is providing the organization with a clear vision of a future state that is distinct from both past and present realities. A second task is creating a management structure designed to carry the organization through the intermediate stages towards a defined future. The third task is communicating the vision and the management structure or system throughout the corporation. The fourth task is continually monitoring and evaluating what is communicated to make certain it is effective.

Success rests on the willingness of the organization's leaders to communicate their vision and personalize their message so it is understood and accepted by the organization's employees.

Alternative Transition Management Structures

Various alternative structures available to help management direct the transition have been outlined by Beckhard and Harris. They include the following:

1. The Chief Executive
2. The Project Manager
3. The Hierarchy
4. Representatives of Constituencies
5. "Natural Leaders"
6. The Diagonal Slice
7. The "Kitchen Cabinet"

1. THE CHIEF EXECUTIVE. The CEO and the CEO's staff assume responsibility for leading the organization through the transition process. While we feel that the CEO must be visibly involved at all phases of the merger-acquisition, the advantages of a highly centralized transition management effort can be offset by its disadvantages. Some highly coordinated, well-defined change efforts can fail to provide the opportunities for general participation and involvement that may be critical for success. In such circumstances, management can appear to be authoritarian and remote thereby further lowering the level of commitment among employees. In small-scale mergers when the interventions of the acquiring firm are limited, such an approach can be used to great advantage.

2. THE PROJECT MANAGER. A staff or line manager may be given responsibility for orchestrating the required changes. This individual operates from the executives' office and uses the assets of the firm's other divisions. He or she serves as a coordinator and an integrator, bringing together all the necessary resources to create change. This lead role is what McKinsey calls a "beachmaster"—the person who reports directly to the acquiring firm's CEO. The head of Corporate Development or a senior line manager is often the person selected to assume this responsibility.

3. THE HIERARCHY. The transition management process is assigned to line managers as a separate or additional responsibility. Beckhard and Harris see this as an appropriate mode for dealing with certain kinds of transitions—presumably well defined and of modest scope. We have found that the magnitude and complexity of most merger-acquisitions is too great to be an "add on" to a manager's existing responsibilities. It is feasible if that individual is given a new job description and assigned as full-time head of the transition effort. Some individuals develop a new career path based on this experience and go on to manage other merger-acquisition efforts in their companies. They also may become specialized consultants dealing with transition management programs.

4. REPRESENTATIVES OF CONSTITUENCIES.   A task force representing the firm's major partners, functions, and constituencies is assigned to manage the change. We have found this to be particularly effective when the task force is chaired by an experienced project manager from the acquiring organization who reports to the CEO on an ongoing basis.

5. "NATURAL LEADERS."   Here the executive manager assembles a group of managers who enjoy the respect and allegiance of the crucial constituencies involved in the transition. This trusted group may not be official representatives, but getting their support may be important since they often can bring the informal organization around to serve the formal organization's goals, since they often hold crucial positions of influence.

6. THE DIAGONAL SLICE.   This approach to providing input allows top management to tap a representative sample of the various organizational functions, locations, and levels, rather than formal group representatives.

7. THE "KITCHEN CABINET."   The informal network of trusted colleagues surrounding the CEO can sometimes provide more objective input than the line managers, who may have vested interests that can distort their perceptions and judgment. This may be a particularly good approach for the executive manager or CEO who wants to maintain control over the transition process.[9]

We have observed that the most well managed transitions have used the representatives of constituencies model. The Allied-Bendix transition, which we will be describing shortly, is a good example of the "representative" approach's effectiveness. In drawing upon the strengths of all the major functions in each organization, a fair and effective transition process can be achieved.

Focusing the Transition Task

Once the transition management approach has been identified, someone must define its scope. In the most ambitious mergers-acquisitions where one organization is completely integrated into another, that is an extremely large task. Noel Tichy describes such fullscale transition efforts as involving three major systems:

1. The technical system (the organization's informational network)
2. The political system (the organization's influence network)
3. The cultural system (the organization's affective network)

From Tichy's perspective, managing a transition means thinking about the impact change has on the technical, political, and cultural systems' social networks.[10] Consequently, the informational system supporting the technical system and its activity is usually reorganized as the flow of information is redirected and rechanneled. The political system's informal and formal influence network is invariably altered, and the shared values and friendships supporting the culture are redefined during the transition process. As Tichy observes,

> The adjustments which take place include breaking and reforming the following network linkages: (1) information links—whom I get information from and whom I transmit it to, (2) influence links—whom I am influenced by and who I influence, (3) affective links—who is friendly toward me and whom I am friendly toward. The major determinants of changes in information links are shifts in the task demands of the technical system. The major determination of a change in an influence network is a shift in the balance of power among organization coalitions in the political sys-

tem. Finally, affective links are most affected by changes in the culture of the organization.[11]

According to this model, management's effort must be directed by a carefully developed strategic plan dealing with the technical, political, and cultural transitions occurring during a major reorganization. Each of the three areas must be understood and managed according to a specific plan that anticipates the specific forms of resistance associated with technical, political, and cultural change.

Successful transition planning calls for a sensitive understanding of the technical, political, and cultural realities in an organization, and the development of a specific plan to deal with each one.

The Collision Of Cultures

There will be a clash between the old culture and the new even under optimal circumstances. As one human resource manager put it, "When we say culture we are talking about the compromise that exists between the competing aims and styles in our firm—culture is a product of conflict and it is always tentative and changing." This is becoming true of many companies, especially during a transition.

Despite the dynamic nature of corporate culture, it is not easy to change in a controlled manner. Reorganizing a culture by a plan takes, by all responsible estimates, at least three years, and many experts see timelines up to at least five years.

Changing an organization's culture requires careful coordination of all management levels. The human resource department and the transition management task force must be directly and actively involved in the corporation's highest strategic levels if they are to support the creation of a new culture. As we stress in the next two chapters, fundamental changes are needed in such areas as reward structures, selection criteria, and training and development programs if cultural change is to be achieved.

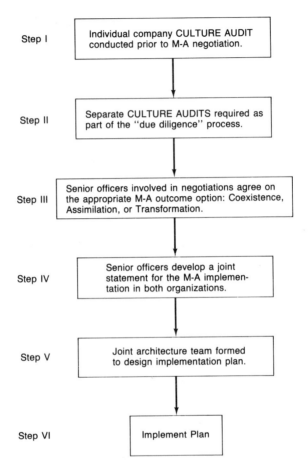

Step I — Individual company CULTURE AUDIT conducted prior to M-A negotiation.

Step II — Separate CULTURE AUDITS required as part of the "due diligence" process.

Step III — Senior officers involved in negotiations agree on the appropriate M-A outcome option: Coexistence, Assimilation, or Transformation.

Step IV — Senior officers develop a joint statement for the M-A implementation in both organizations.

Step V — Joint architecture team formed to design implementation plan.

Step VI — Implement Plan

Figure 7-3 Integrating cultures: sequence of events. (Source: O.D. Resources, 1985.)

During our investigations we learned of many consulting firms specializing in facilitating organizational-cultural change. One such firm, O.D. Resources Inc., works with its clients in coordinating the integration of corporate cultures after a merger. This firm uses a six-step plan beginning with a cultural audit, and moves sequentially toward the development of a detailed implementation plan. The steps are presented in Figure 7-3. Appendix B describes these steps in greater detail.

We find that a cultural audit is an important transition stage task in dealing with the human dimension of the merger-acquisition process. Performing a cultural audit allows a corporation to assess the degree of cultural change needed to make a successful integration of two firms. The magnitude of the tasks and the risks associated with changing an organization's culture will be clearer if managers can estimate how much disruption will accompany changes. The acquiring firm must

1. Define its role, (that is, will it be performing as a financier, functional specialist, restructurer, or architect)

2. Assess the degree of integration needed to achieve objectives between the two organizations' cultures (that is, coexistence, blending, or transformation)

3. Assess the degree of similarity between the two cultures

In performing the third step, the transition team can begin to estimate the degree of change and disruption it must manage.

Performing a cultural audit not only tells the transition managers what but also how much needs to be done. Knowing how much or how little to intervene is seemingly an art form practiced by the most experienced transition managers. In the next chapter we refer to this balance—or too little versus too much—as *minimum essential intervention*. With proper planning and implementation an acquiring firm can avoid excessive or inadequate interventions and increase its probability of success.

Managing the Myths

Blending corporations creates a historical narrative that shapes and builds a new culture. When two firms join together, each brings its own unique history to the match. Corporate history is a living reality. It is the collective memory that prescribes models for good corporate citizenship. The stories that constitute a company's history are often moral tales offering advice on a variety of topics from how hard to work, how much risk to take, how to treat superiors and subordinates, and to how to deal with requests to move. The collective stories retold and used to reinforce the firm's culture are the company's mythology. Myths are the aggregate of people's organizational perceptions, beliefs, and values. These myths exist at a company's core, and they are the central belief system guiding people's past, present, and future behavior.

Corporate myths and the paradigms they offer are severely disrupted during transitions. Numerous terms describe the ensuing state: aftershock, productivity decline, anomie, the neutral zone, and post-merger drift. It is in everyone's best interest to minimize the effects of such adjustment reactions. However, the creation of new myths takes time, and in the meantime what is to be done? Most organizations have been forced to endure costly periods of stagnation while between myths. One manager we interviewed shortly after his organization had been acquired compared his present experience to the drama *Waiting For Godot*. "I feel like one of those characters in a theatre of the absurd performance with no idea of where to go, what to do— so I sit here and wait—but I'm not quite sure for what." What can top management do to avoid such a situation?

An answer may come from social scientists studying cultures that have experienced traumatic social dislocations. One is Thomas O'Dea who has conducted studies of radical social change and transition of minority groups coming to the U.S. His work provide parallels that can help us examine the stress experienced by acquired firms' members. O'Dea found that the groups he studied preserved their integrity and capacity to function by developing what he called an "ideology of transition.[12]" The group leaders validate their authority and vision of the future by providing a rationale for the changes, a belief system, and guideposts to use in the process until it is complete. The transition ideology provides sufficient explanation and direction so new values can be created and instilled, and a new culture can develop. In the moment of chaos between "no-longer" and "not-yet," business must go on.[13] Corporate leaders need to be prepared to articulate an "intermediate vision" that links the past with the present, and the present with the future. The questions raised by Samuel Beckett in *Waiting For Godot* apply to this situation. Who are we in the meantime, and what do we do? While no CEO can usher in the kingdom of heaven, an effective CEO knows that living in limbo is an unpromising and unfulfilling condition.

The successful transition leader offers a better vision of tomorrow and a sense of continuity that can radically improve the life and performance of a company's employees.

Mourning and Melancholia

In his classic paper, "Mourning and Melancholia," Sigmund Freud first described the dynamics of human depression as we now understand it.[14] He made the distinction between mourning—a normal condition of sadness, grief, and lethargy following the experience of loss—and melancholia, a pathological condition extending beyond the normal period of mourning. Melancholia impairs a person's ability to function for an extended period.

Senior managers in reorganized companies can benefit from Freud's insights. By definition, the transition process involves losing the old organization and the attachment people have to it. Thus, a period of mourning is appropriate and necessary. The grief and doubts people express are not a sign of disloyalty or lack of enthusiasm for the new regime. They are a sign that people are preparing to make the psychological transition to the new organization by resolving their previous attachments to the old one. Even in extreme circumstances when the acquired firm's employees welcome the new organization and have an ambivalent or even negative attachment to the previous management, some period of grief and uncertainty is inevitable. Even a bad marriage requires some mourning after the divorce. If the acquiring firm's management takes such expression as a narcissistic blow or sign of disloyalty and ambivalence, and if they interfere with the normal mourning process, they can create a melancholy or depressive organization that fails to produce expected results.

In one classic White Knight rescue of a faltering company, the transition managers felt frustrated because they were not treated as saviors by the acquired employees. As one of the less-experienced transition team members said, "If they are so damned glad to see us, why do they spend all their time talking about the good old days at the company?" Yet this is not really so. Even a negative attachment is an attachment, and its loss must be acknowledged and experienced before new investments and attachments can be made.

Good transition managers must have sufficient understanding of this dynamic so they can listen to gloriously unrealistic tales of the previous management without feeling threatened. Envy and resentment can impair managers' ability to help employees mourn their losses. The most impressive transition managers we interviewed had a somewhat "parental" capacity that let them deal empathically with concerns of acquired employees without being patronizing. They were able to cope with their own reactions of annoyance and frustration, and were able to bear even the narcissistic slight of being begrudgingly accepted.

Successful transition managers need emotional competence to deal with the predictable psychological reactions associated with reorganization and change.

A strategy for dealing with mourning and the resultant post-merger drift is proposed by William Bridges, President of Pontes Associates, a consulting firm that specializes in organizational transition problems. Bridges suggests that, after a disengagement period during which employees mourn the loss of the old company and its ways, there is "a shift from the old task of letting go to the new task of crossing the neutral zone." Bridges defines the "neutral zone" as,

> that wilderness that lies between the past reality and the one that the leadership claims is just around the corner. In the West Indian vernacular, the neutral zone is called 'passing through limbo'—a condition where one is not yet free from the past nor fully into the future. Managing in the neutral zone must begin with an acknowledgment that this zone exists and that it has a constructive function in the transition process.[15]

Bridges describes the neutral zone experience as three conditions:

1. Disorientation—an interim period in which one orientation is no longer adequate and there is not another one to replace it.

2. Disintegration—a sense that anarchy and chaos are overtaking the organization. Bridges cites his findings, which are consistent with our own. "Old issues that individuals and groups have resolved suddenly return to haunt them. Long-dormant anxieties and antagonisms are stirred up, and unless people can understand why this is happening, they are likely to conclude that 'the end is at hand.' "[16]

3. Discovery—as Bridges describes it, "In the ancient rites of passage that used to carry a person through periods of transition, the neutral zone was spent in a literal 'nowhere.' There, in the desert or forest or tundra, the person could break away from the social forces that held his or her old reality in place, and the new reality could emerge."[17]

Individuals and organizations can regress under extreme stress. In such difficult circumstances, the re-emergence of previously resolved issues requires additional attention from managers often already stretched to their limit. This is a vexing and perennial problem for transition managers, who can easily forget that communication and problem-solving are continual and reiterative processes. One transition manager described his extreme frustration to us when an old battle resurfaced between his firm's production and marketing departments. "I thought we'd gone over this a hundred times before and here it was again! Quite frankly I was damned angry and I said so, but this is the way this whole deal (the transition process) has been, two steps forward, then one or one-and-a-half steps backwards."

Another member of the same transition task force mentioned his annoyance at having to communicate the same message several times before it "took." He spoke of how the same issues kept coming up time after time, "like an endless row of ducks in a shooting gallery." For the transition manager in a stressed organization, patience while passing through the neutral zone, is not a virtue, it is a necessity.

In our interviews, we often heard people use words and phrases describing the chaotic qualities of the neutral zone or the transition stage. For example we heard numerous allusions to this environment being like "a jungle," and to their feelings of being "lost in the wilderness," and "trying to find a way through." Under these conditions it is understandable that creativity hardly is at the center of people's attention. However, new realities are created after old ones are destroyed. Chaos and creation are partners. Creative and destructive forces must come into play before old makes way for new. Amidst the pain of disruption there is the promise of something stable and new.

The Role of Ritual

Accepting a new vision and making a new attachment are easier if one lets go of the old ones. The ability to let go is a psychological condition necessary for progress in a transition stage. Recognizing this, some organizations have used rites of passage that are designed to "let go of the old." We have been told of mock funerals—complete with eulogies—that served as public ceremonies addressing the collective experience of an important loss. After one merger, a similar ceremony was held for a discontinued product line. While there was a certain tongue-in-cheek quality to it, management was careful not to be irreverent toward those who had developed or produced the products. In fact, these individuals were the honored guests at a reception following the formal ceremonies. There were many informal opportunities provided for people to talk about parting from their old products and the network of associations that had supported them. This firm's management recognized that such a parting ceremony was a necessary step to take before constructing a viable new culture.

Successful transition managers help the organization understand the inevitable uncertainties and predictable reactions it will experience as it changes, moving through limbo to a new future.

The Allied Transitions

"Almost miraculously, a model of how to put two companies together emerged from the Great Takeover Follies of 1982, which produced the Allied-Bendix merger." With these words Myron Magnet, a *Fortune* editor, describes how Allied CEO Ed Hennessy masterminded one of the most successful transition management programs in modern corporate history.[18] We wanted to know more about Allied's success and we found what we consider a model for successful transition management by studying some of Allied's major acquisition efforts.

Allied-Bendix

While the Allied-Bendix transaction was legally an acquisition, in practice it was to be treated by Allied as a joining of equals. The joint announcement of the new relationship, where all parties were represented, reinforced that message. The deal is still often referred to as a merger within Allied's headquarters in Morristown, New Jersey. The original announcement was planned so key players from both firms joined one another at the same time and location to make carefully planned public statements. The collaborative event's symbolic value foreshadowed what was to become a continual effort to combine the best resources of both firms.

The effort's success is consistently attributed to skillful transition management. Charles Bischoff, a Staff Vice President of Management Resources at Allied at the time of the Bendix takeover, states, "Ed Hennessy's decision to create a transition management task force was the most important single contribution to the success of this venture that I know of." Bischoff, a senior member of the task force, describes his work in the transition effort as, "the most exciting, meaningful time of my career." Bischoff has gone on to become a transition management consultant as a Senior Vice President at Goodrich and Sherwood in Morristown.

The task force was co-chaired—one individual from each firm—appointed by Hennessy and Agee, who was at that

Allied/Bendix Merger Management Task Force		
Function	Bendix	Allied
Co-Directors	VP Human Resources	VP Planning & Development
Finance	VP & Controller	VP & Controller
Human Resources	VP Human Resources Dev.	Director-Mgt. Resources
Legal	Assoc. General Counsel & Asst. Secretary	VP & Secretary
Operations	VP Adm. & Corporate Services	Director, Operations
Planning	VP Strategic Planning & Ventures	VP Planning & Development
Public Affairs	Exec. Dir.-Communications	Director-Corporate Affairs
Technology	VP & General Manager Advance Technology Center	Director-Office of Science & Technology

Figure 7-4   Allied-Bendix merger management task force. (Source: Robert M. Fulmer, "Blending Corporate Families," 1986.)

time CEO of Bendix. Several additional pairs of Allied and Bendix senior managers representing finance, human resources, operations, law, tax, planning, public affairs, and technology were appointed to the task force. Special sub-task forces were formed as needed to deal with issues such as compensation, benefits, and management development. Outside consultants answered specific technical questions. Added to the original core task force membership were representatives from as many other business components as possible, bringing the total membership to 36. Figure 7-4 illustrates the size, composition, and structure of the task force.

The centralized control exercised by the task force made it possible to involve many sub-task force groups without causing confusion. Their efforts and inputs were well coordinated and competently integrated by the experienced members of the task force.

As many managers as possible who were involved in the process's early stages were selected to serve on the task force to help maintain continuity throughout this stage. Dennis Signorovitch, now Director of Allied-Signal's Corporate Information Services group said, "We didn't want to call in a new team when it was time to implement the plan. We knew that unless we provided a great deal of continuity we would have difficulty integrating the two organizations." That is necessary strategy, according to Nick Cameron, currently Senior Vice President of Technology and Business Development for Bendix Aerospace. "You need to use the time you have from the time of the signing to the actual legal merger to take constructive action to begin integrating the new operation," Cameron said. Very willing and experienced senior management made the task force's rapid start-up much easier.

The task force had five months to develop a plan to deal with any integration problems. It worked along with the division managers, whose primary task was maintaining performance during the task force's existence and implementing the plans that later emerged from the task force. The task force's preliminary objectives were to

1. Begin channeling information to decision makers
2. Help form positive attitudes about the merger
3. Communicate both internally and externally about the new company
4. Define common terms to clarify communication and objectives
5. Support any business unit requesting assistance
6. Identify problems threatening the transition effort
7. Identify policy differences that would impede the creation of the new organization
8. Identify overlaps and duplications in staffing so recommendations can be made for downsizing
9. Set timetables for each phase of the integration stage
10. Organize task force members' specific activities so they have clear lines of authority and responsibility
11. Deal with problems by identifying organizational options

Members worked 60 to 70 hours per week, meeting alternately in Morristown and Southfield, Michigan. Despite the tremendous time pressures, members felt continual support from Ed Hennessy. As one member of the team said, "The mission was a tough one, but Ed put every resource we could possibly need at our disposal to get the job done." Charlie Bischoff described, for example, how a corporate jet was assigned to make

8 a.m., shuttles from Morristown to Southfield so members could work there and return to Morristown at night.

The importance of promptly reassuring employees and minimizing disruption was clearly a major part of Hennessy's strategy. Serving as a role model, Hennessy took prompt action himself by speaking to over 5000 management employees in six different Bendix locations in eight weeks. Part of his strategy was to let people "see and feel" him, but it was also to minimize rumors. "Rumor control" proved to be an important function of the task force. They "pounced" on rumors to squash them as quickly as possible. In addition, they regulated the task force members' comings and goings so everyone knew who was seeing whom, when, and why. They avoided speculative gossip by identifying all Allied "visitors."

While not every question could be answered immediately, there were clear timelines set for communicating answers to employees. Major issues, such as key appointments, and who was staying and who was going, were all answered within the initial five months. Setting firm dates for answers was a consistent practice. "In a post-merger environment it is very important for people to perceive that someone is addressing the problems," says Dennis Signorovitch. This practice reportedly reduced anxiety levels by showing that task force members were committed to employees. Firm deadlines were coupled with over-communication—if there can ever be such a condition. Virtually everything the task force did every step of the way was announced. While done to inform and communicate, the hope was to create a sense of trust and impartiality.

The personal leadership displayed by some task force members demonstrated that statesmanship, not gamesmanship, was the desired norm. For example, former Bendix Vice President for Human Resources and task force Co-chairman John Cooke made it clear that he wanted the most capable people from both Allied and Bendix in the new Human Resources Management department. Observers described how he tried to make himself available to everyone, joining people for meals and visiting in their offices to get to know them. While not everyone was retained, there was a general feeling of confidence that the decision-making process used by Cooke and others was fair, equitable, and open.

Another key reason for the transition's success was the liberal transition benefit program. Included in the package were enhanced relocation benefits, increased mortgage interest differential payments, salary bonuses up to 15 percent, comprehensive outplacement services, counseling for spouses, homefinding services, and buyouts and perks to compensate for any losses in assets or benefits.

Reviewing each facet of the Allied-Bendix transition only partially explains its success. Beyond specific programs, measures, and benefits, there was a guiding vision and an ethic that enhanced the value of any specific intervention. There appeared to be genuine respect for the human side of the merger. Nick Cameron validated this perspective. "When you buy a business you are in a sense buying people, so you've got to understand their normal human reactions, their fears, and their anxieties. People need to be able to get their fears out in the open; they shouldn't be covered up. Otherwise we can't address those fears and help them," Cameron said.

David Powell, Senior Vice President for Public Affairs, added his perspective. "In order to bring together two different corporate families you have to have a blend of aggression and humility; the former allows you to be decisive, while the latter makes it possible for you to be sensitive and listen to people," Powell said. Former Bendix managers concur. As one said, "Of course there were negative reactions to being taken over, but it didn't feel like a takeover. We were treated with genuine respect, we were listened to and treated fairly." To demonstrate, Bendix managers held 33 percent of the key management positions once staffing decisions were made. Hennessy made it clear that the best managers from both firms would be selected and that all positions were up for grabs. Bendix managers tried to make the merger work, even some who were not selected for their preferred positions in the new organization.

One of the biggest surprises was a study of employee reactions to the merger. It showed that Bendix employees were more positive than Allied employees. Based on these findings, Myron Magnet observed, "Expecting the worst, Bendix had been pleasantly surprised, whereas Allied employees getting ready to put the Bendix captives into the cauldron, were disappointed to be told by their leaders not to eat them."[19]

Allied-Signal

There are several similarities between the Bendix and Signal transitions, even though Bendix and Signal joined Allied under very different circumstances. Bendix also was a highly centralized and formalized multidivisional firm, while Signal was a very decentralized holding company. Integrating Bendix was easier in these respects because it fit Allied's structure and culture better. Nonetheless, a very similar task force approach was used effectively with Signal. Here, too, the tone quickly established and communicated was one of enthusiasm and cooperative effort by both firms. Signal had more cultural differences and will likely take longer to work through than with Bendix, but these are known and accepted differences. Acceptance is sometimes expressed by mutual joking about Allied management's "pinstripes" and Signal management's Southern Californian style "flower shirts."

A retrospective analysis written by Pieter Schiller, who chaired the task force with John Cooke, describes the success of the Bendix merger as a combination of strong leadership, active senior management, effective communication, prompt action, and careful attention to people. These same basic ingredients also were present in the Allied-Signal transition. The key method for mixing these ingredients again is the transition management task force, this time chaired by two Senior Vice Presidents, Allied's Nick Cameron and Signal's Marc Stern. An internal study comparing the two task forces lists other advantages such as the ability to provide early warnings about issues and to coordinate cross-functional projects and activities. The task force also provided a channel for bypassing layers of management to voice issues and concerns. That helped Signal's managers, who were used to less formal structures. It also helped develop effective working relationships and teams among both firms' managers.

To summarize, the transition process created by Allied for the Bendix merger also has been used effectively under different circumstances with Signal. Their successes lead us to conclude as follows:

The task force approach demonstrates how active management of the transition stage leads to success. If bal-

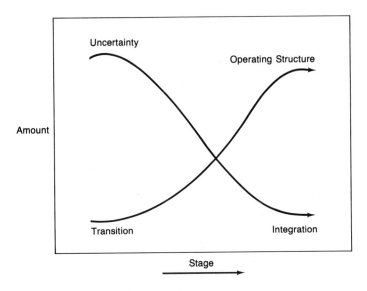

Figure 7-5   Decreasing uncertainty with increasing operating structure.

anced with equally active and effective management before an agreement is negotiated, failure rates for mergers and acquisitions will significantly drop.

Linking to the Integration Stage

For all practical purposes, the implementation stage ends once a planned change agenda has been created. In the Allied cases, it also results in the naming of managers to key positions. The transition management team now must do a well-coordinated "baton pass" to the line operating managers to execute the change agenda. Several sub-task forces may remain to ensure that specific changes requiring cross-functional coordination are executed. The line managers' responsibility is implementing the items they are responsible for on the agenda. Their performance will be evaluated on their ability to accomplish that within a set timeframe. The corporate staff will help as needed and will also monitor the implementation. If an effective baton pass is made, the result will be better implementation and reduced uncertainty. Figure 7-5 illustrates this desirable trend.

Summary

Managing a transition is an exercise in planning and attention to detail. There are no breakthrough technologies or shortcuts available. Talent, time, and resources are the essential ingredients. Experienced and sensitive managers are the crucial commodities. It is imperative to plan in detail. Communicate decisions, involve people as much as feasible, and develop a sensitive approach to employees during a time of stress and dislocation. After that, time is needed to allow the process to reach fruition. The commitment of resources from above is a crucial determinant of success in any transition effort. If the plan is there and the resources are made available, growth can occur.

8

MAKING
IT ALL PAY:
THE INTEGRATION
STAGE

The true difference between building a firm and managing it comes home in the last stage of the merger-acquisition process. Successful merger-acquisition practice requires both the ability to make deals and the ability to manage the outcome of those deals. The two skills should not be confused. Building a firm through shrewd dealmaking is one thing; successfully integrating those acquisitions into an effective firm is another. We have encountered several executives who were excellent, even brilliant dealmakers, yet who had difficulty realizing their acquisitions' full business and financial potential. Why?

Part of the reason certainly has to do with the kinds of faulty assumptions and analyses that can be made very early in the process. Assumptions about synergies and how the acquiring firm would add value to its acquisition may have been weak, and their validity could only be tested later. Contel's proposed acquisition of Comsat in 1987, for example, was based on assumptions about business fit and financial projections that unraveled as the FCC began questioning Comsat's profit margins and accounting practices.[1] As we noted in earlier chapters, one of the inherent difficulties with the process is the inability to fully and safely test early assumptions about the strength of the three pillars. For Contel and Comsat, the deal at least fell apart before its final negotiation.

Without doubt, problems in the early stages of the process are also major factors. Poor strategic planning or fuzzy vision, for example, will lead to poor integration. CooperVision, a diversified healthcare firm, has made over 100 acquisitions since 1979, and the process of buying and selling these businesses during this time has resulted in falling stock market performance and criticism from financial analysts.[2] Parker Montgomery, CooperVision's founder, is accused of being so idiosyncratic about his buying and selling practices that he confuses analysts, the result being CooperVision's perception of drift and lack of direction.

Integration Stage Objectives

The last two chapters focused intensely upon one of this book's core themes: the quality of transition management right after negotiation. These chapters emphasized the need to be clear about the acquiring firm's role and offered specific ground rules for managing the transition stage. The transition stage's major short-term objective, we asserted, was to stabilize performance while creating a process and a positive climate and structure for subsequent change. The long-term objective was to identify issues and create the agenda for change—action plans that would build business, financial, and organizational fit. The primary objective in the integration stage is to execute that change agenda to operationally realize fit within and among these pillars.

From a business fit perspective, this means executing changes that create the synergies thought to exist so value is created from the deal. Business fit, as we have stressed in previous chapters, can only be realized when sufficient investment is made into those businesses—synergies, we restate, are not automatic, and require resources to bring them about. Ultimately, however, business fit becomes a function of organizational fit. As Michael Porter stressed in a 1987 *Harvard Business Review* article, the creation of value through the realization of potential synergies is a function of interrelationships among business units and how those are managed.[3] Shared activities can be found, skills transferred, and leverage created for groups of business units so they can collaborate and build their respective competitive advantages when they are organized and managed effectively.

From a financial fit perspective, this means beating the balance sheet and income statement back into shape, while still investing enough resources in any new business to let business fit be built. To achieve both areas of fit, some businesses and assets may need to be sold or spun off. Having a clear sense of the firm's vision becomes essential at that point to identify core units that are part of the vision. More than one firm has sold a business only to find it necessary to buy it back later.

From an organizational fit perspective, major changes may be necessary in structure, processes and systems, human resources, and culture to let both business and financial fit be built. Building organizational fit is therefore the central focus of the integration stage.

Building fit takes time, and the pressure to show early results can be great. Expectations for early results are created, and the CEO must trade off the firm's long-term vision against short-term expectations. Ed Hennessy, for example, has been criticized in recent months for not boosting Allied-Signal's financial performance faster after the Signal merger.[4] A rule of thumb is that major change—from initial conception to full realization—can take as long as three to five years. Sacrificing a legitimate long-term vision to serve short-term expectations is therefore unrealistic and potentially devastating to integration efforts that need time to fully play out.

If integration is to proceed smoothly, we cannot overstate the importance of line management involvement in the creation of that change agenda. There must be a distinct "baton pass" from the transition team to line management to signal the ending of one stage and beginning of the next. The disbanding of the transition team is another visible signal of the shift. We want to stress the basic difference between these stages by saying the following:

From one stage to the next, the emphasis shifts from managing change in the short term to managing performance in the long term.

In this chapter, we offer specific ground rules for guiding the integration stage and then we identify several areas for integration work. The ground rules were developed from a number of sources, and we draw for help on the growing literature on integration and on a very complicated division-level integration effort—Garrett and Bendix Aerospace—in the Allied-Signal merger.

Ground Rules for Guiding Integration

Five ground rules are offered to help guide integration initiatives. These have to do with (1) the tendency to move too slowly versus too quickly, (2) going too far, (3) the leadership role, (4) the need to prioritize and sequence the targets for change, and (5) the need to balance attention between both firms.

Finding a Balance: Too Slow versus Too Fast

As noted in Chapter 5, process "front-ending" can result in too little attention given to the transition and integration stages. In the transition stage this shows up as dead time—a hiatus—which dampens momentum and breeds uncertainty and anxiety. In the integration stage, this means the implementation effort is prolonged and people may perceive that the process is being undermanaged and is drifting.

Conversely, there may be a tendency to move too quickly and, in effect, overmanage the transition and integration stages. Too much change, too quickly can lead to perceptions of chaos and anarchy, if not managed well, or to the smothering of the acquired firm. Too much change, too quickly, will disrupt the performance of *both* firms—particularly in a large acquisition.

What is the "correct" or appropriate pace of change? This is an extremely difficult question to answer. The answer will vary from case to case, but we have offered the transition role typologies in Chapter 6 as an aid in making a judgment. Obviously, the other firm's performance and the level of urgency for acting must be used as criteria to judge pace.

Moving either too slowly or too quickly is risky, but if you must err, we suggest erring on the side of more slowly than quickly. There is, as Bob Kirk, President of Allied's Aerospace Division, pointed out to us, the very real danger of "creating an unknown from two knowns" when integration efforts move too quickly. Many firms we know refuse to make acquisitions that require them to make radical changes quickly. They first want to get to know their acquisitions' people, technologies, and business characteristics, then introduce change selectively.

The pace at which change will occur needs to be very clearly communicated. In the SantaFe–AV-MED acquisition reported earlier, AV-MED managers and staff needed to be reassured over a series of transition meetings that SantaFe was generally pleased with AV-MED's performance. While some changes would occur, there was nothing so dramatically wrong that these changes would require swift, radical action. AV-MED was waiting for something dramatic to happen while SantaFe was content to move more slowly. After an initial changing of some top managers, SantaFe was prepared to play a "facilitator" role.

Other firms play a "savior" role and utilize the "hammer approach," preferring the initial period of disruption after a deal to make radical change. Wells Fargo moved decisively and swiftly to eliminate several thousand employees in its early 1986 acquisition of Crocker Bank. Crocker has been absorbed and Wells Fargo's performance never faltered. Indeed, Wells Fargo has received applause for its acquisition of Crocker, although it proved disruptive to many employees.

Which approach is best? Aside from relying on the McKinsey typology for guidance, we believe that the acquiring firm's familiarity with the other firm's business should be a major factor.[5] The greater the differences between the businesses, the slower the pace should be. Wells Fargo and Crocker were neighboring banks intimately familiar with each other. Firms less familiar with each other need to move more slowly.

Technological differences are one aspect that makes those businesses different. Bob Kirk at Allied-Signal uses the Garrett-Bendix Aerospace integration as an example illustrating the need to move slowly. The question in thinking about integrating two aerospace divisions is, At what level should the many parts and subsystems they produce be integrated? (1) Should they be kept separate as individual components within subsystems? (2) Combined to create a "black box" of combined subsystems? (3) Combined to create a "platform" of integrated "black boxes"? or (4) Integrated at some still higher level of air-water-ground defense system? The answer does not come quickly and can determine the competitiveness of those divisions in their industries for years to come. To help clarify this point about the pace of change we suggest the following:

Communicate the pace which is set, using realistic targets and milestones to judge progress. Differences dictate caution.

Minimum Essential Intervention

How much integration is enough? Firm decision rules are hard to find, and it is simplistic to say that you simply keep going until the change agenda is exhausted. Encountering both firms' operational and competitive business realities will mean changes to that agenda. In general, the acquiring firm only needs to induce enough change for it to gain mastery over the variables or factors that will most significantly and directly determine success.

This is our rule of minimum essential intervention. You must intervene only to the point where you can control success, but to go beyond that is not necessary and can even be disruptive. This rule recognizes the need to intervene, but it also preserves as much autonomy and control within the acquired firm as possible. It also uses scarce resources efficiently by recognizing the economic trade-off between the marginal cost and marginal return on effort and resources.

The minimum essential intervention rule requires you to know what factors or variables are most important to success. It says that some things are more important to you and must be targeted first, while other things are less important and can be left alone. Acquiring firms generally know why they buy the other firms. For example, one firm may have needed an infusion of new products into its maturing product line. It bought a smaller firm with an active R&D function. Critical to the success of this deal, therefore, is the acquiring firm's ability to retain R&D staff and fund this activity.

Quickly gaining control of the financial reporting and information systems is one of the highest priorities, judging from the practices of most firms. Gaining a full understanding and control over the human resource systems is ranked second, from our experience. The acquiring firm has to know the other firm's management as quickly as possible, and the human resource systems are direct links and ways of communicating to employees and staff about what has just happened to them.

Other areas of immediate concern will depend on the situation. However, Bob Kirk at Allied-Signal suggests focusing efforts to gain control internally first, and only then turning attention to seizing external opportunities. His point means that you get your act together first before taking on the world. You do not want to demonstrate disorganization to customers and investors any more than you have to.

The flipside of this rule is not to do any more than necessary. It means that acquiring firms need to tolerate diversity and not smother the acquired firm, particularly in the transition stage. If you want people to stay with the business, then that means having a light touch. In general, the more people are an important part of the business, the lighter and more sensitive the approach must be during integration. A light touch must, however, be balanced against the firm's condition and the sense of urgency.

A typical and symbolically loaded strategy early in an integration effort is to change the name of the firms in a merger. The formation of UNISYS from the merger of Burroughs and Sperry was done to emphasize the extent to which the integration of the two firms was to go: completely. Allied's acquisition of Signal was also presented as a "joining of equals" and its name change to Allied-Signal expressed the extent to which Allied had moved away from its past toward its high technology vision. Name changes, of course, do not necessarily mean that changes occur deeply within all of the divisions and businesses in those firms. Many may be left intact, while others are broken up and grouped within new divisions.

Minimum essential intervention means that the level of diversity tolerated—even welcomed and cultivated—will be higher than some acquiring firms may be used to. Edwin Halkyard, Allied-Signal's Senior Vice President for Human Resources, told us recently that you need to accept a "multicultural environment" in an organization growing through merger and acquisition.

There are practical reasons why diversity is encouraged. First, Bob Kirk's caution about "creating an unknown from two knowns" is worth remembering. Second, it may well be a misuse of resources to induce more change than necessary. Halkyard uses the example of selling employees on the merits of a merger through extensive and costly programs and communication efforts. At what point is the extra dollar spent to change someone's point of view worth the expense? Is it truly essential, at least in the near term, to have everyone thinking the same way? At what point is the value gained less than the cost of inducing it? This point is worth stressing:

Obliterating differences between firms is not just costly, but potentially damaging; diversity provides the basis for innovation and adaptation over time.

Our basic message, then, is that there are varying levels of integration that can be achieved, and you only need to integrate the two firms up to that point which optimizes business, financial, and organizational fit. You go no further than that point. It may mean in one situation a total merging of identities, while in another, it may mean leaving the acquired firm highly autonomous. It will also mean that some parts of the acquired firm are more tightly integrated than its other parts.[6] No two situations are alike and the overall design of the firm needs to be sensitive enough to tolerate such diversity. We discuss these organization design issues shortly.

Leadership and Meaning

What is important and what is less important during the integration must be clearly communicated by the CEO and consistently reinforced by senior management and staff. We have stressed the CEO's role in Chapter 7, and we want to broaden that discussion by clarifying that role during the integration stage. The CEO's role in the integration stage is to take a broadly defined vision of the firm and begin putting it into action.

The CEO does this by defining a *limited number* of high priority themes or foci for action. Such themes may be "technological leadership" or "cost leadership" and their objective is to encourage related action without dictating all the details for such action. In this sense, the themes act as somewhat focused policies that allow everyone in the firm room to experiment and the discretion to discover how to best move in the direction management envisions. It is, as Linda Smircich and Gareth Morgan call it, leadership as the "creation of meaning.[7]" Leadership that uses the creation and communication of core themes is really a process of selectively reframing perspectives. The themes set a focused direction toward which people in the firm allocate their effort and resources until a fully developed strategic planning process is put into place. More important, they are part of what Laurence Ackerman calls "the psychology of corporation" and have everything to do with defining the firm's core identity.[8]

Through early, consistent, and visible personal behaviors, the CEO communicates the themes that will govern the firm as it moves forward. For Allied-Signal it was "technological leadership" and was reinforced through heavy spending on R&D activities and the spinning-out of many "low tech" businesses in the Henley Group. For NEC, the giant Japanese electronics firm, it was "computers and communications."

We want to emphasize the need to keep the number of themes limited during integration. The firm's tolerance for ambiguity is low and confusion about its identity is still high at this point. During the transition stage, direction needs to be more broadly defined, but the integration stage requires clear signals. Limiting the number of different themes also focuses resources. We emphasize this rule by saying the following:

Keep the menu of major themes limited early in the integration effort, and communicate actively and consistently what they mean.

Prioritize Areas for Integration

Closely related to the previous ground rules is the idea that you need to carefully select and then quickly control the situation's most important variables to manage during integration. Doing what is easiest is not necessarily best.

Again drawing upon Bob Kirk's insights, he ranks four areas for integration work, from relatively easiest to most difficult. Easiest to integrate are the businesses Garrett and Bendix Aerospace operate within. With some effort, these divisions could collaborate to attack a new market or improve competitive position in an existing one. Business units could be grouped and regrouped, and marketing efforts coordinated. But business-level integration requires other changes, as well.

Next most difficult are the two divisions' technologies, since each emphasizes different parts and systems within planes—even different types of planes. Nonetheless, with great care, the most desirable level of integration in their technologies could be found. Integrating technologies at the most strategic level is, in fact, one factor that caused Allied-Signal to go slow with its integration.

Still more difficult to integrate are the two divisions' human resources, particularly their top managements which were still both relatively new to Kirk. Finding the right balance and "chemistry" among his top managers required tremendous sensitivity and study. Indeed, Kirk contends that his most important area for work was the need to identify the best management talent, then build teamwork and balance among these key managers and "align their motivations" by providing sufficient incentives. All other integration areas follow from this. For him, it was this area that provided leverage on changes in the other areas, and he began focusing on this area first. We could not agree more and stress this point by saying the following:

Identifying management talent and harnessing it through effective teamwork is the cornerstone of successful integration work.

Implementing the action plans from the transition stage requires the use of teams which cut across businesses, functions, and levels. Making sure that these teams are composed of the best managers and that these teams are functioning effectively is essential for the plans' success.

In Kirk's view, the fourth and most difficult area for integration is in the two organizations' cultures. While it is popular to talk about changing corporate cultures, the simple fact is that they do not change readily, and such change should not be initiated unless absolutely essential to success. It is better to tolerate cultural differences than start deep interventions which may disrupt changes in the other more critical areas such as business and technology.

Sophisticated senior managers can work with other senior managers as a team knowing that some of their norms and beliefs about how to accomplish things are different. A culture audit like that suggested in the last chapter is useful in identifying those differences. Simply knowing what they are is a positive step. What it takes from both sides is some tolerance and a willingness to suspend judgment about "the right way" until time permits closer attention. We have found that, as long as agreement exists about the vision and direction for the combined firms, cultural differences can be tolerated. Getting that consensus is the most important task. In the meantime, it is necessary to identify any cultural differences and decide how to work with them—even with humor if possible. The issue of cultural differences and their impact is an important one we consider further in the next section.

Balancing Attention between Firms

We encountered in more than one acquisition what we have come to call the "jealous children" syndrome. A major acquisition or merger can be so absorbing for senior management and corporate staff that it can divert their attention away from other parts of the acquiring firm. People in the existing businesses can become resentful, for example, when management training normally provided by corporate staff diminishes and they know that extensive, "lavish" training events for managers in an acquired firm are taking place. They may also find it difficult to get help from staff on their issues and may even find several of their own key managers being pulled away to help on an acquisition. When their budgets are cut to pay for an acquisition, the resentment can become truly divisive.

While so much attention and effort must be given an acquired firm, it is essential for senior management to recognize how the acquisition affects their firm's "silent majority." Surveys, periodic discussion groups, and one-on-one discussions with key managers in existing businesses need to be done to keep everyone in touch with what is going on. The troops back home also need to share the firm's vision so they can appreciate how the acquisition will eventually benefit them.

They also need to know how long the discomfort will last. If it appears it will continue for a long time, it may be necessary to provide additional slack resources to ease their discomfort. You simply cannot keep stretching scarce existing resources without eventually replacing them. The idea that "we are all part of one big family" is hard to sell when an acquisition causes unnecessary and acute hardship for other businesses that continue to need support. Indeed, we suspect that

> **It is the overemphasis on dealmaking rather than managing that gets many actively acquisitive firms into trouble.**

Facilitating Organizational Fit

In Chapter 3 we noted how differences in structures, processes and systems, human resources, and cultures make achieving organizational fit difficult. In the integration stage, any differences which are truly obstacles to achieving business and financial fit must be overcome. These areas collectively determine the organization design. The model presented in Figure 8-1 illustrates how the four components of organizational fit are related to each other.

Structural Fit

How well the two firms' structures fit really is a question of where the acquired firm fits within the overall corporate structure

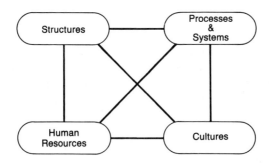

Figure 8-1   The four components of organizational fit.

in terms of reporting relationships and interdependencies with other businesses. The design rule expressed by McCann and Galbraith is to groups units together based on the extent of their interdependence.[9] Galbraith and Kazanjian add that groupings must also take the similarities of their strategies into consideration.[10] The closer and tighter their interdependencies and strategies, then, the closer they should be grouped structurally. If they are not very interdependent, then there is little need to regroup them and they can be kept structurally separate from other tightly linked businesses.

    The modern multidivisional group structure, coupled with sophisticated business and corporate strategy formulation techniques, is the most frequently used device to link and coordinate several businesses. Despite its many shortcomings, the multidivisional structure is a major innovation that has literally helped create the modern corporation. Still, this structure can be unwieldy and insensitive to the needs of newly acquired or merged businesses. One criticism of this design is that it results in businesses being treated too much alike, obscuring the unique features that keep each sensitive to its market.

    What we find is that the multidivisional structure makes sense, and problems attributed to it in mergers and acquisitions appear to have much more to do with the role and capacity of corporate-level staff and the processes and systems used by corporate-level management. Successful mergers and acquisitions depend on a corporate staff that can provide sufficient control over ongoing activities while also providing the high degree of coordination and support needed by new businesses during their integration stages.

The modern Corporate Development function, with its dual focus on strategic planning and merger-acquisition activity is an important innovation in this respect. Planning is useful for both coordination and control purposes, and a well-trained staff also provides a resident capacity for facilitating integration efforts lower in the organization. In addition, Human Resources staff are also playing a much more active role in planning and facilitating change than ever before, and we look more closely at this function's role in the next chapter.[11]

Despite their value, the potential for excessive meddling by corporate staff can be very real. They may choose to play a controlling, rather than facilitative role, for example, which creates barriers between acquired firms and senior management. While the senior managements of both firms may see eye to eye about what norms and tone should prevail during an integration stage, getting these communicated and behaviorally reflected by corporate staff is sometimes not done well. We heard more than one tale about heavy-handed, even arrogant, staff from the acquiring firm violating norms and creating hostility among middle management and staff in the acquired firm. From top management's perspective, relations may look friendly and smooth, while anger and resentment is building lower in their organizations. Rehearsing and reinforcing appropriate norms and tone at several levels of management—particularly among staff—is an essential task in preparing for the transition and integration stages.

Staff also may be so strained trying to manage a newly acquired firm's transition that they have little support left to give to a previously acquired firm's integration stages. As a general rule regarding staff, we offer the following advice:

A highly trained, professional corporate staff plays an essential role in integration efforts by coordinating initiatives and supporting line management. However, senior management must stay involved and in control of these efforts.

Process and System Fit

How the two firms should manage their ongoing interactions, flows of information, and exchange of products and services is the focus for tremendous attention and effort. Changes may be necessary in major processes such as decision making, planning, and budgeting and in major functional systems such as financial controls, human resources, marketing, and production. Changes in decision making and planning are relatively easy to introduce, but changes in information systems and production control systems are not. They may require months, if not years, to fully work through.

Studying a firm's decision making and budgeting processes is very revealing about its values and beliefs, and about how power and influence are distributed within it. Along with structure, changes in these processes are relatively easy to accomplish and should therefore be targeted early for change. Because they can so potently express and reinforce culture and power relationships, changes do need to be very carefully thought through first.

The extent to which participation and consultation in decisions is encouraged, the management level at which a decision can be approved, and who is or is not involved in a decision are all very symbolic of top management's style. They say a lot about who has and does not have power and influence. Experienced managers know this well and use changes in participation to signal shifts in the importance of businesses and individuals. We sometimes wish the messages were less subtle and more explicit, since multiple interpretations are often otherwise possible. If there was ever a time for clarity, it is in the integration stage.

One method we have successfully used to clarify decision making roles and to send clear signals about participation is called Responsibility Charting.[12] One begins Responsibility Charting by identifying decisions that are important to managers but in which they assume unclear roles. In complex organization structures, direct reporting relationships identified on an organization chart simply do not reveal the variety of ways people can participate in decision making, particularly those in staff positions and on teams that may still be in place after a deal. For significant decisions, it is quite likely that as many as 10 to 15 units or groups may be involved in them in some way. For example, one decision we looked at in a Responsibility Charting session to integrate two firms was concerned with purchasing order authorization limits, while another was concerned with pricing decisions for new products. The two decisions varied in importance to the acquiring firm's management; therefore, their participation in the two decisions would vary.

The next step in that session was to identify the "actors" or "participants" thought to be involved in or affected by those decisions. Because the session was done in a group format, considerable discussion ensued about the function and job descriptions for those "actors"—those units and individuals. The managers in both firms learned about what those units actually did, or how job descriptions had been changed in the integration stage.

A decision-making role vocabulary was then created and agreed upon. This vocabulary became a bridge between the two organizations, in a sense. Roles were then assigned to each of the actors for each of the decisions. At the end of the session, there was not only clarity about their respective roles for those decisions, but that group of managers had also learned about key units' functions and created a vocabulary that facilitated their future interactions. A premise in Responsibility Charting is that roles can be negotiated and can vary according to the nature of the decision. The technique can, for example, reinforce an acquiring firm's goal of decentralizing decision making in some functional areas within an acquired firm, while preserving its control over the decisions made in other functional areas.

One tendency is to centralize resource allocations during an integration to control cash flow, particularly if the acquired firm is in trouble. While understandable, a blind grab for all the cash can disrupt performance and sour relationships. In their study of post-merger retention of top management, Hayes and Hoag found that the loss of autonomy and control was the reason why two-thirds of the managers later left acquired firms.[13] When a new financial reporting system and cash management procedures were introduced in one acquisition we knew about, for example, they effectively brought the business of the small acquired firm to a standstill. A better study was needed in the transition stage to identify budgeting process differences and the actual cash needs of the acquired firm. Financial management can be gradually and very selectively decentralized as comfort is built and new reporting systems are introduced and integrated within the acquired firm.

Despite what may be cordial and cooperative negotiations, relations between the two firms can quickly deteriorate when it comes to the design of major functional systems. Inflexibility and unwillingness to cooperate in redesigning a system, whether to save money or time, can stifle the functioning of an acquired firm. We feel that this situation is a major source of trouble, and recommend the following:

> **A collaborative process for initiating design changes in systems should be created. Imposing one firm's systems on the other creates a "win-lose" rather than "win-win" situation. The goal is to take the best from either firm and implement it.**

Human Resources Fit

Deciding who stays and leaves is a critical, difficult task. Reworking those staying into effective management teams is even more difficult. We discussed how these decisions were made in the Allied-Bendix merger, and we generally support that approach. The next chapter also discusses how entry and exit can be better managed.

The major human resources objectives for the acquiring firms we studied in their integration stages were to identify key management talent, place them in the most appropriate positions, and bring them together into effective management teams. As Bob Kirk at Allied-Signal stated—and we emphatically agree—identifying talent and blending it to create an effective top management team is a prerequisite for the integration stage.

The emphasis further down the organization is less on interpersonal and team dynamics and much more on the introduction of changes in reward and compensation, performance review, and career planning and development systems. For these employees, changes in these systems may be the only or most significant impact of the acquisition or merger on them. For this reason, these changes must be flawlessly communicated and introduced. One well-known firm in one of 1986's largest acquisitions made a fatal error, in our opinion, when changes it made in the accounting system resulted in three months of late paychecks for an important group of scientific and technical employees. The late payments soured these valuable employees on their new owners, and it now has to dig itself out of an unnecessary hole.

Intensive management development programs are also designed and introduced to share new knowledge and skills and to build teamwork between managers in the two firms. We say more about management development's role in the next chapter.

In summary, changes in human resource systems have strategic importance because they can directly reinforce or subvert integration efforts. This is a point worth stressing:

Changes in the human resources area deserve the very best management thought and planning to make sure they reinforce, not damage, integration initiatives.

Ideally, during the transition stage, major differences between the firms in these systems are identified and specific areas for change are targeted. Communicating the rationale and timing for these changes as they are implemented keeps employees connected to the transition effort. In one firm we worked with, for example, senior management introduced a change in benefits that they tied back to a need identified in a transition retreat the previous year. The rationale for the change was not only made clear, but it also signaled employees that the implementation plan was at work—the new management was delivering what had been promised, and was in control of the process.

Cultural Change

An early premise of this book was that cultural change could be partially accomplished by changing structure, processes, and human resource systems. These parts of the firm can be used to directly, tangibly, and operationally express the firm's values, beliefs, and symbols—that is, its culture. We have also stated in this chapter that cultures do not change readily, and that it is perhaps best to accept some differences. We even stated that such differences may be useful, and remaking an acquired firm into one's own image is perhaps undesirable. Despite an apparent recognition of their many differences beforehand, for example, the merger of Peat Marwick and KMG Main Hurdman to form the world's largest accounting firm, resulted in several messy and uncomfortable conflicts.[14]

Much of the conflict was the result of very different cultures which were not initially accepted by the other. Resolving these differences will take years, and the fallout, while considerable, may simply be part of the cost of merging professional services firms. Daryl Conner, President of O.D. Resources in Atlanta, would contend that doing "cultural due diligence" in the merger-acquisition process could avoid surprises and help firms better anticipate difficulties.

Such assessment efforts should be embraced as a first step. What should then follow is a dialogue about what shared cultural traits should be developed and reinforced. Here our point in Chapter 6 is worth noting: Change and be prepared to be changed. The goal is to borrow the best of both organizations and meld these into something desirable to all. "What should our firm value? What do we believe?" These questions are answered through many of the mechanisms we have previously discussed: articulating a vision, identifying a set of core themes, and changes in structure, processes, and so on.

We also suggest even creating opportunities to communicate about the desired culture. This entails the creation of stories and myths which are very symbolically powerful communicators about culture. For example, SantaFe Healthcare acquired a small local hospital just a few months after also acquiring AV-MED. Unintentionally, a powerful story was created which eloquently communicated the type of relationship characterized by the new culture. The acquired hospital's financial situation needed clarification, and an AV-MED staff person was brought in from Miami to help SantaFe's corporate management perform its study of the hospital. The CEO later, in a SantaFe–AV-MED transition retreat, publicly praised that person's excellent work. The message communicated to the new hospital's staff, as well as to SantaFe and AV-MED staff, was that employees within acquired firms are full partners, valuable resources, and part of the family.

The benefit gained through such stories is invaluable. Conversely, stories of acquired firms' abuse and neglect can create a legacy not easily overcome. Firms develop reputations about how they treat "captives" which can work against them in future acquisitions. Wells Fargo, despite its sparkling financial success with Crocker, has developed a reputation for dealing harshly with acquired employees because of its initial actions. However, less well known is how some Crocker managers are reportedly finding significant new roles within Wells Fargo. In mergers and acquisitions, perceptions count and must be actively managed.

Summary

This chapter has focused more on how to go about integrating and less about what should be integrated. There are specific areas needing work and we have noted these. The message we have tried to communicate in this chapter is that sensitivity to integration issues means pacing initiatives, knowing how far to go and when to stop, establishing a limited set of themes with which to forge a coherent identity, prioritizing areas for integration, and paying sufficient attention to the rest of the organization to maintain performance and unity. Organizational fit is built by selectively changing and creating fit between the structure, processes and systems, human resources, and cultures of the two firms. The goal is to find a balance among these component parts which best creates business and financial fit. Creating organizational fit may require substantial investments of money and management time and effort. It is in this stage that the price paid for the other firm is justified. Successful firms know this important fact and never skimp on their investments of money, time, or effort in the integration stage.

9

BUILDING CAPACITY

This chapter is directed at the staff and line management who have responsibility for improving their firm's merger-acquisition practice. The need for more actively managing this activity has hopefully been demonstrated in previous chapters. The difficulties inherent in managing the process require systematic, extensive development effort. For example, senior management and corporate staff, primarily with strong finance and strategic planning orientations, tend to dominate the process's early stages. While there are good reasons for bias, the net effects can be dysfunctional. The players "downstream" can suffer by not being involved earlier, and their transition management efforts can be compromised by "upstream" deficiencies. The fragmentation of process stages and the great variety of players make smooth linkages between stages difficult. These and other factors lead us to stress the following:

An active ongoing effort to build the capacity and effectiveness of the process is essential to success.

Corporate development and strategic planning staff do, of course, work to improve the rigor and effectiveness of some stages—particularly the search and screening stages. Their efforts to streamline stages and assure sufficient transition management capacity are vital. These efforts tend to focus on the content or "what" of the process more than on the overall "how" itself. There is, in other words, a concern for what data is produced and its quality, but process facilitation issues seem to receive less attention. The merger-acquisition literature is largely silent about process facilitation issues.

Our observations also confirm that the use—let alone active involvement—of internal organization development (OD) consultants and change management staff for facilitating the process is limited. The use of external consultants is also limited, except for the very specific types of assignments we cited in Chapter 5.

Process facilitation issues are so important that the legitimacy and capacity of internal OD and change management staff need to be built. Only then can they play more active roles. Involvement has been limited for several reasons. First, many of the most actively acquisitive firms such as Allied-Signal have built very sophisticated and well-managed routines. Staff and line managers have gone through the drill many times and feel comfortable with the way they function. In their opinion, prospective deals may fall through for normal reasons, but not because of poor process management.

Second, firms also feel the need to minimize the number of "bystanders" involved. The more players involved, the more unwieldy the process is likely to become. The need for secrecy early in the process is real. The counter argument also has merit that the core group can be too small and its work so secret that it is effectively "decoupled" from the rest of the organization. As the process progresses, it begins to unfold and include other players. We favor having this happen sooner rather than later. The arguments for keeping the group small do have merit only up to a point.

Third, and perhaps most important, the level of specialized knowledge in finance, marketing strategy, and legal issues may limit the number of staff who can meaningfully participate. The presence of senior corporate managers also places a premium on a consultant's poise and confidence. For example, a facilitator may encourage a team to question the benefits of a hotly pursued acquisition. The number of internal consultants with strong "boardroom presence" is limited.

At the end of this chapter a strategy is offered for improving the legitimacy of internal organization development and change management staff. The primary focus for this chapter, however, is on the types of interventions and facilitation needed for the process to work well. Staff and managers other than internal consultants can provide sensitive, effective facilitation. Many highly skilled corporate development staff and senior line managers fill this role. Unfortunately, most typically, specialized financial staff are in charge, and they lack process facilitator training and experience.

An objective facilitator, working closely with a merger-acquisition team, is useful for smoothly introducing new staff or managers into the team, building the team's process awareness, and in designing transition management strategies. Having someone focus solely upon process issues can be very useful. For example, in Japanese negotiation teams one team member may be assigned solely to a listening role to make sure that important but subtle acts are not missed. Still, an existing merger-acquisition team member can play the process facilitator role if provided with the right training. In that case, the internal consultant can be the trainer.

There are two types of development efforts needed: capacity building and process facilitation. The capacity of key individuals, groups, and functional systems must be developed for them to participate more effectively. Functional systems need to be prepared to manage the demands that will be imposed upon them. For example, the human resources function's capacity for playing its important transition stage role must be known. The role of human resources in providing "aftercare" through such programs as employee outplacement, career planning and development, and individual counseling is discussed soon.

The second type of effort is concerned with the facilitation of the process itself. It involves such areas as the psychological, interpersonal, and group dynamics of the merger-acquisition team. Both of these efforts are examined next. To help place them in context, Figure 9-1 illustrates the relation between the level of effort—individual, group, and organization—and the timing of the effort, whether prior to, during, or after a deal. Specific interventions within this matrix are discussed.

Level Timing	Individual/Interpersonal	Team, Task Force, & Group	Multiple Groups/ Organizational

Before Process
Activation
	— Individual team members &
	  staff assessment of skills
	
	— Role negotiation & clarification
	
	— Skill building of members
		— Team building
		
		— Design and manage
		  simulations
		
		— Create baseline data
			— Evaluate capacity
			  of groups to be
			  involved & assist
			  in their development
			
			— Cross-team train-
			  ing & team building
			  to create shared
			  knowledge/skills

During the
Process, Including
Transition
Stage
	— Observation of members and
	  feedback about participation
		— Evaluate & provide
		  feedback about team
		  functioning
			— Link up with counter-
			  parts in other firms
			  to share knowledge
			
			— Coordinate entry/
			  exit of subgroups

Post-Process,
Including
Long-term
Integration
Stage
	— Help personal evaluation of
	  effectiveness
	
	— Interview key players
		— Help team's self-
		  evaluation
		
		— Factor results into
		  new capacity-
		  building efforts
			— Design & guide
			  training activities
			
			— Develop survey data
			  & feed to decision
			  makers
			
			— Team building
			  across firms at
			  multiple levels

Figure 9-1 Levels and timing of process development interventions.

Capacity-Building Interventions

Interventions to build the capacity of key players and systems are of three types (1) knowledge and skill building, (2) improvements in analytic techniques and methods, and (3) functional system improvements.

Knowledge- and Skill-Building Interventions

The specialized knowledge needed about mergers and acquisitions prevents effective participation by many less experienced managers and staff. Even skilled corporate development professionals struggle to keep up with the latest financing strategies and legal rulings. Merger and acquisition work requires both the knowledge of a specialist and the scope of a generalist. The multifunctional and multibusiness nature of an acquisition makes a broad understanding of the organization important. Initially, team members must be thoroughly briefed about their firm's strategies, operations, and performance. Most top management groups are able to stay informed through the normal schedule of staff meetings and quarterly strategic planning reviews, but the firm does need to evaluate how well its key managers are briefed.

Existing internally produced or externally provided management development programs should also be studied to see if they contain useful concepts and techniques for merger-acquisition training. Programs designed to cross-train managers from one functional area in the concepts and methods of another functional area are particularly useful.

There are still too few merger-acquisition training programs around designed for nontechnical managers and staff.[1] The tendency has been to let only corporate finance, planning, and development staff attend programs of this type. We recommend broadening attendance so human resource managers, for example, understand all aspects of the process. University of Michigan professor Noel Tichy noted in a *Fortune* article that, "For years, human resources people have been standing outside a closed door, asking to get in on the important stuff. Now that they are in, some are finding that they don't know what to do, that they can't deliver.[2]" Cross-training builds a common knowledge base which improves communication and interaction between team members.

Beside building knowledge, other skills will need sharpening. Training is recommended in topics such as effective communication and listening, conflict management, negotiations, and change management. Involvement can be both as an individual and as a team member. The finance and human resources functions deserve special attention to receive development in these areas. Staff in these functions are often the first sent into an acquired firm. Intensive coaching and training helps them present the desired tone and professionalism for the transition. Their occasionally insensitive behavior and attitudes have derailed more than one transition.

Developing Analytic Techniques

The value of well-designed techniques for identifying and screening candidate firms speaks for itself. A sophisticated capacity is also needed for quickly evaluating counter-offers and for evaluating the impact of changes in plans. For example, what will the delay in integrating two sales forces do to cash flows and marketing coordination? A well-developed ability to play "what if" games is needed to make such assessments. Computer software to help do this is still limited, but some is available for modeling the impact of stock price changes on the offering price range. Many more sophisticated applications are coming.[3]

Becky Ellenburg at First Atlanta Bank also stresses how important it is for human resources staff to enter an acquired bank in as organized a way as possible. Being able to quickly assess such factors as staffing levels, pay grades, and benefits—even who the insurance carriers may be—is important. Well-designed forms that quickly organize the information she needs create more time for her to listen to the other firm's employees and respond to their questions. High-technology solutions are not necessary in her case.

A major but still undeveloped area is the design and use of surveys and questionnaires designed exclusively for mergers and acquisitions. Well-designed surveys in such areas as organizational climate, employee attitudes, and organization design have great use. For example, a survey used to identify the potential for merging two large state agencies pinpointed specific areas of overlap and ambiguity in responsibilities. In another project, a survey questionnaire was used to monitor employee perceptions about the success of a transition. The survey sampled the perceptions of employees in both firms across several management levels. It also allowed employees less directly involved in the transition to give the team suggestions. One survey outcome was the decision to better inform employees in the acquiring firm about the acquisition.

Good baseline data on employee attitudes, culture, organization design, and performance levels of major systems is invaluable. As Daryl Conner of O.D. Resources said, "You have to know yourself well first, otherwise how can you judge whether changes are for the better or not." Being able to monitor employees' attitudes and concerns before and periodically after a merger or acquisition not only provides good data, but also demonstrates that the acquiring firm is concerned about employees. We stress the use of these tools by saying the following:

The more organized the acquiring firm can become with its techniques for analyzing itself and other firms, the quicker it can respond.

Balanced against the need for better analysis is the need to keep the process flexible and humane. Overdependence on analysis and technique potentially creates rigidity which squeezes intuition and qualitative data out. A human touch is needed. Therefore, it is a good idea to ask whether more analysis is contributing to better success.

Improving Functional Systems

A merger-acquisition process can be compromised when one of the firm's major functional systems fails to handle the demands placed on it. A functional system failure is analogous to a bridge built with one weak foundation. When stressed, the entire bridge is jeopardized. A large merger or acquisition will quickly stress an organization's systems. The question is whether any weaknesses could have been revealed before placing a system under pressure. Trying to overcome weaknesses under the scrutiny of senior managers in both firms—even the media—is not recommended.

Each of the firm's major functional areas needs to be evaluated for its ability to meet the demands that will be placed on it. For example, management information and decision support system hardware and software should be evaluated for their expansion flexibility and compatibility with other systems. Similarly, cash management and financial reporting systems also need examining. Needs in the human resources area are particularly acute. Compensation, management succession, career planning, and management development systems must quickly respond with answers to questions and accommodate large and rapid infusions of new employees.

No firm wants to carry underutilized resources and staff in these functions simply in anticipation of a merger, but all of the major functional systems should at least have plans in place for how they will quickly respond to demands. Functional systems should be changed over a sufficiently long time to prevent excessive stress on them. Time may be available to implement long-term plans, but some systems will have to be changed fast and extensively. For this reason, auditing all major functional systems beforehand is an important organizing step. The goal is to develop throughout these systems a comparably high level of sophistication and capacity. Key issues are the extent a system will be affected, how capable the system is to contribute effectively, and what its development and resource needs are for assuring its effective contribution. This is restated as follows:

> **Investments in major functions to assure their performance in a merger or acquisition are a cost of doing business. While perhaps substantial, these costs must not be avoided.**

Process Facilitation Interventions

A complex chemistry is required to effectively mix many often brilliant merger-acquisition specialists, strong-willed executives, and perhaps only tangentially involved line managers in the pressure-cooker atmosphere of a merger or acquisition. Little wonder that some teams get caught up in counterproductive dynamics. Executing a deal is difficult enough without psychological, interpersonal, and group dynamics becoming major issues. The process breeds uncertainty and stress when time and work are compressed. Personal and organizational stakes may also be great. The "thrill of the chase," sense of power, and competitive spirit which can take hold can create momentum difficult to regulate. A climate that puts a taboo on testing basic assumptions and surfacing contrary information may also be encouraged. Few junior staff will want to try changing the mind of a strong CEO committed to a bad deal. The accounts of the Bendix-Martin Marietta, Texaco-Pennzoil, and many other takeover attempts provide solid evidence of the power of these dynamics.

The intense time and work pressures, uncertainty, excitement, and sense of alienation from the rest of the organization reported to us by some team members can have effects that last for weeks afterward. While demanding to the extreme, we found few of these members who resisted getting involved in a later deal. An important role can be played by a skilled process facilitator before, during, and after the merger-acquisition process to minimize these effects.

Involvement Before the Process

A facilitator can play an important and active team-building role when a team is first formed and when new members join it. Team-building interventions establish members' confidence in each other and in the team. Several specific activities help accomplish this outcome:

1. Building a shared understanding of each member's skills, including their strengths and weaknesses
2. Clarifying each member's role and responsibilities
3. Articulating how decisions are to be made and differences resolved

4. Setting ground rules and norms concerning commitment to the team and work quality and also for sharing concerns
5. Building communication, listening, and conflict management skills

The facilitator can also take the team away from the work setting for intensive sessions. These sessions can be punctuated with briefings by internal staff and merger-acquisition experts on various issues, industry trends, and the firm's present activities.

We particularly like the use of a facilitator in designing and guiding simulations of acquisitions, particularly when the initial contact and offer stage is emphasized. One-on-one preparation of the functional staff who first enter the acquired firm is important for developing their communication and listening skills.

Involvement During the Process

A facilitator can also observe team meetings and intervene when the process appears to get bogged down or side-tracked. Feedback would be provided individually and collectively to team members about their communications, how they test ideas and assumptions, and manage conflict. This is a difficult role to fill. Few merger-acquisition teams we know of allow this role to be played by a third-party facilitator. They prefer instead to have a regular team member play that role. Training members in these skill areas beforehand is one way to make sure those skills are within the team. Our only concern is that *someone* should pay attention to group dynamics, and who does it is less important than making sure it is done.

Once a transition team is formed, the facilitator can work with its leader to manage team dynamics and coordinate and monitor its work. Given the great number of involved subgroups, coordinating their work is a major undertaking. The support role is frequently filled by planning or human resources staff, and an internal facilitator with excellent change management skills should also be involved.

Finally, a great deal of classic organization development work can be done during the transition stage. Help can be provided to groups from both firms in comparing perceptions of each other, exploring similarities and differences, and developing action plans for reducing undesired differences. For example, McKinsey & Co. consultants played a useful role in the Allied-Signal merger by showing Allied's management how its divisionalized structure differed from Signal's holding company design. This difference translated into different decision-making and management styles, and cultures.

Involvement Afterwards

A facilitator can help in the post-hoc analysis of a merger or acquisition. Systematically learning from experience is a key feature of successful firms. However, regaining management's attention to "Monday morning quarterback" an acquisition is difficult. An internal facilitator can help by interviewing players and holding a half-day debriefing session where everyone can compare notes and make changes in procedures and strategies.

Considerable training and team building will occur over the following few months as functional areas and business units start to integrate systems and activities. Internal training staff will be helping coordinate these efforts.

Creating Aftercare Capacity

We call the resources and budgets allocated for post-merger–acquisition management of human resources *aftercare*. Interventions designed to build human resource capacity and minimize disruption to employees are essential. The evidence strongly suggests that poor management of human resources after a deal is a major source of failure. Sophisticated aftercare practice is rapidly growing, although cases of blatant mistreatment of the acquired firm's employees are still encountered. Three types of aftercare programs are currently being provided by human resource functions in more sophisticated firms. These are (1) career planning, (2) stress management, and (3) outplacement services.

Career Planning Programs

Ideally, career planning is a joint responsibility of the employee and firm. They should coordinate their planning efforts so the needs of both can be met. For the ideal to happen, a two-way flow of communication must occur so each can be aware of the other's needs. In reality, few employees have a realistic understanding of the long-term needs of their organizations, nor of the organization's intentions for them. In one study, fewer than one-third of one large corporation's employees had a realistic understanding of their position in the organization—including their potential for promotion.[4] It is impossible to make informed choices in this situation. Valuable employees who have the most options can assume the worst and leave. Less-valued employees can assume they will be promoted and remain.

The predictable aftershock of a merger or acquisition can complicate a career planning process even more because it disrupts traditional career paths and large numbers of new employees enter the system. We stress the following in these situations:

The essence of career planning after an acquisition or merger is prompt identification of management talent and creation for them of a new vision for their careers in the organization.

High-quality performance appraisal and management assessment systems are critical in this effort. They provide performance information for career development and management succession plans. They also provide feedback to managers about the expectations of the new organization.

A merger or acquisition also provides senior management excellent opportunities to test the talents and motivations of new managers. A manager's knowledge and skills can surface when a special study is requested or when they are asked to participate in the transition management team. Creating these "opportunities" is standard practice, and the results are factored into the firm's career and succession plans for these managers.

An acquisition is a unique opportunity for talented managers to surface if they had been suppressed by their previous leaders who then leave after the deal.

Prioritizing the opportunities that may come their way is tough for employees. Transitions require employees to be clear about their own values and what they want for themselves, despite the insecurity the transition can bring. Transitions are critical career events for individuals because they provoke self-assessment and questioning. Ed Schein's concept of "career anchors" is useful for managers caught in a merger.[5] A career anchor is the sense of one's talents, motives, needs, and values that guides and constrains their career choices and gives career identity.

When used diagnostically along with other instruments, a firm can help a manager safely and effectively through a self-assessment. The results can be the basis for a new career development plan. In general, the goal is to provide timely, relevant information to both the new firm and the employee about each other and help the employee avoid a prolonged and unnecessary period of self-doubt and debilitating insecurity. Frequently, employees are left "flapping in the wind," wondering whether they will fit into the new organization. To prevent this situation, the human resources group must work quickly to build and communicate information that helps them make informed career decisions.

Career actions tends to be swiftest for the high performers who are promoted, and for low performers who are outplaced. Unfortunately, the bulk of the work force fits between these two groups and is not the focus for early decisions. This group is composed of "solid citizens" who remain, but are plateaued for a relatively long time—even permanently—until new human resource systems are implemented.[6] They will get the work done, but also will need reassurance and reassessment during the integration stage if they are to get back on track and loyal to the new firm. Ference, Stoner, and Warren illustrate in Figure 9-2 how a work force can be segmented into distinct groups which can become targets for specific career interventions.[7] While the "solid citizens" will need some attention, for

Current Performance	Likelihood of Future Promotion	
	Low	High
High	Solid Citizens (effective plateauees) Organizationally Personally Plateaued Plateaued	Stars
Low	Deadwood (ineffective plateauees)	Learners (comers)

Figure 9-2 Identifying work force groups for interventions. (Source: Ference, Stoner, and Warren, 1975.)

example, the "learners" are a high-risk group because they will be lost to the organization unless actively developed.

From a career planning perspective, the demands on a firm's human resources function can be tremendous. High performers must be quickly identified and their commitment gained through attractive career plans. While not large, this group is an important one. How they are treated is one of the greatest aftercare issues. However, the bulk of the work force is composed of "solid citizens" who will absorb the most time and resources. Because its members constitute the core of the work force, not taking care of them well can be disastrous. The low performers become the focus for another aftercare program. Balancing attention leads us to the following conclusion:

"Triage" may need to be practiced with employees. Setting resource and attention priorities for different classes of employees is essential.

Outplacement Services

The most visible consequence of a merger or acquisition is often the gearing up of an outplacement service for managers in "redundant" positions. Outplacement is a distasteful ordeal for firms and individuals. Softening the blow for these employees, and smoothing their exits makes sense from both ethical and managerial perspectives. There are winners and losers in mergers and acquisitions, and cutting salaries and benefits through staff cutbacks is a major source of anticipated savings to pay for a deal. However, one of a firm's most visible and important characteristics is how it treats an acquired firm's employees. Reputations become well known. Knowledge about how the firm treats acquired employees precedes many deals. In more than one case, a bad reputation has helped ruin a deal. Frank Lorenzo's attempted takeover of TWA is one example.

During the downsizing effort that followed Allied's merger with Bendix, severance packages were offered and vigorous efforts were made to place employees. As one former Bendix employee stated,

> Despite the fact that I felt some bitterness about losing my job, once I accepted the fact I was able to move ahead and find another position. They (Allied) were very good about providing me with all the resources and help I needed with my job search, they also treated me with respect which I appreciate. If I had to lose my job at least I didn't have to lose my self-respect. They made that part easier by treating all of us in my position very well.

Jannotta, Bray & Associates was used by Allied and Bendix to minimize the impact of the negative experience for outplaced employees and to protect the morale of those remaining. By all accounts the effort succeeded. While a tremendous amount of planning and involvement was required, Joe Jannotta, chairman of the firm, feels that it was worth it because "we helped structure and organize their job searches at a time when they were very stressed and vulnerable." Counseling, contacts, office space, and telephones were provided. Jannotta's company also helped design a special program for spouses to help them deal with their concerns. While help can be provided to spouses in their own job searches if they are a two-career family, most of the attention is on the family's ability to handle the trauma of career dislocation.

The range of services provided by outplacement services is impressive. For example, New York's Goodrich and Sherwood Company assists corporations in handling in general termination process and in specific areas such as termination interviews. They also assist employees with self-assessments, job market research, interviewing, and follow-up counseling for several months after the person accepts a new position. The comprehensiveness and depth of these services are designed to get employees back on track as quickly as possible. They help the firm fulfill a social responsibility that it recognizes but does not have the internal capacity to perform.

Stress Management Services

Acquiring firms are also increasing their commitment to stress management programs, employee assistance programs (EAPs), and other services that help employees and their families deal with stress and anxiety. The "post-merger syndrome," as it is called, lowers productivity and breeds morale problems. Some performance drops right before and after a deal are inevitable, but without care they can be prolonged.

Illness and absenteeism rates caused by mergers have not been researched. However, corporate mental health clinics and EAPs report sizable increases in referral utilization rates during periods of corporate reorganization. As Personal Performance Consultants' Regional Director Todd Foster told us, "We see increases in the rate of utilization of our services that include referrals for alcohol and drug abuse, particularly cocaine, as well as stress, depression, and anxiety disorders. We also see many nonspecific cases, one example being a manager who came dragging into our offices recently complaining about being 'emotionally worn-out.'" Foster emphasizes that while the stresses associated with a merger do not cause disorders, they can bring latent problems to the surface.

Employees need to verbalize complaints, appraise their situation, and develop new coping responses, all of which can occur through stress management programs, counseling, and psychotherapy. Disruption during the transition can be minimized without simply pretending that everything is just great.

The costs are not trivial for such programs. Hundreds of thousands of dollars can be spent. The money can be well spent, but frequently a short-term cost-cutting mentality prevails. Employees are either asked to "tough it out" or programs and services are underbudgeted. The human resources function ap-

propriately has a growing and major responsibility in mergers
and acquisitions, and it must be given the resources and capacity
to succeed. Our position is simple:

> **You have to devote the relatively small resources needed
> to make the integration a success or watch much greater
> sums be wasted when it fails. Investments in people
> pay for themselves many times over.**

Building the Facilitator's Legitimacy

Traditionally, internal organization development and consulting
staff have been involved only in the very late stages. While useful
at these late points, we feel that the most senior and experienced
of these individuals should be used much earlier. Still, 80 percent
of internal staff's effort will be used in later stages. However,
that remaining 20 percent is far from trivial, and can make the
other 80 percent more effectively spent.

Some firms have a history of using internal organization
development staff in senior management activities. In other firms,
such staff may not even exist. External consultants can be used,
and close relationships with a specific consulting group may
already exist. Consultants need legitimacy and a clearly demonstrated capacity for them to be used in an area as sensitive
and important as mergers and acquisitions.

To build legitimacy, facilitators and consultants should,
as a first step, learn as much as possible about the merger-
acquisition process. Gaining this knowledge also will mean
understanding the basics of corporate strategic planning. A
knowledge of the strategy implementation literature is also important. Diving head-first into highly technical, financially oriented books, articles, and publications is not required. These
topics are too deep to allow that. Besides, this information is best
acquired on an "as needed" basis. Simply reading the articles
and books in our annotated bibliography is a good start. At-
tending specialized management development programs on
merger-acquisition management is also helpful, but finding the
right ones require some looking. We are generally not impressed
with the programs in the market as we wrote this book.

Once an understanding of the process and basic issues is gained, expressing to senior management an interest in observing stages of the process should follow. Based on these observations, a proposal can then be presented to management for providing more facilitation in the process. The goal is to work upstream in the process as far as possible.

Finally, we want to encourage the development of a professional network of internal consultants who are active in their firms' merger-acquisition practice. Getting involved in such a network and helping it develop will build the level of skills and knowledge about this area. Merger-acquisition activity is not that different from many well-developed forms of facilitation and intervention, but it is different enough to require study and preparation.

10

LESSONS
LEARNED

Despite the diversity and complexity of the mergers and acquisitions we have studied, there are some consistent lessons to be learned. What follows is a summary of what we have discussed in this book. There is no easily available format for such a synthesis, so we decided to organize these findings with reference to different groups of readers. Our findings are listed in three categories (1) lessons for top management, (2) lessons for human resource managers, and (3) lessons for individual employees.

Lessons Reviewed

Lessons for Top Management

Understand your purpose and motives.

Know exactly how you plan to add value to the acquired company and what role you plan to assume with the new venture.

Test your key assumptions at the earliest opportunity.

Plan as thoroughly as possible for life after the deal.

Appraise a prospective target's financial, business, and organizational fit to be certain that compatibility can be achieved.

Maintain an integrated overview as much as possible, and avoid the process's "front-ending" bias and fragmentation.

Make plans for implementation based on a realistic appraisal of the financial, managerial, and productive capacities of both organizations.

Conduct negotiations on a positive sum approach; "winning" in negotiations can mean you lose later.

Respect and empathy should guide your interactions with your counterparts.

Expect to lose key management personnel even though you are trying to retain them.

Pay close attention to the process and its pitfalls.

Limit the amount you undertake and keep the change agenda manageable.

Actively manage but don't overmanage.

Create a transitional ideology and a climate for the acceptance of change.

CEOs must actively sell a vision of a new shared future.

Top management must stay involved during the implementation and integration process.

The acquiring company must make substantial investments in transition management capacity.

Establish and maintain open lines of communication.

Lessons for Human Resource Management

Human resource management should be involved in the merger-acquisition process as early as possible.

Manage the psychological forces so they work for you.

Provide participative roles in the integration process as often as possible.

Make the fullest possible use of both organizations' management education capacities.

Deal with disparities in compensation, benefits, and incentive programs quickly and equitably.

Lessons for Individual Employees

"Managing up" is the key to survival and success.

Assume responsibility for managing your career.

Make sure you are aware of all the resources at your disposal and use them.

Lessons for the Top

Understand your purpose and motives.

Know exactly how you plan to add value to the acquired company, and what role you plan to assume with the new venture. The possible range of roles and strategies outlined in Chapter 6 include the following:

1. Being a *director* who adds selected new management capability with modest goals for improvement for the new organization
2. Being a *facilitator* who removes barriers to growth and builds a larger organization through the acquisition
3. Being a *savior* who takes charge and turns around a less productive firm
4. Being a *transformer* who takes the acquired company and develops a new strategy and organization that adds new capabilities and profitability to an industry

Jim Balloun, Managing Director of McKinsey's Atlanta office, offers the following observation: "too often acquirers fail to define their role adequately, and so they buy a company and basically leave it alone. Failing to define how they will add value to the new organization, they manage it ineffectively and are subsequently disappointed with the outcome of the venture."[1] This is particularly true in unrelated mergers where the other industry is not known well. As Peter Drucker notes, successful acquisitions, since the time of J.P. Morgan a century ago, have followed five rules, the first of which is that an acquisition will succeed only if the acquiring company thinks through what it can contribute to the business it is buying. Relying on the contribution and synergy from the acquired company leads to disappointment.[2] (See the Annotated Bibliography for a synopsis of Drucker's observations.)

Test your key assumptions at the earliest opportunity.

In a recent large-scale merger it was assumed that the organizational fit was good and that the two firms' employees would join harmoniously; so the decision was made to postpone doing employee attitude and opinion surveys to appraise peoples' reaction to the reorganization. Soon thereafter there was a rapid turnover of top executive talent, three high-level managers had heart attacks, and there were high absenteeism rates throughout the company. As one senior officer later commented, "It would have been a hell of a lot cheaper to have run those surveys early and find out about all of the people fit problems we had before they hit us—I really think we could have managed them if we had checked all of this out earlier." This is clearly one of the key lessons we have learned and have stressed throughout this book.

Careful and comprehensive planning is a prerequisite for success.

Planning that anticipates post-merger problems and helps prevent major upheavals is particularly crucial. As an ongoing activity, the highest quality corporate development programs consistently analyze acquisition targets so timely decisions can be made without sacrificing careful appraisal. We described these organizing and screening stages in Chapter 3. In observing a number of corporate development programs we find that in many cases what might appear to outsiders as a rapid opportunistic buy—a reactive response to new circumstances—is often, in reality, a proactive response based on long-term comprehensive analysis and screening of prospective targets. The firm was able to move quickly and confidently at the right time.

Central in these considerations is how the acquirer will manage and integrate the new firm into its existing operation. Allied's mergers with both Bendix and Signal were such transactions. Allied had appraised both firms, their products, operations, management, and culture before the merger so when the circumstances were right they were able to act quickly and efficiently. While the amount of information available to a prospective acquirer is limited, a long-term planning perspective makes it possible to have accessible as much information as possible.

> **Appraise the financial, business, and organizational fit and general operating style of a prospective target to see if compatibility can be achieved.**

In Chapter 3 we described the need to appraise and anticipate problems in financial, business, and organizational fit. Organizational fit is particularly difficult to assess and easy to neglect, yet it is often the decisive factor that determines a merger's success or failure. Determining whether a prospective partner has a business or operating style compatible with your own is a crucial part of any sound assessment. Such "intelligent screening"—a term used by Booz-Allen Hamilton—must provide a critical understanding of one's own as well as the prospective acquiree's business style. Richard Davis suggests that five characteristics related to business style need to be understood:

1. Management's position on risk taking
2. How long an organization will tolerate waiting for a return on investments
3. How profits are shared between management and stockholders
4. Delegation of authority and responsibility in the company's operation
5. The relative importance of functional areas within the business[3]

Maintaining an integrated overview is essential.

As we pointed out in Chapter 4, the multitude of specialized experts involved in making a deal contributes to one of the major problems found in mergers and acquisitions, process fragmentation. Multiple participants with different vocabularies and contrasting perspectives and forms of analysis make it difficult for both the acquiring and acquired companies to maintain a clear focus and sense of direction. Some observers refer to this phenomenon as segmentation, adding that it, "produces conceptually and operationally different analyses and a disproportionate attention to strategic fit over organizational fit, thereby decreasing the possibility of successfully combining the businesses.[4]"

A generalist's perspective needs to be maintained to oversee and orchestrate a successful merger-acquisition. Such a perspective is gained through the lessons of experience. It is no surprise that some of the most successful firms in the merger-acquisition game are also the most experienced. They also appear to be the ones who have the greatest ability to oversee the entire process and orchestrate all the merger's phases to create a smoothly operating system. In the absence of such experience, external consultants can broaden a company's understanding of the merger-acquisition process and help the organization build internal capacity to gain the understanding and expertise necessary to manage the new organization. Even the most experienced firms, such as GTE, GE, and Allied-Signal, make use of major consulting firms as a way to gain a second opinion and outside perspective on their acquisition efforts.

Implementation plans must be based on a realistic appraisal of the financial and managerial capacities of both organizations.

Too often when strategic assumptions are made people assume that capacity will somehow emerge and implementation will be easy; those involved in a merger-acquisition negotiation can simply negotiate in good faith and thus reinforce trust and communication. Such a negotiating atmosphere *can* lead to mutual problem solving and gain. But it is unlikely, since such an ideal state is never fully attainable. The alternatives, however, are risky. For example, insofar as the negotiations resemble courtship or combat—the two most prevalent models—one can expect that not all information will be disclosed and, therefore, many important issues will not be clearly understood or easily resolved. In such an atmosphere there is a great deal of tacit bargaining going on—both parties agreeing not to disagree—thus postponing the resolution of key issues until the post-merger period when they may be much harder to resolve. At the very least, completing unresolved negotiation issues after the deal has been made limits the range of available solutions and may consume resources needed for integration purposes. Achieving as much closure as possible in the formal merger-acquisition negotiations, particularly about how post-merger management issues will be resolved, enhances the prospects for later success.

Respect and empathy should guide one's efforts.

The other company's business style and organizational culture have most likely evolved for very valid reasons. While those stylistic differences may be troublesome in some respects, they may have contributed to that organization's success. When the more formally attired executives of Allied met with their more informally dressed counterparts at Signal the contrast provoked the usual jokes and comments about mellow Californians and uptight easterners, but the humor apparently was taken well; mutual respect and tolerance prevailed. For their part, Allied recognized that the informal and decentralized style of Signal contributed to its creative vitality and accomplishments. Allied's respect and understanding of those characteristics, and the need to preserve them, has contributed to the success.

Charlie Bischoff, Allied's Vice President of Human Resource Management at the time of the Bendix acquisition offers the following observations: "if you don't view the (acquisition) process as a merger of relative equals and you come in with an acquiring aura, you are going to have real problems." In retrospect, Bischoff attributes Allied's success in its acquisitions to the mutual respect developed between Allied and its acquired firms. The respect displayed by Ed Hennessy is, in Bischoff's view, a crucial component of that success: "the top guy's behavior and words have to communicate that respect and set the tone for the entire transaction."

Expect to lose key management personnel while trying to retain them.

As mentioned in Chapter 4, numerous studies have shown that attrition in the post-merger phase is usually high. Drucker puts the matter succinctly: "it is fallacious to assume you can buy management through an acquisition.[5]" Nevertheless the majority of acquisitions presume that a critical number of top managers will remain. Creating incentives for managers of both organizations encourages them to stay and become stakeholders in the new organization. Turnover is difficult to predict and impossible to control: The most experienced firms are capable of planning for the worst while hoping for the best. Offering substantial promotions or enhanced benefits seems to be the most common way of accomplishing this.

Understand the process and its pitfalls.

The process has a life of its own, one that sets in motion forces that tend to accelerate the flow of events.[6] Once the flow of information becomes public and the media become involved, the process escalates. The key players can become pawns forced to commit themselves to a course of action they may find questionable. The need to save face and to appear decisive and commanding may, ironically, sweep the leaders up in a process where their control and judgment are diminished. In such circumstances, decisions can be made in haste and judgments can suffer from premature closure. It is important to try to maintain sufficient reflective distance to question the unfolding process and shift its velocity if necessary. This can be facilitated by soliciting feedback within the organization and by inviting outside review from a variety of external resources.

Understanding the process and its potentially harmful effects and controlling it through well-timed, carefully conceived decisions and communications are key.

Limit the amount you undertake and keep the agenda manageable.

Controlling the process becomes much easier when a merger-acquisition's labor-intensive demands are realistically anticipated. A well-managed deal may require the key internal players to give their undivided attention and full energy. Organizations, like living organisms, can suffer from stimulus overload that diminishes the capacity to perform adaptively. Experienced executives set priorities for their corporate development programs so they can commit the organization's full resources to the immediate merger-acquisition effort.

Actively manage but don't overmanage.

Achieving a proper balance between undermanaging and overmanaging may be both an art and a science. The most common error is undermanagement where an acquiring company invests large amounts of capital and then takes a laissez-faire approach as if it had no strategy for adding value to the acquisition. Conversely, numerous acquisitions have failed because a larger firm suffocated a smaller one with its complex, demanding controls and procedures.

Successful acquisition efforts involve gaining early control of a limited number of crucial variables ranging from specific, such as gaining control of the cash accounts, to general, such as taking over the strategic planning and critical path schedules.[7] The most important lesson regarding the degree to which one should manage a new acquisition is *the rule of minimum essential intervention.* Intervene enough to direct the new organization toward the goals you have set, but do not manhandle a new partner.

Create a transitional ideology.[8]

Moving an organization into a new era involves the creation of a new belief system that reflects the venture's objectives and strategies. Information must be provided that clearly outlines these objectives in a fashion consistent with (but not the same as) previous strategies and operating procedures. The transition team coordinates management's efforts during the transformation process when old practices and procedures coexist with new ones. Preserving old cultural symbols and mores can be very valuable to acquired firm's employees as the need for continuity and stability can be great. This is not to say that change cannot or should not be expected. On the contrary, the change process can be facilitated and resistance can be diminished if respect for the previous organization is shown. This often includes assimilating some of the practices from the acquired company's culture. In a regional bank merger the acquiring bank encouraged the old president to stay on to facilitate the change process; in addition, the acquired bank kept its name and identity. While this was done, in part, to maintain good customer relations in the small community, it was also done to help employees maintain a sense of continuity and commitment to the new order. If properly handled, the acceptance of change can be built into the ongoing process so people can work together to move beyond the previous period of stability.

The CEO must articulate and actively sell a vision of a shared future.

A major source of anxiety during and after the deal's closing is uncertainty about what the future holds. The acquiring CEO can minimize this uncertainty by articulating clearly, consistently, and frequently his or her vision of the two firms' shared future. This vision need not, and likely cannot, be precise in every detail, but it can communicate a broad sense of direction and purpose, as well as an approximate timeframe.

Ed Hennessy strongly advocated the view that Allied's acquisition of Signal was really a merger, not an acquisition, that would enable the combined firm to better position itself in high technology industries. The new corporation drew upon personnel from both companies to form a new blended corporate staff.

Top management must stay involved during implementation and integration.

Nowhere can the "remoteness" of management be more costly than in a merger-acquisition effort. We have observed that the laissez-faire approach taken by some corporations after a merger or acquisition does little to create the momentum necessary to bring about changes needed to recover the premiums paid for the acquired firms. This does not mean that the acquiring firm must manhandle the new acquisition; it means rather, that senior management must stay informed and provide the requisite resources and direction. Historically, acquiring firms' managements have tended to underestimate the capital and human resources required to achieve a new acquisition's optimal performance.

Invest in transition management capacity.

Economizing on such expenses as operating costs and new staffing needs can be hazardous, especially during the delicate post-merger stage. As one corporate officer told us, "If you have to ask how much it costs to fund a transition/integration effort, you probably can't afford it, so don't make the acquisition in the first place!" The most successful transition management teams are well supplied with both funds and staff. The teams have been trained and developed. The transition managers are assigned to the post-merger integration effort on a full-time basis. They structure and guide the process so they can restabilize the newly formed organization as quickly as possible. By committing both time and capital to the post-merger management effort, the corporate chiefs stay well informed and highly involved. This allows the CEO to orchestrate the merged firms' collective energies effectively through the transition management team.

Establish and maintain open lines of communication.

No amount of planning can prevent problems and conflicts from arising. However, they can be successfully resolved if clearly articulated channels of communication provide employees with an ongoing flow of accurate information.

During the implementation and integration stages, some of the most crucial information flows from the bottom up, as problems become evident in day-to-day operations. While such problems are inevitable it is critical that they are reported promptly and accurately so that quick action can be taken. If management has not established realistic goals and expectations based on a sound appraisal of the new organization's actual capacity, there may be reticence to pass information upwards since reports of performance shortfalls are unwelcomed. Good communication flow is dependent on realistic strategies that in turn rest on a sound appraisal of the organizations' true capacity. The most tragic example of how unrealistic strategy can adversely affect communication is the NASA Challenger explosion. In planning an unreasonably high number of missions in order to attract congressional dollars, NASA placed enormous pressure on its employees and those of its suppliers. Attaining the proposed number of launches was impossible and the consequent "failure" led employees to avoid communicating upwards to prevent criticism from superiors. The slowdown or stoppage of information flow led to a fatal launch decision.[9] In the majority of successful acquisition management programs, we have observed there is a central clearinghouse for coordinating the flow of information. It is clearly identified and the individuals responsible are known throughout the organization. The human resource function is often responsible for serving in this role. The specific features of a sound information coordination program are described in Chapter 5.

Defining terms and developing a shared vocabulary is also an important part of establishing a good communication process in a post-merger environment. Semantic problems can be extremely costly. When two organizations decide they will form a new corporate division that will be "marketing driven," this does not mean they reached a manageable agreement. A mutual assumption that all parties have a common understanding of such a phrase has led to extremely expensive misunderstandings. In a merger of two consumer products companies, one proceeded to double the size of its sales department in keeping with its understanding of the new marketing strategy. Executives from the other firm were stunned by the announcement of the new hirings since they assumed the funds to achieve the state would be used to increase the advertising budget.

In contrast, we have been impressed with the efforts made by a number of companies to prevent such misunderstandings. Management newsletters are used in some cases to spell out precisely what the acquirer means by such terms as "sales driven" or "product line enhancement," so a lexicon of crucial words and phrases is placed in the hands of every employee. While such communiqués serve broader needs for communication (and contribute to the development of new transitional road-maps), they also prevent misunderstandings due to semantic ambiguity.

Finally, it is important to develop a strategy for communication that is specific to each phase of the merger-acquisition. As the process of a merger-acquisition unfolds, employees' needs for information shift. Initially, basic clarification is called for; insofar as possible the firm should provide information describing what is happening and why, and how will it affect employees. After the formal announcement and before the actual formation of a new corporate entity, other forms of communication are required. Marsha Sinetar, a Consulting Psychologist of Sinetar and Associates, stresses that information that helps employees "organize their work and their roles" is particularly vital. Such communication provides "timelines for the merger and for systems to transfer services, people and technical knowledge.[10]" Finally, when the new organization is formed, more specific information about compensation, benefits, incentives, working conditions, and performance appraisal, as well as information about day-to-day operations, must be provided. Designing mechanisms for this communication and using outside resources for information and support must be carefully planned and executed.

Lessons for Human Resource Management

Human resource management should be involved in the merger-acquisition process as early as possible.

The most successful mergers we observed were ones that addressed the issues of organizational fit and human resource systems integration early in the process. A high degree of involvement of human resources executives is a notable characteristic of successful mergers and acquisitions. They are involved in defining screening criteria, performing in-depth analyses of candidates, and playing a key role in the transition teams. Charles Bischoff, who served as Allied Staff Vice President for Management Resources, played a tremendously varied role during the Bendix acquisition such as evaluating specific candidates for positions and mediating between two functional areas that were in conflict over how they were to be integrated.

A merger's impact on employee retention, morale, compensation, and benefits is not easy to resolve, but the probability of successfully coping with these problems is enhanced if they are anticipated. Involving the human resource and OD functions early is the best way to prevent unexpected people trauma. Mergers and acquisitions demonstrate the need for human resource management to play a proactive role as a strategic function (not just an operational or managerial one).[11]

Manage the psychological forces and emotional climate so they work for you.

The energies and forces unleashed by an organizational upheaval such as a merger-acquisition can play both a constructive and destructive role. For example, the anxiety created can, up to a certain point, serve an energizing function. However, the level of anxiety that develops needs to be limited. The organization can help set those limits by creating temporary systems and structure while building more lasting ones. Task forces and ad hoc committees can be used to deal with immediate questions about reporting relationships and new procedures, as well as with more general concerns like job security.

Ambiguity is the opposite of structure and contributes to free-floating anxiety and the perception of organization drift. Thus, by providing information in a timely, accurate fashion, the organization can create the clarity and structure necessary to make productivity possible. Supplying information is one of the most important tasks of the transition management team and the human resource management (HRM) function during the integration phase. The most common error we have observed is a well-intentioned effort to provide reassurance by prematurely communicating information that proves to be inaccurate or incomplete. This is the equivalent of top management's temptation to make promises it cannot keep. While the motivation is often laudable, the effects are harmful since confidence and trust are undermined. Predictable and otherwise manageable psychological distress is exacerbated and made more intractable by such management practices. In successful transition management, the flow of information is carefully handled so (1) many questions and concerns are anticipated and addressed through the constant flow of information provided by a variety of media and (2) unanticipated questions are responded to with a specific date by which the answer will be given.

Managing information flow is a crucial part of dealing with the psychological reactions to a merger-acquisition. Clear, consistent information helps to keep people informed, productive, and committed. Conversely, rumors can tear at the fabric of an organization. In one tragic situation the top managers of a valuable division resigned because they had "inside information" leading them to believe erroneously that the division was to be closed or divested. In contrast, the human resource management department of a high technology firm installed red phones in specified locations in a new building where a joint venture enterprise was started so anyone could call an information-rumor control center.

Provide participative roles in the integration process as much as possible.

The psychological contract between employees and their organization becomes more tentative during a period of reorganization.[12] Providing opportunities to participate and help manage the transition process is the kind of involvement that helps reaffirm employee commitment. The payoff can be substantial because the best employees—that is, the most involved and responsible ones—have the greatest need to participate. Allowing them to participate as much as possible contributes to their level of satisfaction and enhances the probability they will maintain their contract to continue actively contributing to the firm. In contrast, depriving people of the opportunity to respond actively and positively to upheaval can create trauma, particularly for the most valued and conscientious employees. The need to actively master what would otherwise be "passive trauma" has long been noted in psychological literature.[13] The effects of trauma can be diminished if individuals are given opportunities to respond actively to the situation. Conversely, the absence of such opportunities increases the probability that serious stress symptoms and/or depression will erupt. The other obvious advantage of providing meaningful roles for a maximum number of people is that the firm gains the benefit of their opinions and expertise. In most cases the outcome of a merger-acquisition is dependent on the collective intelligence and goodwill of the people who work for the organizations.

Make the fullest possible use of the management education capacities of both organizations.

Such programs are designed to disseminate information in a clear, cogent, and standardized format, and in so doing they are powerful socialization forces. Management education can provide a conceptual framework to aid understanding of the merger-acquisition process and its purpose and aims, and can, therefore, contribute to the development of a transitional ideology and all of the psychological benefits it offers. Robert Fulmer, previously a director of management education at Allied-Signal, and now President of his own New Jersey-based executive education firm that provides programs to major corporations, describes the contribution that can be made by the training function during a postmerger transition. "Management development is a valuable means of reducing resistance to the merger, and it assists the process of building a positive blended corporate culture for the managers involved in a merger." According to Fulmer, the skillful use of management development proved to be "a major asset in attempting to achieve the goal of a united corporation in the Allied-Bendix acquisition.[14]"

The role of education in post-merger management is rapidly developing. Both corporations and business schools are initiating research and training efforts. For example, Fulmer now teaches the first graduate-level course in post-merger management at Columbia University's School of Business.

Deal with disparities in compensation, benefits, and incentive programs quickly and equitably.

Task forces or transition teams that represent both organizations provide a vehicle to resolve potential inequities in a reasonable and efficient manner. These issues are of sufficient import and sensitivity that perception is as important as reality.

We have addressed this issue in Chapter 4 in some detail. Our point in restating it here is to emphasize the need to act quickly in dealing with these matters since they will have an immediate impact on employees' decisions to remain or leave the organization. A highly visible task force that provides representation of all parties is often the best hedge against perceptions of favoritism and unfairness. For example, blending compensation programs in a public forum with open communication does not guarantee general acceptance, but it is a powerful catalyst in bringing about such agreement.

Lessons for Individual Employees

Managing up is the key to survival and success.

Getting information from above is vital when you are reassessing your position with your firm. It is the only way you can realistically understand your future prospects. By gathering as much information as possible from trusted superiors and associates, you can begin to answer critical questions so you can make intelligent career planning choices. Based on a survey of acquired firms' executives, John Hardy has designed an eleven-point checklist to help managers assess their level of vulnerability after a merger. His list includes the following:

1. Did the new owner buy your company for management talent, including yours?
2. Are you the key executive in a profit center of vital interest to the new management?
3. Are you flexible enough to report to a new group of executives, function in a new organization structure (that is, a decentralized one), and do things "their" way?
4. Are your executive skills transferable within the new structure?
5. Was your company acquired for nonmanagement reasons (for example, special financial advantages, manufacturing facilities, or its distribution set-up) of which you are a part?
6. Is your salary high in relation to the compensation scale of the purchasing company?

7. Is the salary for your job high relative to the "market" for similar positions?
8. Is your function duplicated in the parent company?
9. Were you publicly against the merger?
10. Are you in a staff position?
11. Are you a "self-made" man with long tenure?

The degree of vulnerability for a person is indicated by the sum of negative responses to the first five questions and positive responses to any of the remaining six questions.[15]

Assume responsibility for managing your career.

If you are not managing your career, who is? It is imperative that employees take a proactive stance during post-merger integration. Career management at its best is a joint venture between the individual and the organization. Well-conceived mergers and acquisitions provide a broad array of resources for career planning purposes, including individual counseling, counseling for spouses and families, testing programs, outside consultants, contacts with recruiters, and outplacement programs. Making full use of these services facilitates an adaptive response in what may be a critical situation.

The need for self-knowledge is paramount during any time of career crisis, but perhaps especially during a merger, since staying on the job may necessitate a career change because the organizational setting and expectation are likely to change. Taking a reflective look at your talents, needs, and values so you reappraise your "career anchor"—the core of attributes that provides you with an occupational identity—enhances the probability of your making the right choices at a critical juncture.[16]

Annotated
Bibliography

The literature on managing mergers and acquisitions is scattered through a wide range of periodicals. For these reasons we thought it would be helpful for the practitioner and student alike to provide abstracts of some of the more helpful writings that have informed our efforts in this book. The list is by no means complete, but it does offer a synopsis of the major writings in the field to date. We have organized the bibliography alphabetically by author because no other system of classification proved workable. Even though these articles were written with different audiences in mind (top management, human resource management, acquirers, and acquired), the commonality of interests among all parties appears such that it seemed misleading and counterproductive to segment the literature along such lines.

ARNOLD, JOHN D., "Saving Corporate Marriages: Five Cases," *Mergers & Acquisitions*, Winter 1983, pp. 53–58.

The tendency of acquiring companies to impose their own notions of what is good for an acquired organization (without input from the latter) is a recurring event in floundering corporate marriages. Economic and financial considerations can cloud the judgments of the parties concerned who can easily overlook the fundamental human resource issues that will ultimately determine whether the merger is fully successful. Concern over these issues must be built into the negotiations so discussions address not only the price and terms of the merger but also the degree of autonomy and authority the acquired company will have after the acquisition.

CALLAHAN, JOHN, "Chemistry: How Mismatched Managements Can Kill a Deal," *Mergers & Acquisitions*, March-April 1986, pp. 47–53.

Irreconcilable cultural and psychological mismatches between managements—particularly between CEOs—can disrupt the most well-planned integration efforts between two firms. When basic chemistry between merger partners does not exist it can create problems that cannot be undone during the post-acquisition process. Chemistry is defined as the ability of merging managements to get along and cooperate productively on behalf of the combined company.

Important checkpoints to keep in mind include the following:

1. Frequent discussions on how well the adjustment is progressing during the initial months, with emphasis on assignments, roles, responsibilities, decisions, achievements, problems, goals, and objectives. Free-flowing communication is essential.

2. Determine if the new roles are compatible and if there is a need for tailoring or fine tuning.

3. Assess the degree to which the principals are open, trustful, and objective, and how conflicts are handled.

4. If the long-term prognosis is not favorable, plans should be made for separation with respect and honor, and the new organization should be protected from trauma and turmoil.

5. If the operation has been successful, celebrate its health by acknowledging those who have contributed to it, appreciating their contributions, analyzing the contributing factors, and continuing to apply these influences for success in future acquisitions.

In assessing the chemistry between two organizations, one can be more sensitive to the issue of organizational fit and thereby avoid making the fallacious assumption that the product, marketing strategies, and financial figures are so good that the deal cannot fail.

DAVIDSON, KENNETH M., *Mega-Mergers: Corporate America's Billion-Dollar Takeovers*. Cambridge, Mass.: Ballinger, 1985.

This book provides a review of the players, the strategies, the laws, and the consequences of the current wave of mergers. It describes the acquisition process, including decision making and strategy setting. The economic and social consequences are reviewed and outlined.

DAVIS, R. E., "Compatibility in Corporate Marriages," *Harvard Business Review*, July-August 1968, pp. 86–93.

Companies seeking to gain operating synergy through an acquisition or merger would do well to assess the business style of the target company before the merger to prevent serious post-merger problems. This is particularly necessary if the two organizations are expected to achieve a high degree of integration as a precondition for accelerated growth. Appraising the business style of a company involves understanding five factors:

1. Management's position on risk taking.
2. The time an organization will tolerate waiting for a return on investments.
3. How profits are shared between management and stockholders.
4. The delegation of authority and responsibility in the company's operation.
5. The relative importance of functional areas within the business.

While proponents of the acquisition may emphasize the operational compatibility of the combined organizations, the more intangible issue of the two firms' compatibility should also be taken into full consideration.

DRUCKER, PETER, "The Five Rules of Successful Acquisition, *The Wall Street Journal*, October 15, 1981.

Five rules for successful acquisition have been followed in all successful acquisitions since the time of J.P. Morgan a century ago.

1. An acquisition will succeed only if the acquiring company thinks through what it can contribute to the business it is buying. Relying on the contribution and synergy from the acquired company leads to disappointment.

2. Successful diversification through acquisition requires a common core of unity: shared markets, technology, or (on occasion) similar production processes. Financial ties are insufficient to engineer a successful merger.

3. No acquisition works unless the people in the acquiring company respect the product, the markets, and the customers of the company they acquire. The acquisition must be a "temperamental fit."

4. The acquiring company must be prepared to supply the top management talent for an acquired company within one year. It is fallacious to assume you can buy management through an acquisition.

5. In order to retain management it is necessary to offer members of management from both organizations substantial promotions to demonstrate that the merger offers them personal opportunities.

———, "Curbing Unfriendly Takeovers," *The Wall Street Journal*, January 5, 1983.

The fear of unfriendly takeover is particularly widespread in "strong, prosperous, medium-sized companies—those with sales of $75 million to $400 million and excellent long-range growth prospects." These businesses are the ones with the greatest need for long-term strategies and heavy investments in the future. Ironically managers who best serve those needs are the ones who place themselves and their companies at the greatest risk for an unfriendly takeover. The challenge is trying to develop measures that will curb unfriendly takeovers without hampering constructive merger-acquisition activity and diminishing the availability of venture capital funds for new business.

DULL, JULIA H., "Helping Employees Cope With Merger Trauma," *Training*, January 1986, 23, no. 1, pp. 70–72.

To a large extent it is the employees who determine whether a merger will work. A merger or acquisition is a threat to the employees of at least one of the companies. How such a threat is handled can be a deciding factor in the merger's success.

Activities and programs that address emotional needs are the responsibility of both companies. However, the acquired company may have to bear the entire burden as the acquirer is often insensitive to the acquired employees. The following suggestions are offered:

1. Timing—employees should hear the news first internally; this tends to decrease shock and increase trust.
2. Meetings—frequent and regular throughout transition.
3. Anonymous feedback—telephone merger hotline.
4. Train managers—that is, seminar on coping with change and uncertainty, loss of control, retaining key people.
5. Technical job training.
6. Family assistance program.
7. Stress reduction.
8. Introductory meetings, team building.
9. Orientation programs to the acquiring company to build identification with the new organization and trust.
10. Explain new roles.
11. Help those who will lose their jobs.
12. Post-merger team building from the top to the bottom.

EHRBAR, ALOYSIUS, "Have Takeovers Gone Too Far?" *Fortune*, May 27, 1985, pp. 20–22.

Even giant corporations feel vulnerable to raiders these days, and a lot of managers would feel more comfortable if the government would raise new bars to unfriendly acquisitions. But intervention would be bad for stockholders and the economy. Takeovers, in some instances, accelerate needed change by bidding for control of corporations whose managers are adjusting too slowly to the new environment; and the competition for corporate control pushes all managers to exploit their assets more effectively.

FARLEY, JAMES B., and EDWARD H. SCHWALLIE, "An Approach Toward Successful Acquisitions," *The Texas Business Executive*, Fall-Winter 1981, pp. 32–39.

The authors (of Booz-Allen Hamilton) describe six key steps in a successful acquisition:

1. integration with a strategic plan
2. "intelligent" screening
3. evaluation of targets using both creativity and analysis
4. understanding value and price
5. anticipating the post-acquisition phase
6. efficient implementation

FOX, JOHN, "Planning—The Key to Successful Mergers and Acquisitions," *Management Review*, September 1967, pp. 12–18.

The success of a particular merger-acquisition is directly related to the quality of the planning done. A checklist for developing merger goals is provided. A variety of considerations are briefly described including timing, pricing, tax considerations, and post-merger operations. In discussing the latter point, it is suggested that post-merger change be orchestrated by a liaison team with representatives from the marketing, production, and financial areas.

FULMER, ROBERT, and RODERICK GILKEY, "Blending Corporate Families: Management and Organization Development in a Post-merger Environment," *The Academy of Management Executive*, (in press).

This paper draws upon psychotherapeutic and family systems theory to outline some of a successful merger's key features. Individual case examples are used to illustrate the major points. Much of the material is collected from the authors' own experiences with the Allied-Bendix and Allied-Signal merger-acquisitions. The success in these ventures is attributable in part to a clear understanding of the roles and rules in the new relationships (through the use of an integration task force), the use of outside counsel, seminars dealing with both the content and process of the merger, and mechanisms for listening and collecting data about employee reactions.

GAIENNIE, L. RENE, "Handling the Personnel Problems of a Corporate Merger," *Personnel*, November 1956, pp. 267–72.

Two major tasks confronting management in a merger situation are

1. Maintaining good communications within the company and with the general public.
2. Installing internal operating controls.

Establishing internal controls can be summarized in six steps:

1. Developing an adequate organizational structure
2. Writing job descriptions
3. Working out a consistent compensation system
4. Selecting employees to staff the organization
5. Developing policies and procedures in certain special areas of personnel administration
6. Training the new team to meet the established requirements

GREENHALGH, LEONARD, "A Process Model of Organizational Turnover: The Relationship With Job Security as a Case in Point," *Academy of Management Review*, 1980, 5, no. 2, pp. 299–303.

This study proposes that there are five stages during the employment relationship's life cycle where the decision to participate and contribute to the organization is made. At each stage the employee assesses his or her situation and decides to stay or exit. A major factor in such assessments is job security, with its perceived absence leading to the decision to leave the organization or, in cases where there is not an alternative source of employment, a decision to withhold contribution (a "psychological quit"). The five stages include

1. Choosing the organization
2. Entering into the employment contract (the point of entry)

3. Staying on through the induction crisis when one gets a sense of the organization from the inside
4. Continuing to participate during the "differential transit" when the organization and its limitations become thoroughly known to the employee
5. Making the decision to contribute and reaffirm the psychological contract that was made at the point of entry.

———, "Maintaining Organizational Effectiveness During Organizational Retrenchment," *The Journal of Applied Behavioral Science*, 18, no. 2, 1982, pp. 155–70.

Work force planning must be incorporated as an integral part of planning for organizational change. To avoid job insecurity problems including costly turnover, loss of morale and productivity, and breaches in the social contract that exists between employers and employees, work force planning must be done directly by the strategic decision makers. There is a great need for effective communication regarding the effects of organizational changes on job security before rumors begin. "Failure to take these steps can result in the irony of reducing organizational effectiveness through the introduction of changes intended to increase it."

HACKETT, JOHN T., "Developments, Trends & Useful Proposals for the Attention of Managers," *Harvard Business Review*, January–February 1974, pp. 17–19.

In questioning the premise of mergers and acquisitions, the author asks if there is not a limit to growth that should be considered by companies thinking about enlarging. Three major disadvantages of expanding are cited:

1. An inability to achieve adequate financial control and planning.
2. The difficulty of maintaining a responsive and timely decision-making process.
3. A decline in the ability to realize the creative and innovative potential of individuals in large organizations.

It is suggested that dividing existing organizations into smaller, independent enterprises may help solve some of the problems associated with overexpansion.

HAYES, R. H., "The Human Side of Acquisitions," *Management Review*, November 1972, pp. 41–46.

When one company acquires another, new human relationships are formed among those in the buying and selling organizations. This human element can dramatically affect the deal's success and the participants' happiness. Development of a good communication program is critical in minimizing management problems after the acquisition.

Potential sellers who wish to remain after the acquisition should consider the following points:

1. Deal directly with the top management of the acquirer.
2. Get to know the acquirer's top management on both a social and a business basis.
3. Contact the top management of other divisions to identify their management style.
4. Do not accept offers from firms whose management style seems incompatible with yours.
5. Review all factors that could become points of contention.

HOUSTON, BRYAN, "Let's Put More Esprit in de Corporation," *Harvard Business Review*, November-December 1972, pp. 55–61.

Corporate health and strength is evidenced by the presence of esprit de corps, an innovative product or service, a sense of the "now" (keeping pace with accelerating change), and an understanding of cash flow—"the navigational system of business."

HOWELL, ROBERT A., "Plan to Integrate Your Acquisitions," *Harvard Business Review*, November-December 1970, pp. 146–56.

A conceptual scheme is outlined which allows executives to conceptualize an acquisition in three stages: (1) investigation and selection, (2) negotiation, and (3) integration. The scheme is based on strategic considerations which classify acquisitions as being either financial, marketing, or manufacturing depending on the goals defined and tactics used. The key tasks and central issues associated with each stage of an acquisition are outlined.

In the investigation and selection stage the issues are determining the breadth of the search to be conducted, the source of leads to be used, the focus and depth of the analysis to be done, and the method to assign responsibility for the decision.

In the negotiation phase, three approaches to achieving agreement can be utilized:

1. Provide an incentive to the acquired management not only to stay with the company but to achieve high subsequent performance.
2. Offer an employment contract as a middle-ground alternative to assure that the new acquired management will stay with the parent company.
3. Buy the acquisition outright either for cash or an exchange of stock with no continuing formal commitment to the acquisition's management.

In the integration stage of a merger successful completion will depend on how management organizes acquisitions relative to the parent company, utilizes opportunities for functional integration, and establishes systems for planning and control. Different types of acquisitions (financial, marketing, or manufacturing) call for different forms of corporate organization which are described in some detail. While the types differ, their benefits can be cumulative and synergistic in nature—for example, marketing acquisitions can produce both financial and manufacturing benefits.

IMBERMAN, ARLYNE, "The Human Side of Mergers," *Management Review*, June 1985, pp. 35–37.

One of the most essential factors in a merger's success is employee morale. It is critical to consider employees' anxieties and desire for information. Of the employees that do not jump ship, those remaining worry about (1) job loss, (2) relocation, (3) new and unsympathetic management, (4) arbitrary decisions, and (5) loss of status and power. Long-term employees often suffer from depression, uncertainty, and disillusionment. The need for communicating before and after the merger with employees is crucial.

A thoughtfully conceived employee and public relations plan is essential for a long and happy corporate marriage. The effort should include the following:

1. National and local press, both companies' employees, affected local communities, suppliers, customers, and shareholders.
2. Informing key managers on both sides of the company's new strategy and corporate philosophy.
3. Keeping employees informed regarding
   a. company policies, goals, objectives, and direction
   b. company history
   c. corporate expertise and areas of dominance
   d. new chain of command
   e. matters of personal concern.
4. Printed materials to provide an ongoing flow of information.
5. Interpersonal exchanges with management.
6. Formation of teams to inform and reassure, and to bridge the gap between management and employees.
7. Encouraging employees to say what they think and feel.

Companies whose managers have had the foresight to cushion the blows—and elucidate the potential benefits—have been well rewarded for their efforts.

KITCHING, JOHN, "Why Do Mergers Miscarry?," *Harvard Business Review*, November-December 1967, pp. 84–101.

Based on interviews of twenty-two high-level executives whose companies have been involved in a total of 181 acquisitions or mergers, a series of findings are presented that are referred to as objective and subjective. In the former category incidents of failure are reported by type, with concentric acquisitions accounting for the highest frequency of failure (47%), followed by conglomerate acquisitions (42%), horizontal (11%), and vertical (0%). Mismatches in size are frequently associated with failures: in 84% of the failures, the acquired company's sales volume is less than 2% of the parent company's at the time of acquisition. Cited most frequently as accompanying features of such failures are an underestimation by the parent company of the financial and managerial needs of the newly acquired organization. The authors also studied the functions that produced the largest dollar payoff from synergy after acquisition. Finance is the function in which synergy produces the greatest payoff, followed by marketing. Production and technology are the least productive, at least in the short run (two to seven years).

The subjective results that describe the causes of success and failure in acquisitions can be summarized in six points:

1. Managers of change—it is the quality of management that determines the success or failure of a venture.
2. Skills for the task—"the sum of management skills must be greater than the joint management task." Frequently, businesses underestimate the demands a merger will make on management time. Three ways of safeguarding against such an error are
   a. Have a policy based on recognition of the problem
   b. Have a good method of appraising subsidiary company management before the purchase is made
   c. Make an independent audit of subsidiary management's competence before the merger takes place.
3. Management relationships—the most successful acquisitions seem to have three characteristics in the relations between the parent and acquired companies:
   a. The parent company appoints a top executive to "ride herd" immediately after the acquisition
   b. Reporting relationships are made clear, and any changes are made on a carefully planned basis
   c. The system of controls is immediately put into operation;

from the outset, the major emphasis is on information reporting rather than on budgets.

4. Reactors versus planners—a major finding of this study is that there is a "distinct difference in the success rate of companies with a strategy for growth and diversification, of which an acquisition program may be only a part, and that of companies which merely react to opportunities to buy."

5. Effective criteria—having acquisition criteria that, both consistently and strenuously applied, is a major factor in successful acquisitions.

6. Analysis of future needs—successful companies make a careful analysis of their acquired company's requirements for parent company funds.

Finally, a set of specific recommendations that follow from these results are offered.

LEIGHTON, CHARLES M., AND ROBERT G. TOD, "After the Acquisition: Continuing Challenge," *Harvard Business Review*, March-April, 1969, pp. 126–138.

While most buyers deal with the legal and financial aspects of an acquisition, they often fail to thoroughly consider how to operate and manage the new company afterwards. The authors suggest nine guidelines for management planning. The first three are relevant during the pre-acquisition phase.

1. Get group management in at the outset.

2. X-ray the candidate (that is, know all the relevant details before the deal is made).

3. Minimize anxieties (which calls for close collaboration among all management personnel).

4. Fight the prima donna urge (managers from the acquiring company should try to blend in).

5. Sell yourself as the helmsman (by demonstrating its usefulness to the president of the acquired company, the new management team can establish joint leadership and mutual

respect and influence, bringing both the acquired and acquiring companies into mutually advantageous collaboration.

6. Motivate to the hilt (profit incentives for both the president and group management team are encouraged).
7. Humanize management controls (sell improved financial monitoring systems in a gentle discreet fashion).
8. Cross-fertilize aggressively (dovetail resources and abilities thoroughly and continually.
9. Make the group manager a "man for all seasons"—that is, a consultant, ambassador, coordinator, innovator, and boss.

LEVINSON, HARRY, "A Psychologist Diagnoses Merger Failures," *Harvard Business Review*, March–April 1970, pp. 20–28.

While the cause of most merger failures is attributed to rational technical problems, unrecognized psychological issues are frequently more often the real culprit. Psychological fear and psychological obsolescence (for example, rigidity and lack of adaptiveness) often underlie and influence the decision-making process that leads to unsuccessful mergers. Minimizing the likelihood of such outcomes involves first recognizing that there are two basic problems: (1) the executive's anxieties, and (2) the task of meshing two organizations that are productively coordinated. Four ways of counteracting the negative psychological factors associated with mergers include

1. Introspective assessment on the part of management
2. Analyzing the projected assumptions of the parent organization about the anticipated partner
3. Asking what the other company is all about psychologically
4. Assessing the differences between the two organizations and the importance of those differences

These four factors should be openly discussed in the appropriate setting so the acquiring company is fully informed about its own motivations and goals as well as those of the potential new partner.

MAGNET, MYRON, "Help! My Company Has Just Been Taken Over," *Fortune*, July 9, 1984, pp. 44–51.

This article asserts that after the financial and legal processes have been completed in a merger or acquisition, "the real work of putting two companies together begins." Case material is presented which supports the view that managing the human aspects of the transaction has a great deal to do with how well it ultimately works out. Three basic principles provide guidelines for successfully engineering such transitions

1. Let acquired employees know where they stand right away
2. Adopt special procedures to manage integration (for example, a transition task force representing both organizations)
3. Involve the acquired company's managers so they will work for the merger's success

————, "Acquiring Without Smothering," *Fortune*, November 12, 1984, pp. 22–30.

Smart managers know that the value of an acquired company resides not just in its assets, but also in the unique way it operates. Prioritizing and knowing what is wanted from the deal, holding inference to a minimum, and talking a lot are characteristics of successful dealmakers. The leaders of the companies that have acquired without smothering are strong on patience, tact, and the ability to live with the messiness that accompanies diversity.

MARKS, MITCHELL L., "Merging Human Resources: A Review of Current Research," *Mergers & Acquisitions*, Summer 1982, pp. 38–44.

A review of the literature addressing the impact of mergers on individuals and institutions is provided. Topics presented include

1. The management of the merger process
2. Organizational issues in mergers
3. Personal issues in mergers. This comprehensive synthesis highlights the most important studies while describing the general limitations of the research methods employed thus far.

————, and PHILIP MIRVIS, "Merger Syndrome: Stress and Uncertainty," *Mergers & Acquisitions*, Part I, 20, no. 2, pp. 50–55.

The variety of stress symptoms that affect organizations and individuals during a merger is described in detail. A number of suggested strategies and interventions are explained. The authors note that executives have a double responsibility during such transitions: that of managing their relationship with a new partner and managing their own organization and the stress it is experiencing.

MCLEAN, ROBERT, "How to Make Acquisitions Work," *Chief Executive*, April 1985, Morgan-Grampian Ltd.

Three major points are emphasized in this paper:

1. The price paid for an acquisition should be based on the capacity of the acquirer to add value to the acquisition.
2. The strategy for adding value and transferring skills should be realistic and sound.
3. "Post-acquisition management should balance the changes necessary to add value with careful integration of the two cultures."

The results of Dr. Roland Burgman's research on more than 600 acquisitions in the U.S. are cited. Those findings include the following:

The higher the premium paid, the less successful the acquisition tends to be.

The greater the acquiree's functional understanding of the acquirer, the better the prospects for success.

Retention of the acquired company's top management is also associated with success.

Sheer size tends to increase an acquisition's success prospects—perhaps, it is suggested, because of the amount of forethought and analysis involved.

MILES, MARY, "Rebuilding After a Restructuring. Which Will It Be for You After a Corporate Merger, Acquisition or Restructuring, Pain or Gain?," *Computer Decisions*, January 28, 1986, 18, no. 3, pp. 52–54.

A corporate restructuring can be a golden career opportunity or a disaster. There are many factors which determine your fate:

You must be perceived as a vital part of the team to fare best.

You need to rebuild operations to conform to new priorities with reduced staff.

Knowledge is power. The more you know about both organizations, the better able you'll be to provide needed information (that is, the best way to integrate systems).

Important to maintain or forge clear lines of communication with top-level decision makers. If no shared vision exists, you may have to actively forge it.

Take care of yourself—stress can wreak havoc physically and emotionally.

Be ready to jump at career options—keep your resume polished.

Keep your staff's spirits high. Good lines of communication can ease the pain and anxiety.

Under the best circumstances, restructuring is a time of upheaval and confusion. But it can also be a time to broaden skills and move up the corporate ladder. This can be achieved by cultivating business skills, expanding technical aptitude, preparing for realignment (rather than waiting for it to come barreling through your department), and by offering your staff guidance and giving top management your support.

MIRVIS, PHILIP, AND MITCHELL MARKS, "Merger Syndrome: Management by Crisis," *Mergers & Acquisitions*, Part II, 20, no. 3, pp. 70–76.

The post-merger management style of many acquired companies often consists of a crisis management approach that emphasizes the centralization of control and formalization of communications. While this may create a comforting illusion of control for stressed management teams, it also creates distance, ambiguity, and conflict with employees who can come to feel poorly informed and disregarded. Management should try to overcome the tendency to respond to the merger crisis with a "defensive retreat" that isolates them from employees. Instead, a variety of proactive measures can be instituted, including team building, openly communicating (including conducting employee surveys and actively dealing with grievances), and establishing internal task forces and social support systems (for example, personal and career counseling). Such means allow a firm to minimize the inevitable presence of "merger syndrome" and facilitate the smooth integration of the organization.

PRITCHETT, PRICE, *After the Merger: Managing the Shockwaves.* New York: Dow Jones-Irwin, 1985.

This book describes the psychological and organizational effects evident after a merger. Included in this review are the major causes of managerial turnover and what to do about them. A three-way evaluation of an acquired company's management staff is strongly advocated so the acquiring company can make effective decisions in reorganizing the management of its acquisition. Suggestions are provided that describe how to realize a merger's motivational potential. Finally, the author offers guidelines for successful merger-acquisition for the leaders of both the acquiring and acquired companies.

PROKESCH, STEVEN E., " 'People Trauma' in Mergers," *New York Times,* November 19, 1985, pp. 27, 29.

This article documents, through an extensive series of interviews, the human costs of mergers that lead to morale problems, loss of productivity, and turnover. While these effects are known to be present in upper management it is becoming increasingly clear that they also occur in the ranks of middle management.

REIBSTEIN, LARRY, "After a Takeover: More Managers Run, or Are Pushed, Out the Door," *Wall Street Journal*, Nov. 15, 1985.

This article addresses the question of why executives are bailing out—or getting pushed out—faster and more frequently than ever. In one Lamalie Associates' survey almost half the executives of acquired companies in 1984 sought new employment within one year; in contrast, in 1981 only 20% of a comparable group of senior executives tried to leave their companies. This change is attributed to the increasing number of hostile takeovers "which often create a sour climate and a clash in management styles; the increasingly steep stock price premiums in buyouts that give managers holding the stock greater freedom and mobility; a lessening of corporate loyalty; and the proliferation of so-called golden parachutes." The increase in movement of top level executives has taken the stigma out of moving or being replaced so corporate nomads are becoming more frequent.

SCHOONMAKER, ALAN, "Why Mergers Don't Jell: The Critical Human Element," *Personnel*, September-October 1969, pp. 39–48.

A strategy for analyzing the human elements that can contribute to a merger failure is discussed. Included in the analysis are self-analysis (What are your motives for undertaking an acquisition? What will the effects be on your organization?), preliminary investigation (which includes an assessment of management quality, the probability of retaining key executives, anticipating the complexities of the integration, and balancing the compensation systems), dealing with the negotiation phase (getting enough information to make decisions, making the best possible deal, and establishing a basis for a good post-merger integration), announcing the merger (for both the stockholders and the employees), and, finally, post-merger integration (encouraging participation, avoiding arbitrary decisions and respecting existing social norms).

SEARBY, FREDERICK W., "Control Post-merger Change," *Harvard Business Review*. September-October 1969, pp. 139–45.

Post-merger management is the greatest single determinant of success in many corporate acquisition programs. The author reviews and summarizes the tasks involved in an acquisition. To avoid the danger of half-success in an acquisition, three areas need to receive particular attention: organization (which is conducted by a merger manager who reports to the parent company's CEO), leadership (which is provided by a merger committee and the merger manager who work together to communicate, clarify, and develop a written strategy with long-term goals for both companies), and timing (which involves assessing when to promote or delay important organizational changes). A four-step planning process is outlined that includes the following:

1. Specific and realizable objectives should be developed before the merger is consummated.
2. The key variables should be brought under control immediately following the merger.
3. Programs should be thoroughly designed to achieve the merger's objectives.
4. Controls to measure the results of actual performance against plan should be installed.

More general advice is offered stating it is essential that decisions be based on careful factual analysis to insure that all possible alternatives are considered so actions taken are based on fact rather than fallacious assumption.

SINETAR, MARSHA, "Mergers, Morale and Productivity," *Personnel Journal*, November 1981, pp. 863–67.

In imposing a major life change on employees, mergers can seriously undermine their self-esteem and morale. The psychological reactions can include shock, disbelief, grief, anger, anxiety, and depression, all of which can lower performance levels. "Management needs to recognize the merger as a process—not just an event" and involve itself in pre-planning and preventive efforts. The author suggests that there are three major phases in a merger that require different forms of communication to help employees. In phase one—the pre-merger phase, prior to and immediately following the formal announcement—employees need direct communication that reassures (in the sense of answering, as much as possible, the question, What's next for me?) and brings order to their work (by continuing with a business-as-usual policy). During phase two—the post-merger process, after the formal announcement and before the formation of a new corporate entity—communications are required that help employees organize their work and their roles. Timelines for the merger and for systems to transfer services, people, and technical knowledge should be communicated. In addition, a newsletter from an outside or "neutral" source that addresses the psychological issues and needs of people in transition is suggested as are work improvement teams that can troubleshoot and problem-solve during this phase. In phase three—the transition phase—when the new company starts up, more directive communication is required that serves to integrate personnel, information systems, and the new management team.

REFERENCES

Chapter 1

1

CLEMENS P. WORK, "Merger Mania," reprinted in *Eastern Flight Review Magazine*, February 1986, pp. 27–35.

2

LAURIE MEISLER, "Mergers & Acquisitions: The Fireworks Aren't Over Yet," *Forbes*, June 2, 1986, (advertising supplement).

DAVID KIRKPATRICK, "Deals of the Year," *Fortune*, January 20, 1986, pp. 26–30.

H. JOHN STEINBREDER, "Deals of the Year," *Fortune*, January 21, 1985, pp. 126–30.

ELLYN E. SPRAGINS, "The Corporation Shopping Spree Roars On and On," *Business Week*, July 21, 1986, pp. 110–14.

3

GEORGE ANDERS and PHILLIP L. ZWEIG, "Friendly Takeover Offers Prevail Amid Insider Scandal: Investment Bankers Reassess Tactics as Commercial Banks Enter Field," *Wall Street Journal*, February 25, 1987, p. 6.

GARY WEISS with JAMES ELLIS and JONATHAN B. LEVINE, "The Top 200 Deals: Merger Mania's New Accent," *Business Week*, April 17, 1987, pp. 273–92.

STUART WEISS, "Deal Mania: Tax Reform Is No Tranquilizer After All," *Business Week*, March 30, 1987, pp. 66–67.

4

PAUL B. BROWN and JOHN A. BYRNE, "Let's Do a Deal," *Business Week*, April 18, 1986, pp. 265–86.

5

JOSEPH MCCANN and WILLIAM CORNELIUS, "How Acquisitions Fit The Growth Strategies of Rapidly Growing Firms," *Mergers & Acquisitions,* July-August 1987.

6

JOHN W. HUNT, STAN LEES, JOHN J. GRUMBAR, and PHILIP D. VIVIAN, *Acquisitions—The Human Factor* (London: Egon Zehnder International, 1987).

7

JANICE CASTRO, "The Canadians Come Calling," *Time,* November 17, 1986, pp. 68–9.

FRANK J. COMES, JONATHAN KAPSTEIN, RICHARD A. MELCHER, and ELIZABETH WEINER, "Europe Goes on a Shopping Spree in the States," *Business Week,* October 27, 1986, pp. 54–55.

LESLIE HELM and JONATHAN B. LEVINE, "Japan's Giants Go Shopping for U.S. Startups," *Business Week,* November 3, 1986, pp. 46–49.

WILLIAM J. HOLSTEIN with LARRY ARMSTRONG, ROBERT NEFF, and RICHARD BRANDT, "Japan's Bigger and Bolder Forays Into the U.S.," *Business Week,* November 17, 1986, pp. 80–81.

WILLIAM J. HOLSTEIN, "Hoechst's Puzzling Return to Commodity Chemicals," *Business Week,* November 17, 1986, p. 65.

AMY BORRUS and RICHARD A. MELCHER, "British High Tech Wants to Catch Merger Fever," *Business Week,* December 16, 1985, pp. 40–41.

GREGORY L. MILES and MATT ROTHMAN, "Holmes À Court Thinks Even USX Is Fair Game," *Business Week,* September 1, 1986, p. 26.

LOUIS KRAAR, "Australia's Acquisitive Recluse," *Fortune,* September 2, 1985, pp. 78–82.

CHERYL DEBES with AMY BORRUS, "An Aussie Raider's Heady Bid to Buy a British Brewer," *Business Week,* September 23, 1985, pp. 53–54.

SHAWN TULLY, "Electrolux Wants a Clean Sweep," *Fortune,* August 18, 1986, 60–62.

R. DUANE HALL, *Overseas Acquisitions & Mergers* (New York: Praeger, 1986).

8

STEVEN P. GALANTE, "Selling the Firm to Foreigners Adds to Adjustment Problems," *Wall Street Journal,* January 6, 1986, p. 23.

9
WORK, "Merger Mania."

10
CLEMENS P. WORKS, "Banished Species," *Manhattan Inc.*, February 1987, p. 26.

11
JOHN A. BYRNE and JONATHAN B. LEVINE, "Corporate Odd Couples: Joint Ventures Are All the Rage—but the Matches Often Don't Work Out," *Business Week*, July 21, 1986, pp. 100–105.

KATHRYN R. HARRIGAN, *Strategic Flexibility* (Lexington, Mass.: Lexington Books, 1985).

KATHRYN R. HARRIGAN, *Strategies for Joint Ventures* (Lexington, Mass.: Lexington Books, 1985).

JAMES R. NORMAN, "Matt Simmons: Doctor to the Oil Fields' Walking Wounded," *Business Week*, November 4, 1985, pp. 82–83.

12
Statistic reported to us from Jim Balloun, McKinsey & Co., Atlanta.

13
MICHAEL E. PORTER, "From Competitive Advantage to Corporate Strategy," *Harvard Business Review*, May-June 1987, pp. 43–59.

Chapter 2

1
LEWIS BEMAN, "What We Learned From the Great Merger Frenzy," *Fortune*, April 1973, pp. 70–73.

2
KENNETH DAVIDSON, *MegaMergers* (Cambridge, Mass: Ballinger, 1985).

3
ALFRED D. CHANDLER, *The Visible Hand: The Managerial Revolution in American Business* (Cambridge, Mass.: Belknap Press, 1977).

4

STAN CROCK, ELIZABETH EHRLICH, and NORMAN JONES, "How the Tax Code Is Feeding Merger Mania," *Business Week*, May 27, 1985, pp. 62–64.

JOHN CRUDELE, "Merger Lag Is Linked to Doubts on Tax Law," *New York Times*, February 3, 1986, sec. 4, p. 1.

DANIEL HERTZBERG, MONICA LANGLEY, and JAMES B. STEWART, "Changing the Rules: Attacking Junk Bonds, Fed Becomes a Player in the Takeover Game," *Wall Street Journal*, December 9, 1985, p. 1.

BRUCE INGERSOLL, "SEC Endorses Major Changes in Merger Fights," *Wall Street Journal*, March 14, 1984, p. 4.

"Feeding Merger Mania," *Business Week*, May 27, 1985, pp. 62–64.

DAVID A. VISE, "From Boardroom to Courtroom," *Washington Post National Weekly Edition*, February 10, 1986, p. 9.

"Closed Loopholes That Open Merger Problems," *Business Week*, October 18, 1982, pp. 173–76.

"Game Point Should Go to Volcker," *Business Week*, January 20, 1986, p. 100.

5

WILLIAM GLASGALL, JAMES R. NORMAN, and SCOTT TICER, "ARCO Enters Oil's New Era," *Business Week*, May 13, 1985, pp. 24–25.

6

ANTHONY BIANCO and CHRIS FARRELL, "Power on Wall Street: Drexel Burnham Is Reshaping Investment Banking—and U.S. Industry," *Business Week*, July 7, 1986, pp. 56–63.

RON ROSENBAUM, "The Great Gatsby of Wall Street: Why Fred Joseph of Drexel Drives Old Corporate America Crazy," *Manhattan, Inc.*, August 1986, pp. 61–70.

HOWARD RUDNITSKY and ALLAN SLOAN, "Taking in Each Other's Laundry," *Forbes*, November 19, 1984, pp. 207–22.

7

GERALDINE BROOKS, "Some Concerns Find That the Push to Diversify Was a Costly Mistake," *Wall Street Journal*, October 2, 1984, p. 33.

JUDITH H. DOBRYZYNSKI, "Gulf & Western Unloads a Grab Bag," *Business Week*, June 24, 1985, p. 44.

MARILYN A. HARRIS with RESA W. KING, TODD MASON, and JOHN P. TARPEY, "The Unraveling of Harry Gray's Grand Design at United Technologies: Dumping Mostek and Picking a New CEO May Mark the Start of a More Cautious Era," *Business Week*, November 4, 1985, pp. 76–78.

SCOTT TICER, ". . . and Wickes Believes It's Full of Gold," *Business Week*, June 24, 1985, p. 45.

STEWART TOY, "Splitting Up: The Other Side of Merger Mania," *Business Week*, June 1, 1985, pp. 50–55.

8

MICHAEL E. PORTER, "From Competitive Advantage to Corporate Strategy," *Harvard Business Review*, May-June 1987, pp. 43–59.

H. IGOR ANSOFF, *Corporate Strategy* (New York: McGraw Hill, 1965).

H. IGOR ANSOFF, T. A. ANDERSON, F. NORTON, and J. F. WESTON, "Planning for Diversification Through Merger," *California Management Review*, 1, no. 4 (1959), pp. 24–35.

E. RALPH BIGGADIKE, *Corporate Diversification: Entry, Strategy, and Performance* (Cambridge, Mass.: Harvard University Press, 1979), based on 1976 dissertation.

ALFRED D. CHANDLER, *Strategy and Structure* (Cambridge, Mass.: The MIT Press, 1962).

KENNETH N. M. DUNDAS and PETER R. RICHARDSON, "Implementing the Unrelated Product Strategy," *Strategic Management Journal*, 3 (1982), pp. 287–301.

DAVID REMNICK, "Grace Under Pressure: There's Trouble Brewing at His Company, and Peter Grace Is Feeling the Heat," *Manhattan, Inc.*, January 1987, pp. 55–63.

9

REMNICK, "Grace Under Pressure."

10

THOMAS J. PETERS and ROBERT H. WATERMAN *In Search of Excellence* (New York: Harper & Row, 1983).

11

"America's Restructured Economy," *Business Week*, June 1, 1981, pp. 55–100.

12

ANTHONY BIANCO, "Deal Mania: The Tempo Is Frantic, and the Future Prosperity of the U.S. Is at Stake," *Business Week*, November 24, 1986, pp. 74–83.

JUDITH H. DOBRZYNSKI with JOAN BERGER, "For Better or for Worse?," *Business Week*, January 12, 1987, pp. 38–40.

JUDITH DOBRZYNSKI, "More Than Ever, It's Management for the Short Term," *Business Week*, November 24, 1986, pp. 92–93.

BRUCE NUSSBAUM and JUDITH DOBRZYNSKI, "The Battle for Corporate Control," *Business Week*, May 18, 1987, pp. 102–9.

BRUCE NUSSBAUM, "The End of Corporate Loyalty?," *Business Week*, August 4, 1986, pp. 42–49.

13

See, for example, the following:

DAVID HALBERSTAM, *The Reckoning* (New York: Morrow, 1987).

WILLIAM J. HAMPTON and JAMES R. NORMAN, "General Motors: What Went Wrong," *Business Week*, March 16, 1987, pp. 102–10.

WILLIAM J. HAMPTON, "GM Wants Hughes to Help It Into the 21st Century," *Business Week*, June 17, 1985, p. 35.

DORON P. LEVIN and DALE D. BUSS, "GM Plans Offer to Pay $700 Million to Buy Out Its Critic H. Ross Perot," *Wall Street Journal*, December 1, 1986, p. 1.

TODD MASON, RUSSELL MITCHELL, and WILLIAM J. HAMPTON, "Ross Perot's Crusade," *Business Week*, October 6, 1986, pp. 60–65.

14

JENNIFER LINDSEY, "Acquisition Crazy," *Venture*, March 1985, pp. 63–65.

15

JOHN BUSSEY, "Recharged Firm?: Gould Reshapes Itself Into High-Tech Outfit Amid Much Turmoil," *Wall Street Journal*, October 3, 1984, p. 1.

16

"U.S. Steel's New Name Is USX Corp.," *Atlanta Constitution*, July 9, 1986, p. 2.

MARK IVEY, GREGORY L. MILES, STEVEN PROKESCH, and WILLIAM C. SYMONDS, "The Toughest Job in Business: How They're Remaking U.S. Steel," *Business Week*, February 25, 1985, pp. 50–56.

THOMAS F. O'BOYLE, "U.S. Steel, in Bid to Expand Energy Business, Agrees to Acquire Texas Oil for Stock Valued at $3.56 Billion," *Wall Street Journal*, October 31, 1985, p. 3.

LINDA SANDLER, "U.S. Steel Stock Is Sold by Many Institutions in Wake of Its Plan to Buy Texas Oil and Gas," *Wall Street Journal*, December 6, 1985, p. 63.

WILLIAM GLASGALL, TODD MASON, GREGORY L. MILES, and WILLIAM C. SYMONDS, "U.S. Steel Moves Closer to Becoming U.S. Oil," *Business Week*, November 11, 1985, p. 34.

KENNETH M. DAVIDSON, "Megamergers: A Scorecard of Winners and Losers," *Wall Street Journal*, January 20, 1986, p. 16.

17

ANTHONY BIANCO, "Jerry Tsai: The Comeback Kid," *Business Week*, August 18, 1986, pp. 72–80.

18

BILL ABRAMS and JOHNNIE L. ROBERTS, "General Electric to Acquire RCA for $6.28 Billion; Combined Firm's Revenue Would Top $40 Billion," *Wall Street Journal*, December 12, 1985, p. 3.

HOWARD BANKS, ed., "What's Ahead for Business," *Forbes*, August 25, 1986, p. 25.

MARILYN A. HARRIS, ZACHARY SCHILLER, RUSSELL MITCHELL, and CHRISTOPHER POWER, "Can Jack Welch Reinvent GE?: He's Getting the Industrial Giant Ready for the 21st Century," *Business Week*, June 30, 1986, pp. 62–67.

PETER PETRE, "What Welch Has Wrought at GE," *Fortune*, July 7, 1986, pp. 43–47.

DOUGLAS R. SEASE, "GE Is Seen Using RCA to Supply Cash Needed to Defend Its Best Export Lines," *Wall Street Journal*, December 26, 1985, p. 2.

19

TERI AGINS and WILLIAM M. CARLEY, "People Express Merger Might Cause Problems: But Purchase of Frontier Will Produce Stronger Airline," *Wall Street Journal*, October 14, 1985, p. 6.

AARON BERNSTEIN and CHUCK HAWKINS, "Frank Lorenzo, High Flier: Buying Eastern Will Give Him Control of the Nation's Largest Airline," *Business Week*, March 10, 1986, pp. 104–12.

REGGI ANN DUBIN, "At TWA, the AGE of Icahn Is About to Begin," *Business Week*, September 2, 1985, pp. 31–32.

CHUCK HAWKINS and PATRICK HOUSTON, "Republic Will Help Northwest Put the Heat on United," *Business Week*, February 10, 1986, p. 27.

MARK IVEY, "People Express Wins the Duel for Frontier Air," *Business Week*, October 21, 1985, p. 42.

KENNETH LABICH, "Why Bigger Is Better in the Airline Wars," *Fortune*, March 31, 1986, pp. 52–55.

JAMES R. NORMAN, "The Future Belongs to the Giants: Texas Air's Deal With TWA Is the Latest Step Toward a Few Big Carriers," *Business Week*, July 1, 1985, pp. 20–21.

20

JOHN CRADDOCK, "Banks Have Found Managing Mergers a Tough Trick," *Florida Trend*, May 1985, pp. 51–54.

SCOTT SCREDON, "Bank Mergers Start to Sizzle in the South," *Business Week*, July 1, 1985, pp. 25–26.

JOHN TAYLOR and MATT WALSH, "What Deregulation Has Wrought," *Florida Trend*, October 1986, pp. 67–84.

"Renaming the Cast at SunTrust Bank," *Florida Trend*, October 1985, p. 29.

PHILLIP L. ZWEIG, "Rise in Regional Mergers Frustrates Big Bank," *Wall Street Journal*, January 20, 1986, p. 6.

21

JAMES E. ELLIS, JONATHAN B. LEVINE, MARK MAREMONT, RANDY WELCH, and JOHN WILKE, "The Baby Bells Take Giant Steps," *Business Week*, December 2, 1985, pp. 94–104.

"Bell Units Weigh Diversity," *Mergers & Acquisitions*, Winter 1985, pp. 7–8.

22

DAVID STARKWEATHER, *Mergers in the Making* (Ann Arbor: American Health Administration Press, 1983).

23

REBECCA AIKMAN and SCOTT SCREDON, "The Fever Hits Health Care," *Business Week*, April 15, 1985, pp. 40–42.

MICHAEL L. MILLENSON, "A Merger for What Ails You," *Orlando Sentinel*, April 7, 1985, sec. 3, p. 1.

JANE A. SASSEEN, "Quality Care's Bid to Stand Out in the Crowd," *Business Week*, July 22, 1985, p. 87.

24

ANTHONY BIANCO, "Can the Corporate Raiders Be Stopped in His Tracks?," *Business Week*, December 23, 1985, p. 65.

ANTHONY BIANCO, "The Raiders: 'They Are Really Breaking the Vise of the Managing Class'," *Business Week*, March 4, 1985, pp. 80–91.

KENNETH DREYFACK, "Baytree Investors: The Tangled Roots of a Take-over Company," *Business Week*, May 12, 1986, pp. 84–85.

ALOYSIUS EHRBAR, "Have Takeovers Gone Too Far?" *Fortune*, May 27, 1985, pp. 20–24.

ELIZABETH EHRLICH, "Twilight for the Lone Ranger," *Business Week*, January 27, 1986, pp. 38–39.

ELIZABETH EHRLICH, "Getting Rough with the Raiders," *Business Week*, May 27, 1985, pp. 34–35.

HOWARD GLECKMAN and RONALD GROVER, "Icahn Ponders Dismem-bering His New Airline," *Business Week*, March 17, 1986, p. 56.

MARILYN A. HARRIS, GEOFF LEWIS, and TODD MASON, "Raider Asher Edelman Gets Trapped in the Executive Suite," *Business Week*, April 1, 1985, pp. 64–65.

LAWRENCE MINARD, "Millions for Defense, Not One Cent for Tribute," *Forbes*, April 8, 1985, pp. 40–42.

JAMES R. NORMAN, "What the Raiders Did to Phillips Petroleum," *Business Week*, March 17, 1986, pp. 102–3.

TOM O'HANLON, "What Does This Man Want?," *Forbes*, January 30, 1984, pp. 78–86.

IRWIN ROSS, "Irwin Jacobs Lands a Big One—Finally," *Fortune*, July 8, 1985, pp. 130–36.

HAROLD SENEKER and ALLAN SLOAN, "How Posner Profited Even Though His Companies Didn't," *Forbes*, April 8, 1985, pp. 42–45.

ALLAN SLOAN, "Why Is No One Safe?," *Forbes*, March 11, 1985, pp. 134–39.

JAMES B. STEWART and MICHAEL WALDHOLZ, "Internal Affair: How Rich-ardson-Vicks Fell Prey to Takeover Despite Family's Grip," *Wall Street Journal*, October 30, 1985, p. 1.

FORD S. WORTHY, "What's Next for the Raiders," *Fortune*, November 11, 1985, pp. 20–24.

25

BILL SAPORITO, "Black & Decker's Gamble on 'Globalization'," *Fortune*, May 14, 1984, pp. 40–48.

CHRISTOPHER S. EKLUND, "How Black and Decker Got Back in the Black," *Business Week*, July 13, 1987, pp. 86–90.

Chapter 3

1

BENJAMIN J. STEIN, "Where Are the Stockholder's Yachts?: But John Kluge Pockets Billions From Metromedia's LBO," *Barron's*, August 18, 1986, pp. 6–7.

2

"Roger Smith Takes on GM's Critics," *Fortune*, August 18, 1986, pp. 26–27.

DAMON DARLIN and MELINDA GRENIER GUILES, "Whose Takeover?: Some GM People Feel Auto Firm, Not EDS, Was the One Acquired," *Wall Street Journal*, December 19, 1984, p. 1.

3

LESLIE WAYNE, "A Costly Merger for Occidental," *New York Times*, January 23, 1983, p. F1.

4

DAN COOK with EDITH TERRY and AMY DUNKIN, "Is Campeau in Over His Head at Allied Stores?," *Business Week*, February 9, 1987, pp. 52–53.

5

CHUCK HAWKINS, "People Is Plunging, but Burr Is Staying Cool," *Business Week*, July 7, 1986, pp. 31–32.

GEORGE RUSSELL and FREDRICK UNGEHEUR, "Air Pocket in the Revolution," *Time*, July 7, 1986, pp. 42–44.

"Frontier Still Hoping to Work Out Sale," *Atlanta Constitution*, August 27, 1986, sec. 2, p. 2.

6

KATHLEEN DEVENY and ELIZABETH EHRLICH, "Leveraged Buyouts: There's Trouble in Paradise," *Business Week*, July 22, 1985, pp. 112–13.

DOUGLAS R. SEASE, "ESOPs Weren't Meant to Be Bailouts," *Wall Street Journal*, December 2, 1985.

7
STRATFORD P. SHERMAN, "Ted Turner: Back From the Brink," *Fortune,* July 7, 1986, pp. 25–31.

8
CAROL J. LOOMIS, "The Comeuppance of Carl Icahn," *Fortune,* February 17, 1986, pp. 18–25.

9
"Roundtable: Putting the Deal Together," *Mergers & Acquisitions,* Fall 1982, pp. 22–28.

10
ELLEN FARLEY, "Columbia Pictures: Are Things Really Better With Coke?," *Business Week,* April 14, 1986, pp. 56–58.
KEITH HERNDON, "Head of Coca-Cola's Film Production Arm Resigns," *Atlanta Constitution,* April 10, 1986, sec. 4, p. 2.

11
JAMES E. ELLIS, "Dart & Kraft: Why It'll Be Dart and Kraft," *Business Week,* July 7, 1986, p. 33.

12
FORD S. WORTHY, "A Health Care Merger That Pains Hospitals," *Fortune,* June 24, 1985, pp. 106–10.

13
JOHN MARCOM, JR. and EILEEN WHITE, "IBM-MCI Pact Portends Big Changes," *Wall Street Journal,* June 27, 1985, p. 2.

14
JOHN KITCHING, "Why Do Mergers Miscarry?," *Harvard Business Review,* November-December, 1967, pp. 84–101.

15
LYNN ASINOF, "Small Firms Turn to Big Business for Capital, Markets, Technical Aid," *Wall Street Journal,* November 5, 1985, sec. 2, p. 1.
LAURIE P. COHEN, "Failed Marriages: Raytheon Is Among Companies Regretting High-Tech Mergers," *Wall Street Journal,* September 10, 1984, p. 1.

16
SANDRA D. ATCHISON, "Kraft Is Celestial Seasonings' Cup of Tea," *Business Week*, July 28, 1986, p. 73.

17
SANDRA D. ATCHISON, "Why Nabisco and Reynolds Were Made for Each Other," *Business Week*, June 17, 1985, p. 34.

18
ROBERT BATT, "When Oil Firms Merge, MIS Groups Follow Suit—but Not Without Problems," *Computerworld*, July 19, 1982, p. 13.

19
JOHN W. HUNT, STAN LEES, JOHN J. GRUMBAR, and PHILIP D. VIVIAN, *Acquisitions—The Human Factor* (London: Egon Zehnder International, 1987).

20
STUART GANNES, "IBM Dials a Wrong Number," *Fortune*, June 9, 1986, pp. 34–40.

21
JAMES H. HUGUET, JR., "Blending Sales Forces After the Acquisition," *Mergers & Acquisitions*, Summer 1984, pp. 52–57.

22
VIJAY SATHE, *Culture and Related Corporate Realities* (Homewood, IL: Richard D. Irwin, 1985).

Chapter 4

1
JAMES B. YOUNG, "A Conclusive Investigation Into the Causative Elements of Failure in Acquisition and Mergers," *Handbook of Mergers and Acquisitions* (Englewood Cliffs, N.J.: Prentice-Hall, 1981).

2
JAMES W. BRADLEY and DONALD H. KORN, *Acquisition and Corporate Development* (Lexington, Mass.: Lexington Books, 1981).

RICHARD J. BERMAN and MARTIN R. WADE, III, "The Planned Approach to Acquisitions," *Handbook of Mergers and Acquisitions* (Englewood Cliffs, N.J.: Prentice-Hall, 1981).

ROCHELLE O'CONNOR, *Managing Corporate Development* (New York: The Conference Board, Inc., 1980).

3

DANIEL J. POWER, "Acquisition Decision Making," *Mergers & Acquisitions*, Summer 1983, pp. 63–67.

IVAN E. BRICK and LAWRENCE J. HABER, "Breakthrough: New M & A Research Findings," *Mergers & Acquisitions*, Summer 1983, pp. 62–63.

4

International Technology Corporation, *Our Mission* (Torrance, CA, 1986), p. 12.

5

See Farley and Schwallie article in the annotated bibliography at the end of this book.

6

MARK L. FELDMAN, "The SWAT Team Approach to Acquisition Analysis," *Mergers & Acquisitions*, Winter 1985, pp. 61–63.

7

O'CONNOR, *Managing Corporate Development*.

8

PAULA DWYER, "The Baby Bells: Ready, Get Set, Diversify," *Business Week*, September 1, 1986, pp. 29–30.

JONATHAN B. LEVINE, "The Baby Bells' Weak Sister Is Growing Into a Bruiser," *Business Week*, September 8, 1986, pp. 69–70.

9

JEROLD L. FREIER, "Acquisition Search Programs," *Mergers & Acquisitions*, Summer 1981, pp. 35–39.

"Roundtable: Searching for the 'Right' Company," *Mergers & Acquisitions*, Summer 1982, pp. 22–30.

10

KENNETH M. DAVIDSON, *MegaMergers* (Cambridge, Mass.: Ballinger, 1985).

PETER PETRE, "Merger Fees That Bend the Mind," *Fortune*, January 20, 1986, pp. 18–23.

SUSAN DENTZER with CAROLYN FRIDAY, DOUG TSURUOKA, and ELAINE SHANNON, "Greed on Wall Street," *Newsweek*, May 26, 1986, pp. 44–46.

11

TRISH HALL, "For a Company Chief, When There's a Whim There's Often a Way," *Wall Street Journal*, October 1, 1984, p. 1.

12

ARTHUR M. LOUIS, "Does Gannett Pay Too Much?," *Fortune*, September 15, 1986, pp. 59–64.

13

MARK MAREMONT, "The Duo That Makes Hanson Trust a Power to Reckon With," *Business Week*, September 8, 1986, pp. 38–39.

14

CHARLES FIERO, "Electronic Access to 10,000 Transactions," *Mergers & Acquisitions*, Winter 1984, pp. 21–22.

15

ALFRED RAPPAPORT, "Strategic Analysis for More Profitable Acquisitions," Strategy and Tactics in Mergers from the *Harvard Business Review*, 19, July–August 1979, pp. 91–102.
See also the material provided by the Alcar Group Inc., Skokie, IL.

16

STEVEN E. PROKESCH and TERESA CARSON, "Fluor: Compound Fractures From Leaping Before Looking," *Business Week*, June 3, 1985, pp. 92–93.

17

WILLIAM B. GLABERSON, TERRI THOMPSON, and JAMES R. NORMAN, "Texaco Has Several Options—All of Them Grim," *Business Week*, December 23, 1985, pp. 27–28.

18

LEE SMITH, "The Making of a Megamerger," *Fortune*, September 7, 1981, pp. 58–64.

19

"Dealmakers Cut Failure Rate," *Mergers & Acquisitions*, Spring 1985, p. 23.

20

KATHLEEN A. HUGHES, "In Mergers, Manners Can Matter a Lot," *Wall Street Journal*, October 4, 1982, p. 35.

L. J. DAVIS, "Deals II," *Vanity Fair*, June 1984, p. 20.

Chapter 5

1

KENNETH M. DAVIDSON, *MegaMergers* (Cambridge, Mass.: Ballinger, 1985).

DUANE MICHAELS, "The Dealmakers," *Fortune*, January 24, 1983, p. 56.

RICHARD PHALON, *The Takeover Barons of Wall Street* (New York: Putnam, 1981).

2

JONATHAN ALTER, "Civil War at CBS," *Newsweek*, September 15, 1986, pp. 46–54.

3

ANTHONY BIANCO, "The Dynamos Who Made Oppenheimer a Power in Megamergers," *Business Week*, December 10, 1984, pp. 132–33.

ANTHONY BIANCO, "The King of Wall Street: How Salomon Brothers Rose to the Top—and How It Wields Its Power," *Business Week*, December 9, 1985, pp. 98–104.

TIM METZ, "Goldman Sachs Avoids Bitter Takeover Fights but Leads in Mergers," *Wall Street Journal*, December 3, 1982, p. 1.

BILL POWELL, "The New Dealmakers," *Newsweek*, May 26, 1986, pp. 47–52.

JEROME ZUKOSKY, "Trial by Fire for Merrill's Dealmakers," *Business Week*, September 30, 1985, p. 52.

4

TIM METZ, "Merger Masters: Outside Professionals Play an Increasing Role in Corporate Takeovers," *Wall Street Journal*, December 2, 1980, p. 1.

5

DAVIDSON, *MegaMergers*.

6

PETER W. BERNSTEIN, "Profit Pressures on the Big Law Firms," *Fortune*, April 19, 1982, p. 91.

DAVIDSON, *MegaMergers*.

BRIAN DICKERSON, "Law Firm Knows the Ropes of Takeovers," *Miami Herald*, December 6, 1982, p. 13.

MARTIN LIPTON and ERICA STEINBERGER, *Takeovers and Freezeouts* (New York: Law Journal Seminars Press, 1979).

RICHARD VILKIN, "Advising Risk Arbitrageurs Challenges M & A Lawyers," *Legal Times of Washington*, June 1, 1981, p. 28.

7

EDWARD JAY EPSTEIN, "Raiders' Nadir?: Poison-Pill Paralysis Sets In for the Boys in Bungalow Eight," *Manhattan, Inc.*, September 1986, pp. 25–28.

JOSEPH G. FOGG, III, "Takeovers: Last Chance for Self-Restraint," *Harvard Business Review*, November-December 1985, pp. 30–40.

MURRAY L. WEIDENBAUM, "The Best Defense Against the Raiders," *Business Week*, September 23, 1985, p. 21.

HAROLD M. WILLIAMS, "It's Time for a Takeover Moratorium," *Fortune*, July 22, 1985, pp. 133–36.

8

RICHARD PHALON, "Tipping the Takeover Balance of Power," *Mergers & Acquisitions*, Winter 1982, pp. 52–56.

9

EDWARD JAY EPSTEIN, "Inside Out: The SEC's Hot Pursuit of Outsider Information," *Manhattan, Inc.*, August 1986, pp. 17–19.

WILLIAM B. GLABERSON, "Why Wasn't $1 Million a Year Enough?: A Lot More Than Greed Led to the Insider Trading Scandal," *Business Week*, August 25, 1986, pp. 72–74.

Testimony of Felix G. Rohatyn, U.S. Congress, Senate. Committee on Banking, Housing and Urban Affairs, Subcommittee on Securities, June 6, 1985.

Testimony of Andrew C. Sigler, U.S. Congress, House. Committee on Energy and Commerce. Subcommittees on Telecommunications, Consumer Protection, and Finance, May 23, 1985.

10
Statement of Wayne E. Glenn, U.S. Congress, House. Committee on Energy and Commerce. Subcommittee on Telecommunications, Consumer Protection, and Finance, June 12, 1985.

11
CAROLYN FRIDAY and DAVID PAULY, "A Fatal Flight Takes Its Toll: TWA Workers Finally Grapple With Harsh Reality," *Newsweek*, September 8, 1986, pp. 38–40.

12
JAMES E. ELLIS, CHUCK HAWKINS, and MARK IVEY, "Will Frontier's Fall Ground People Express, Too?," *Business Week*, September 8, 1986, pp. 22–23.

JOHN FRANK, CHUCK HAWKINS, and MARK IVEY, "A Fight at United May Seal People's Fate," *Business Week*, August 25, 1986, pp. 40–41.

13
Testimony of Robert F. Harbrant, U.S. Congress, House. Committee on Ways and Means. Subcommittee on Oversight and Select Revenue Measures, April 16, 1985.

14
AARON BERNSTEIN, "A Union's Novel Attempt at Shaping a Buyout," *Business Week*, September 8, 1986, p. 31.

15
TRISH HALL, "When Food Firms Merge, Effects Reach Into Aisles of Supermarkets," *Wall Street Journal*, June 13, 1985, p. 33.

PATRICIA SELLERS, "When Clients Merge, Ad Agencies Quake," *Fortune*, November 11, 1985, p. 101.

16
CHRISTINE DUGAS and RICHARD MELCHER, "Saatchi & Saatchi's Expansion: Too Much, Too Fast?" *Business Week*, October 6, 1986, pp. 33–36.

STEPHEN KOEPP, "The Not-So-Jolly Advertising Giants," *Time*, November 17, 1986, p. 73.

17
MYRON MAGNET, "What Merger Mania Did to Syracuse," *Fortune*, February 3, 1986, pp. 94–98.

18
See the annotated bibliography for several articles related to process management.

19
See also DAVID B. JEMISON and SIM B. SITKIN, "Corporate Acquisitions: A Process Perspective," *Academy of Management Review* 11 (1986), pp. 145–63.

20
See annotated bibliography for articles and books on post-merger management, especially those by Leighton and Todd, Magnet and Pritchert.

21
JEMISON and SITKIN, "Corporate Acquisitions," p. 151.

Chapter 6

1
GENE F. BRADY and DONALD L. HELMICH, *Executive Succession* (Englewood Cliffs, N.J.: Prentice-Hall, 1984).

2
JAMES BRIAN QUINN, "Strategic Goals: Process and Politics," *Sloan Management Review*, Fall 1977, pp. 21–37.

3
JONATHAN ALTER and BILL POWELL, "The Showdown at CBS," *Newsweek*, September 22, 1986, pp. 54–59.
GEORGE RUSSELL, "Corporate Shoot-Out at Black Rock," *Time*, September 22, 1986, pp. 68–72.

4
ROBERT DUNCAN and GERALD ZALTMAN, *Strategies for Planned Change* (New York: Wiley, 1977).

5
ROGER HARRISON, "Choosing the Depth of Organizational Intervention," *Journal of Applied Behavioral Science* 6 (1970), pp. 181–202.

6

PAUL TILLICH, *The Courage to Be* (New Haven: Yale University Press, 1958).

7

KAREN COOK, "Imperfect Binding: The CBS-Ziff Magazine Merger Proves That There Is More Than One Way to Tackle an Issue," *Manhattan, Inc.*, April 1986, pp. 31–39.

JIM JUBAK, "Retaining Staff After the Sale: Open Communications and Shared Goals Preserve UCS' Crew," *Venture*, August 1985, p. 98.

JONATHAN B. LEVINE, "How IBM Is Getting the Most Out of Rolm: Respect for the Phone-Switchboard Maker's More Casual Culture Has Paid Off," *Business Week*, November 18, 1985, pp. 110–11.

CAROL J. LOOMIS, "The Morning After at Phibro-Salomon," *Fortune*, January 10, 1983, pp. 74–79.

MYRON MAGNET, "Acquiring Without Smothering," *Fortune*, November 12, 1984, pp. 22–30.

TODD MASON and RUSSELL MITCHELL, "How General Motors Is Bringing Up Ross Perot's Baby," *Business Week*, April 14, 1986, pp. 96–100.

THOMAS MOORE, "Culture Shock Rattles the TV Networks," *Fortune*, April 14, 1986, pp. 22–27.

MONCI JO WILLIAMS, "Shearson Lehman: The 'Mismatch' May Be Working," *Fortune*, March 31, 1986, pp. 32–34.

CAROL HYMOWITZ and KEN WELLS, "Takeover Trauma: Gulf's Managers Find Merger Into Chevron Forces Many Changes," *Wall Street Journal*, December 5, 1984, p. 1.

8

JAMES S. BALLOUN, *The Acquisition Management Framework*, McKinsey & Company, Inc., December 13, 1985.

9

O.D. RESOURCES, *Managing the Human Aspects of Mergers and Acquisitions* (Atlanta: O.D. Resources, 1986).

Chapter 7

1

NOEL TICHY, *Managing Strategic Change: Technical, Political, and Cultural Dynamics* (New York: John Wiley & Sons, 1983).

2

JAMES S. BALLOUN, *The Acquisition Management Framework*, McKinsey & Company, Inc., December 13, 1985.

3

PRICE PRITCHETT, *After the Merger: Managing the Shockwaves* (New York: Dow Jones-Irwin, 1985).

4

LARRY REIBSTEIN, "After a Takeover: More Managers Run, or Are Pushed Out the Door," *Wall Street Journal*, November 15, 1985, p. 33.

5

See LEONARD GREENHALGH article in the annotated bibliography.

6

RICHARD BECKHARD and REUBEN HARRIS, *Organizational Transitions*, Second Edition (Reading, Mass.: Addison-Wesley Publishing Co., 1987).

7

BECKHARD and HARRIS, *Organizational Transitions*.

8

TICHY, *Managing Strategic Change*.

9

BECKHARD and HARRIS, pp. 76–78.

10

TICHY, *Managing Strategic Change*.

11

TICHY, p. 340.

12

THOMAS O'DEA, "Religion in Times of Social Distress," in William Sadler Jr., (ed.), *Personality and Religion* (New York: Harper Forum Books, 1970).

13

PAUL TILLICH, *The Courage to Be* (New Haven: Yale University Press, 1958).

14
SIGMUND FREUD, "Mourning and Melancholia," 1917, *Standard Edition* (London: Hogarth, 1957).

15
WILLIAM BRIDGES, "Managing Organizational Transitions," *Organization Dynamics*, 1980, p. 29.

16
BRIDGES, "Managing Organizational Transitions," p. 30.

17
BRIDGES, p. 30.

18
MYRON MAGNET, "Help! My Company Has Just Been Taken Over," *Fortune*, July 9, 1984, pp. 44–51.

19
MAGNET, "Help! My Company Has Just Been Taken Over."

Chapter 8

1
JULIE AMPARANO, "Contel Seeks to Terminate Merger Accord," *Wall Street Journal*, April 15, 1987, p. 16.
TOM HALLMAN, "Comsat May Comprise With Contel," *Atlanta Journal*, May 3, 1987, p. 3.
ROBERT SNOWDON JONES, "Analysts Critical of Contel-Comsat Merger," *Atlanta Constitution*, October 1, 1986, sec. 2, p. 3.

2
JOAN O'C. HAMILTON and JUDITH H. DOBRZYNSKI, "Inside Parker Montgomery's Tangle of Troubled Companies," *Business Week*, February 23, 1987, pp. 110–11.

3
MICHAEL E. PORTER, "From Competitive Advantage to Corporate Strategy," *Harvard Business Review*, May-June 1987, pp. 43–59.

4

JUDITH H. DOBRZYNSKI and LAURIE BAUM, "Will All That Restructuring Ever Pay Off for Ed Hennessy's Allied?" *Business Week*, February 2, 1987, pp. 78–80.

5

JAMES A. YUNKER, *Integrating Acquisitions* (New York: Praeger, 1983).

6

PAUL SHRIVASTAVA, "Postmerger Integration," *The Journal of Business Strategy*, Summer 1986, vol. 7, no. 1, pp. 65–75.

7

LINDA SMIRICICH and GARETH MORGAN, "Leadership: The Management of Meaning," *Journal of Applied Behavioral Science*, vol. 18 (3), 1982, pp. 257–273.

8

LAURENCE D. ACKERMAN, "The Psychology of Corporation: How Identity Influences Business," *The Journal of Business Strategy*, pp. 56–65.

9

JOSEPH E. MCCANN and JAY R. GALBRAITH, "Interdepartmental Relations," in P. Nystrom and W. Starbuck (eds.), *Handbook of Organizational Design*, vol. 2 (New York: Oxford University Press, 1981), pp. 60–84.

10

JAY R. GALBRAITH and ROBERT K. KAZANJIAN, *Strategy Implementation: Structure, Systems, and Process*, second edition (St. Paul, Minn.: West Publishing, 1986).

11

JOHN HOERR, "Human Resources Managers Aren't Corporate Nobodies Anymore," *Business Week*, December 2, 1985, pp. 58–59.

12

JOSEPH E. MCCANN and THOMAS N. GILMORE, "Diagnosing Organizational Decision Making Through Responsibility Charting," *Sloan Management Review*, Winter 1983, pp. 3–15.

13

ROBERT H. HAYES and GERALD H. HOAG, "Post Acquisition Retention of Top Management," *Mergers & Acquisitions*, Summer 1974, pp. 8–18.

14

LEE BERTON, "Peat-KMG Merger Proposal Strained as Units in Some Countries Drop Out," *Wall Street Journal*, January 6, 1987, p. 7.

LEE BERTON, "Accountants' Merger Tests Idea of Meshing Partners World-Wide," *Wall Street Journal*, April 22, 1987, p. 1.

Chapter 9

1

See, for example, the programs provided by organizations like the Strategic Planning Institute in Cambridge and major colleges like Wharton and Columbia.

2

WALTER KIECHEL III, "Living With Human Resources," *Fortune*, August 18, 1986, pp. 99–100.

3

See, for example, the software package developed by The Alcar Group Inc., which is the most widely used software designed for this use.

4

JAMES E. ROSENBAUM, *Career Mobility in a Corporate Hierarchy* (New York: Academic Press Inc., 1984).

5

EDGAR SCHEIN, *Career Dynamics: Matching Individual and Organizational Needs* (Reading, Mass.: Addison-Wesley, 1978).

6

EDGAR SCHEIN, *Career Anchors: Discovering Your Real Values* (San Diego: University Associates, 1985).

7
THOMAS P. FERENCE, JAMES A. F. STONER, and E. KIRBY WARREN, "Managing the Career Plateau," *Academy of Management Review*, October 1977, 602–12.

Chapter 10

1
JAMES S. BALLOUN, *The Acquisition Management Framework*, McKinsey & Company, Inc., December 13, 1985.

2
PETER DRUCKER, "The Five Rules of Successful Acquisition," *Wall Street Journal*, October 15, 1981, p. 28.

3
RICHARD DAVIS, "Compatibility in Corporate Marriages," *Harvard Business Review*, July-August 1968, pp. 86–93.

4
DAVID JEMISON and SIM SITKIN, "Corporate Acquisitions: A Process Perspective," *Academy of Management Review* 2, no. 1 (January 1986), p. 148.

5
DRUCKER, "The Five Rules of Successful Acquisition."

6
JEMISON and SITKIN, "Corporate Acquisitions."

7
JAMES BALLOUN, interview, November 1985.

8
THOMAS O'DEA, "Religion in Times of Social Distress," *Personality and Religion* (New York: Harper Forum Book, 1970).

9
MICHAEL BRODY, "NASA's Challenge: Ending Isolation at the Top," *Fortune*, May 12, 1986, pp. 26–32.

10
MARSHA SINETAR, "Mergers, Morale and Productivity," *Personnel Journal*, November 1981, pp. 863–67.

11
NOEL TICHY, "Managing Change Strategically: The Technical, Political, and Cultural Keys," *Organizational Dynamics*, Autumn 1982, pp. 59–80.

12
LEONARD GREENHALGH, "A Process Model of Organizational Turnover: The Relationship With Job Security as a Case in Point," *Academy of Management Review*, 5, no. 2 (1980), pp. 299–303.

13
ANNA FREUD, *The Ego and Mechanisms of Defense* (New York: International Universities Press Inc., 1946), pp. 109–22.

14
ROBERT FULMER, "Managing Mergers With Training and Development," *Personnel Journal* (in press), and personal interview.

15
JOHN HARDY, "How to Face Being Taken Over," *Harvard Business Review*, November-December 1969, pp. 44–54.

JOINING FORCES: CRITICAL QUESTIONS FOR MANAGEMENT CONSIDERATION

A. **Strategic Planning Process**
1. How well articulated is our strategic plan?
2. Who or what do we want to be? By when?
3. Has an assessment of strategic capability been performed? What are our most critical strengths and weaknesses? Threats and opportunities?
4. What are our action priorities? Action timeframe?
5. How do mergers-acquisitions fit within the plan? How adequate are our key resources (for example, financial) for executing deals?

B. **Merger-Acquisition Process Capacity**
1. How well are we organized to pursue and execute deals?
   (a) Who are "key players" (internal and external) and what is the extent of their role or responsibility clarity, skills and abilities, time commitments, and level of team development?
   (b) Has leadership overall and across merger-acquisition stages been firmly fixed?
   (c) How adequate are the resources devoted to the process?

2. How well have we developed the screening process?

  (a) What is the depth and breadth of our search?

  (b) How do we select targets? What are our criteria and what is their validity? What assumptions are implicit or explicit in these?

3. How well developed and sophisticated is our analysis process?

  (a) Major models, tools, and techniques utilized? Who is involved?

  (b) Level of analysis of the "three pillars?"

    (1) Financial Fit: (a) price/valuation range, (b) terms and conditions to be set?

    (2) Business Fit: (a) anticipated benefits/synergies, (b) actions or resources needed to realize?

    (3) Organizational Fit: (a) cultures, (b) structure, (c) systems, processes, policies?

  (c) What are the critical assumptions we are making concerning each pillar? How can these be quickly and safely tested?

4. Have we thought through how we make an offer and negotiate?

  (a) Who assumes leadership?

  (b) Preparation for first and subsequent contacts?

  (c) Clarity of ground rules (disclosure, "friendliness")?

5. How will we manage the transition process (implementation and integration stages)?

  (a) Strategic role selection (McKinsey Model)? Depth and timing of intervention needed?

  (b) Organization of the transition team(s)?

  (c) Control over preconditions (governing assumptions, communication channels, information access, resources)?

  (d) Identification and adequacy of resources devoted to transition?

  (e) Clarity/consensus about opening moves or first steps?

6. Adequacy of opportunities for feedback and learning for overall process development?

B

THE
CULTURAL
AUDIT

STEP I. The first step toward managing the human aspects of merger-acquisition projects is to understand what the culture is in your own company and how it affects the success or failure of M/A activities. Organizations that anticipate the possibility of acquiring other companies, being acquired themselves or engaging in a merger should conduct a *cultural audit* before entering any M/A negotiation.

Audits, are commissioned to identify how well a company's current culture matches with the type of culture required for success in the future. Such an *audit* is conducted in nine steps.

STEP II. When an organization has completed a *cultural audit* for itself and has learned the value of this type information, similar information about a prospective M/A partner becomes extremely important. For example, cultural data from prospective M/A partners may become part of the information requested when conducting "due diligence" investigations.

When such information brings out significant differences between the cultures in question, the negotiations are not automatically in jeopardy. In fact, in many situations, it is the difference in the cultures that forms the attraction companies have for each other. Synergy only occurs from integrating diverse perspectives and, therefore, some differences are essential for success. It is critical, however, for the executives involved in the negotiations to understand what cultural similarities and differences exist between their companies so they can make more informed decisions about the blending of these cultures.

STEP III. Once an exchange of *cultural audit* information has taken place, the senior negotiating executives can determine what form of working relationship the two cultures should have with each other (coexistence, assimilation, or transformation) and what will be the cost to achieve the desired cultural mix. Cost estimates of M/A agreements that do not include the resources necessary to blend the cultures are grossly underestimated.

STEP IV. This step involves the writing and distribution of an "Implementation Guideline" statement that defines the type of cultural blending desired during M/A implementation. Once cultural guidelines for the M/A effort are identified and key decisions are made (Step III), the senior officers involved in the negotiations must develop a broad-based statement that can be disseminated throughout both organizations and serve as a vehicle for articulating the cultural goals of the M/A agremeent.

The development of this "Implementation Guideline" statement cannot be delegated to subordinates of the senior negotiators. CEOs and any others directly involved in the negotiations must personally invest in the task of finding the right words to describe the kind of culture they hope to achieve through the M/A agreement. Such a task is not easy and can be time consuming, but the reward will be well worth the investment. When the organization has not only a clear statement to relate to, but one that has the full commitment of all the negotiating senior executives, the trauma of implementation is dramatically reduced.

STEP V. Now managers from key functional areas in both organizations can begin to focus on the tactical aspects of the implementation plan. This joint group has the primary architectural responsibility for the plan's development and implementation.

STEP VI.   The final step in blending two previously separate cultures is to implement the plan. It will be important for all those responsible for implementation to remember that there are three speeds at which people change. The *physical* speed is the fastest. If all you expect out of people is for them to behave differently, you can legitimize such shifts rather quickly. There is, however, usually a time lag before people understand *intellectually* why they need to behave differently. Finally, the last movement to occur is an *emotional* commitment to the change. Not all organizational changes require the time for all three elements to shift, but with blending cultures it is an absolute necessity. You must build into the implementation process enough time for physical, intellectual and emotional changes if a successful new culture is to emerge.

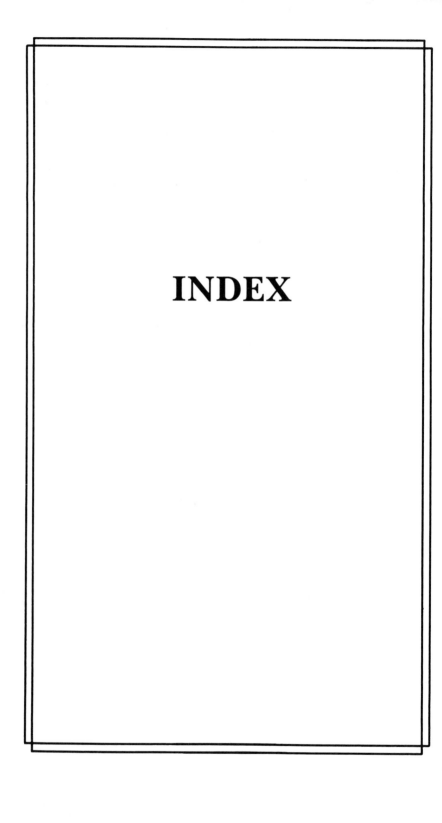

INDEX